Job

Westminster Bible Companion

Series Editors

Patrick D. Miller
David L. Bartlett

Job

JAMES A. WHARTON

 Westminster John Knox Press
Louisville, Kentucky

Book design by Publishers' WorkGroup
Cover design by Drew Stevens

First edition
Published by Westminster John Knox Press
Louisville, Kentucky

This book is printed on acid-free paper that meets the American National Standards Institute Z39.48 standard. ♾

PRINTED IN THE UNITED STATES OF AMERICA

99 00 01 02 03 04 05 06 07 08 — 10 9 8 7 6 5 4 3 2 1

Library of Congress Cataloging-in-Publication Data

Wharton, James A., 1927–
    Job / James A. Wharton.
        p.   cm. — (Westminster Bible companion)
    Includes bibliographical references.
    ISBN 0-664-25267-2 (alk. paper)
    1. Bible. O.T. Job—Commentaries.   I. Title.   II. Series.
    BS1415.3.W58   1999
    233'. 1077—dc21   98-53719

Contents

Series Foreword

This series of study guides to the Bible is offered to the church and more specifically to the laity. In daily devotions, in church school classes, and in listening to the preached word, individual Christians turn to the Bible for a sustaining word, a challenging word, and a sense of direction. The word that scripture brings may be highly personal as one deals with the demands and surprises, the joys and sorrows, of daily life. It also may have broader dimensions as people wrestle with moral and theological issues that involve us all. In every congregation and denomination, controversies arise that send ministry and laity alike back to the Word of God to find direction for dealing with difficult matters that confront us.

A significant number of lay women and men in the church also find themselves called to the service of teaching. Most of the time they will be teaching the Bible. In many churches, the primary sustained attention to the Bible and the discovery of its riches for our lives have come from the ongoing teaching of the Bible by persons who have not engaged in formal theological education. They have been willing, and often eager, to study the Bible in order to help others drink from its living water.

This volume is part of a series of books, the Westminster Bible Companion, intended to help the laity of the church read the Bible more clearly and intelligently. Whether such reading is for personal direction or for the teaching of others, the reader cannot avoid the difficulties of trying to understand these words from long ago. The scriptures are clear and clearly available to everyone as they call us to faith in the God who is revealed in Jesus Christ and as they offer to every human being the word of salvation. No companion volumes are necessary in order to hear such words truly. Yet every reader of scripture who pauses to ponder and think further about any text has questions that are not immediately answerable simply by reading the text of scripture. Such questions may be about historical and geographical details or about words that are obscure or so loaded with meaning that one cannot tell at a glance what is at stake. They may be about the fundamental meaning of a passage or about what connection a particular text might have to our contemporary world. Or a teacher preparing for a church school class may simply want to know: What should I say about this biblical passage when I have to teach it next Sunday? It is our hope that these volumes, written by teachers and pastors with long experience studying and teaching the Bible in the church, will help members of the church who want and need to study the Bible with their questions.

The New Revised Standard Version of the Bible is the basis for the interpretive comments that each author provides. The NRSV text is presented at the beginning of the discussion so that the reader may have at hand in a single volume both the scripture passage and the exposition of its meaning. In some instances, where inclusion of the entire passage is not necessary for understanding either the text or the interpreter's discussion, the presentation of the NRSV text may be abbreviated. Usually, the whole of the biblical text is given.

We hope this series will serve the community of faith, opening the Word of God to all the people, so that they may be sustained and guided by it.

Introduction:
Thoughts on the Interpretation of Job

THE FUNCTION OF JOB

The book of Job comes to us from the margins of biblical faith, not from its center. No word appears here about the God who called Sarah and Abraham, who liberated Israel from slavery, who made covenant with them at Sinai through Moses, who proved faithful when they proved faithless, who bore them on eagle's wings to the land of promise, who judged and restored them, who made everlasting promises. For Christians, nothing in Job suggests that God so loves this grotesquely unfair world that God *gave* . . .

We can call Job marginal in the sense that no distinctive doctrine, whether Jewish or Christian, is based on texts found in the book. Yet Job is not at all marginal when it comes to the excruciating questions raised for faithful Jews and Christians "when bad things happen to good people," as Rabbi Harold Kushner put it in the title of his remarkable book. There are times for all of us, I think, when these questions fill the whole horizon of faith, perhaps especially in this generation. Instant communications confront us daily with appalling suffering and injustice on a global scale. When this excruciating unfairness strikes us directly and personally, no faith question is more central than the agonized "Why?" addressed to God.

Jews and Christians have always lived among people for whom biblical faith was either unknown or shrugged off as irrelevant. Outsiders to the biblical story have often raised hard questions, not only about the God of whom the Bible speaks but perhaps more devastatingly about the questionable ways in which biblical faith communities have actually behaved, presumably on the basis of the faith they profess.

Job, however, raises these familiar questions about God's righteousness and ours in a much more serious way: not from outside the Bible but from within. For this reason, I suppose, the book of Job is much easier to read

1

if you happen to be an outsider to biblical faith. You are then free to dismiss Job's God as an absurd relic of an ancient culture. You can still value Job as a masterpiece of ancient literary art. You can cherish the book for the light it throws on the universal human quest for meaning and order in a world that consistently mocks both. You may even salute the author of Job as a surprisingly modern skeptic born millennia ahead of time, one who designed the book to demonstrate the absurdity of God and all religious constructs that take God seriously.

People who are serious about biblical faith, in contrast, do not enjoy the luxury of reading the book of Job at arm's length, in this disengaged and relatively comfortable way. Jewish and Christian interpretations of Job differ widely, not only from each other but also within each of the two traditions. Yet all distinctively Jewish or Christian interpretations of Job have one urgent thing in common: *Somehow*—and this is a crucial word—somehow, Job's outrageous questions about undeserved suffering must be put to *our* God, to God our contemporary, to the God we are committed to worship and serve. Biblical faith is not mature until it has faced the harshest realities of human experience clear-eyed and cold sober, as Job requires us to do. By comparison with this costly dialogue with God, questions put to biblical faith from the outside sound sophomoric.

Throughout the long history of Judaism and Christianity, faithful interpreters of Job in every generation have confronted us with Job's incandescent questions. A variety of efforts have been made to derive answers to these questions, whether from the book itself or from the biblical witness as a whole. Yet none of these "answers" has ever succeeded in providing an acceptable religious consensus. The questions remain vivid in every generation, crying out for fresh responses from those who are called to love God with everything they have and to love neighbor as self. Love for God, as well as love for neighbor, forbids us to accept any religious "solution" that makes human suffering and injustice somehow "acceptable" or "understandable."

This leads me to the conclusion that the function of Job, from the time of its inclusion among the Holy Scripture of Judaism and of Christianity, has *never* been to provide answers to the questions it raises. Rather it has functioned, for Jews and Christians alike, as a means of keeping the questions urgent and contemporary for all who set out to honor and serve the God of whom the Bible speaks.

If this is so, people of biblical faith cannot approach the reading of Job as a literary or religious puzzle to be solved. Every reading of Job demands all the resources of faith we possess, not only to face the contemporary reality of these questions head on but to wrestle them through with confidence that—again, *somehow*—biblical faith invites us to address our most outraged and heartbroken cries (even outcries against God) to God, and not to another. Indeed, at the simplest and most important level, Job has provided faithful people with this slim comfort: Joblike questions born of Joblike pain do not exclude us from the biblical story. Job resounds with our cries of the heart and honors them as an authentic dimension of faithfulness.

It is from this perspective that I invite you to look over my shoulder as we read Job together. The reflections on Job recorded here, together with the responses I find myself making, are not intended to replace yours. At best, they may stimulate you to make the questions of Job your own, in a fresh way, and to work out responses appropriate to your experience of life and of God. If we do this faithfully, then I think the book of Job will have accomplished for us its unique and proper function as Holy Scripture.

THE STRUCTURE OF JOB

Before we plunge into the reading of Job, it may be useful to have an overview of the whole book. (The table of contents is helpful for this.) First, whoever wrote this book had a remarkable eye for literary architecture. Like a pair of bookends, chapters 1 and 2 stand at one end and chapter 42:7–17 stands at the other end of the massive argumentations that make up well over 90 percent of Job. You do not have to be a Hebrew scholar to recognize the sharp difference between the storytelling style of these two "bookends" and the rhythmic, poetic style of the arguments that fall in between. Modern translations honor this difference by printing each kind of literature in the appropriate style, whether narrative (like most of Genesis) or poetic (like the Psalms).

In fact, if you read Job 1:1 through 2:10 and then jump directly to Job 42:12–17, you get an almost complete story of Job's former state, how he endured the horrendous test imposed on him, and how God rewards such faithful endurance by restoring Job's former blessings twice over. Job might have been a very short book with a very simple message: God may test us severely with sufferings beyond all human comprehension, but God ultimately rewards patient and trusting endurance with blessings beyond measure.

The structure of Job, however, shows that for the author of this book, the simple piety of such a story is not enough. The mighty poem that stretches between the tragic beginning and the happy ending of this story confronts us with a Job who is outraged by innocent suffering, not only his own but that of others. Job is anything but patient when he makes his case against his friends' pious arguments, and even more important, against God.

It is easy to see why many students of Job tend to think that something very like the simple story of Job 1:1–2:10 and 42:12–17 was already well known and popular among religious people long before the present book ever took shape. We can't know for certain that this is so, but the only allusions to Job elsewhere in the Bible point in that direction: Ezekiel 14:14, 20; James 5:11. Each of these texts offers Job as an example of unswerving righteousness and patient endurance without a hint of Job's titanic struggle with God.

It seems possible, then, that the author of Job may have used the story of Job's proverbial faithfulness under pressure to set the stage for a series of mighty poems designed to explore a wide range of questions about the righteousness of God and the righteousness of people as they emerge in real human experience.

Job 2:11–13 and Job 42:7–9 (or perhaps vv. 7–11), then, serve to link the simple story to the elaborate poetic material (Job 3:1–42:6) that lies in between. It is as if the author were saying to us: "Here is the well-known story of the patient sufferer. Let us now explore the struggles that lie beneath the surface of such a breathtaking example of faithful endurance."

The largest and most obvious structural pattern of the poem is found in Job 3—27. It begins with the agonized "Why?" that comes welling up out of Job's pain (chap. 3). Each of the friends named in Job 2:11 (Eliphaz, Bildad, and Zophar) protests in turn against what Job is saying, in each case followed by a counterprotest by Job (Job 4—14). Readers sometimes feel that the issues between Job and his friends are reasonably clear by this time, but the poet has other ideas. This is only round one of the contest. Job's protest in chapters 12, 13, and 14 is three times longer than the opening one in chapter 3. This triggers a second round of arguments from Eliphaz, Bildad, and Zophar, each followed by a response from Job (Job 15—21).

Modern readers of Job are typically weary at this point, sensing that everything in this mutual harangue has already been said twice over. A certain Joblike patience is required (for modern readers, at least) to read Job 22—25 and discover that a third such round appears to have begun.

But chapters 26 and 27 break the pattern of the first two rounds in a confusing way. None of the speeches in Job 26 or 27 is assigned to Zophar, whose name is not mentioned in this third round. Even more puzzling is what we now hear Job saying in chapters 24, 26, and 27. Some of the statements here (especially 24:18–25; 26:5–14; 27:7–23) seem to fit into the arguments of Job's friends much more convincingly than they do into the arguments of Job. This has led most students of Job to conclude that the third round has been scrambled, whether deliberately or accidentally, in the long history of editing and recopying the text of Job. The reordering that the translators and editors of the *Jerusalem Bible* suggested is only one among several scholarly attempts to reconstruct this third round of speeches after the familiar pattern of rounds one and two. Zophar is restored to the debate in this way; Bildad is given a speech of appropriate length; and the arguments of Job and his friends sound much more like those we have heard before.

It is worth noting that earlier editions of the Revised Standard Version (RSV) tried to deal with this problem in a more modest but equally speculative way. At Job 24:18 these older editions inserted the words *You say*, suggesting that Job is quoting the arguments of his friends at this point, not advancing his own. The New Revised Standard Version (NRSV), following the tendency of many contemporary scholars, has dropped such attempts on the grounds that there is simply no textual evidence for them. This does not allay the suspicion that we do not possess chapters 25—27 in the form they may once have had, but it does honor the Hebrew text in the form that has come down to us.

It is possible that chapter 28 is a hymn to transcendent Wisdom and a self-contained masterpiece in its own right. After the long, often bitter disputations between Job and his friends, this poem comes as a little oasis of serenity. It does not join the argument about Job's innocence or guilt. It does not deal with the question of whether God rewards the righteous and punishes the wicked in this life. It simply points beyond all human quests for wisdom to God, who alone "understands the way to [wisdom] and . . . knows its place" (28:23).

Job's final defense of his integrity with respect to God and people (chaps. 29, 30, and 31) has a unique significance for the book as a whole. My experience with study groups has been that they are so overwhelmed by the arguments and counterarguments of Job 3—27 that Job 29—31 only sounds like more of the same old thing. In this book I invite you to read these chapters afresh, in close connection with chapters 1:1–2:10, as if we had not heard the hectic arguments that lie between. These "last words" (31:40), from beginning to end, are strictly between Job and God. The reader is privileged to eavesdrop.

Chapters 32—37 are the quite unexpected speeches of a new character, young Elihu, who is not referred to elsewhere in the book of Job, either in the beginning (Job 2:11) or at the end (Job 42:7, 9). This study invites you to reflect on what Elihu says but also to ponder how his speeches function in the book of Job, coming as they do after Job and his friends have fallen silent and before God answers Job out of the whirlwind (38:1ff.). However, Elihu's speeches intrude in a somewhat disconnected way, without clear indications as to how they relate to what comes before and what follows.

Chapters 38—41, of course, present God's daunting "answer" to Job, in two stages: 38:1–40:2 and 40:6–41:34. Job responds twice (40:3–5; 42:1–6), each time in a tone of voice we have not heard Job use since 1:21 and 2:9–10. This book invites you to reflect on the speeches of God and Job's responses in ways that are especially crucial for the interpretation of Job.

The prose epilogue (42:7–17) brings us back to the simple story with which Job began. This study invites you to reflect on how the "happy ending" of Job may relate to the issues raised in all the speeches, as well as in the prologue.

My hope is that this introduction and the outline in the table of contents may serve as a kind of road map for reading Job. Modern readers are often frustrated when they read Job straight through, from beginning to end. This is partly because the extended arguments between Job and his friends begin to sound repetitious. Worse still, it often seems that Job and his friends are simply talking past each other rather than debating issues the other has raised. (Modern "discussions" often suffer from the same ailment.) This study illustrates from the speeches of Eliphaz how useful it can be to follow one argument through from beginning to end. We do this by reading chapters 4—5, 15, and 22 without interruption, as a comprehensive statement of Eliphaz's argument against Job. This will be useful when we come to the speeches of Bildad, Zophar, and Elihu, to see whether they contribute anything fresh to the case against Job.

THE NAMES OF GOD IN JOB

The most distinctive name for God in the Hebrew Bible is what is sometimes called the "tetragrammaton" (four-letter word), after its four consonants: YHWH. It is this name, according to Exodus 3:13–16, that was revealed to Israel through Moses as the personal name by which Israel was to know "the God of your ancestors, the God of Abraham, the God of Isaac, and the God of Jacob" (Exod. 3:15–16). Like no other appellation for God, then, YHWH denotes God as the one who is known to Israel through its memory of a unique story that began with Abraham and Sarah, continued throughout the biblical period, and still presses forward toward its conclusion. Like no other designation for God, YHWH is the name that demands Israel's total respect and awe, to the point that it became literally "ineffable" within the community of faith, not to be spoken aloud even in the public reading of the sacred text. To ensure this respect, the curators of the Hebrew Bible retained the consonants YHWH but supplied the name with vowel pointings indicating a quite different word, *adonai* (meaning "lord"), which was to be spoken aloud in its place. Only unknowing or uncaring Christian translators of the Hebrew text attempted to combine the consonants of YHWH with the vowel pointing of *adonai* to produce the curious and quite inaccurate hybrid "Jehovah." While there is a scholarly consensus that the appropriate vocalization of YHWH is "Yahweh," the NRSV has chosen (wisely, I think) to retain something of the ancient respect for the divine name by translating YHWH as "LORD" (= *adonai*). Since *adonai*/lord is commonly used in the Hebrew text as a title in its own right, the NRSV renders the word LORD, in capital and small capital letters, when it is used as a substitute for YHWH.

Armed with this clue, ordinary readers of Job in the NRSV can detect instances where the uniquely Israelite name for God occurs in Job. The results of such a study are surprising. YHWH occurs twenty-four times in the prologue (1:1–2:13) and the epilogue (42:7–17) of Job, whereas only five or six occurrences of this divine name appear in the rest of the book: in the introductions to God's speeches "out of the whirlwind" in 38:1, 40:1, and 40:6; in the accounts of Job's response in 40:3 and 42:6; and in what may be an altered text in 12:9. With the possible exception of 12:9, the name YHWH never appears in the great series of poems that stretches from 3:1 to 37:34. "Generic" names for God (that is, appellations widely known in other cultures or names that have no special rootage in Israel's story with God) dominate the vast bulk of the book of Job (*Elohim, Eloah, El Elyon, El Shaddai*).

This strange state of affairs has fueled the notion that the book of Job was not originally an Israelite work at all, that it was "appropriated" for Israel's faith by the authors of the present prologue and epilogue, who inserted YHWH into the text at the points indicated above. Others have argued that Job is indeed a product of Israel's own wisdom traditions, granted that literature of this sort is characteristically "international," that is, closely related to similar traditions well documented in other cultures. On that reading, the overwhelming preponderance of "generic" names for God in Job can be understood as a stylistic matter, deliberately casting the poems of Job in the context of universal questions about divine and human righteousness. These alternative theories represent only the tip of a scholarly iceberg of research into this and other riddles that make the book of Job so endlessly fascinating from a purely academic standpoint.

For our purposes it is important to note that none of the research into the names of God in Job has proven convincing enough to affect the interpretation of the book in significant ways—not for the biblical faith communities. For Jews and Christians, the concentration of references to YHWH at the beginning and end of Job makes it quite impossible to separate what is said of God in this shocking book from the God we worship and serve as our contemporary. From the perspective of my own theological tradition, this does not mean that every sentence in Job is to be taken as a direct revelation of who God is and how God deals with people. Like all scripture, in my view, Job is to be read as a very human witness to what is going on in the story between God and the world. No word of scripture, however glorious, can possibly contain the fullness of God's truth. Yet in my view God is able, even through the human words of scripture, to disclose to the community of faith everything we really need to know about who God is, about who we are in relation to God and to one another, about what on earth God is up to, about what God wants from us, and about what we may expect from God. It is in the lively interchange between the witness borne to God in scripture and our own very real human circumstances that faith is born and the quest for contemporary understanding and faithfulness takes place. If I find anything in Job especially off-putting, or even appalling, then this is a matter I must take up with YHWH, not with any human court of opinion, whether literary or philosophical.

I draw a second implication from the identification of YHWH as the God with whom Job has to deal. Since YHWH, more than any other appellation, names God as the chief actor in the entire biblical story, biblical faith communities have no option except to put what we hear of God in Job in direct conversation with what we hear of God from the whole of scripture. No two parts of scripture ever bear witness to God in precisely the same way—compare Genesis and the Psalms, Leviticus and the Song of Solomon, the Gospel of Mark and the book of Revelation. According to an ancient rule, scripture is always to be interpreted in the light of scripture. It is only when we remember YHWH as the God of Abraham and Sarah, of Moses and Zipporah, of David and Bathsheba, of Isaiah and Jeremiah, and of Ezra and Mark and Paul that we can hear the unique testimony borne to YHWH in the book of Job in its clearest meaning for contemporary faith.

Literary scholarship warns us against making fanciful connections between texts that are quite simply unrelated, whether literarily or conceptually. Faith communities need to listen carefully to this warning, lest we impose on scripture a theological uniformity it does not possess. We have not heard Job's witness to YHWH faithfully unless we have heard it in all its uniqueness, in all its striking difference from other biblical witnesses. Yet at the point where contemporary faith must think, and decide, and act, there can be no artificial separation between what is known of God from one text and what is known from another. It is at this level, where faith decisions must be made on the basis of the best we know of YHWH our contemporary, that the whole witness of scripture must be brought to bear on our understanding of Job.

The upshot of all this for this book is that wherever the word *God* appears, it is not intended as a generic term for "the deity" by any conventional understanding of the word. Rather, I have opted to let the word *God* stand for all the names for God that appear in Job, without distinction. The reader should know, however, that my own working definition of the word *God* is YHWH, that is, the God who is uniquely attested as the chief actor in the whole biblical story, from Genesis to Revelation; the God I am called by faith to worship and serve. As Job 42:7–8 indicates, it is altogether possible to be dead certain about one's religious convictions and nevertheless fail to speak "what is right" about God. It is the glory and the terror of biblical faith that God alone is the ultimate judge of whether or not our witness to God is faithful. It is in that spirit, in reliance on the grace of God, that this interpretation of Job is offered.

"MY SERVANT JOB"

The Hebrew word for servant or slave is as commonplace in that language as it is in English. In each language its meaning may range from the menial (a farmer's goatherd) to a high public official (a king's prime minister). In either case, the servant is one whose duty it is to carry out the will of the master.

The references to "my servant Job" in 1:8; 2:3; and 42:7–8, however, belong to a fascinating set of texts in which God identifies a specific person as "my servant" in direct discourse:

Abraham (Gen. 26:24)
Moses (Num. 12:7–8; Josh. 1:2–7; 2 Kings 21:8)
Caleb (Num. 14:24)
David (2 Sam. 3:18; Psalm 89:3, 20; Isa. 37:35)
Isaiah (Isa. 20:3)

Eliakim (Isa. 22:20)
Nebuchadrezzar (Jer. 25:9; 27:6; 43:10)
Zerubbabel/The Branch (Hag. 2:23; Zech. 3:8)

In every case, the individual is singled out and commissioned by God to carry out the divine will, in varying ways (including Nebuchadrezzar, a worshiper of the Babylonian god Marduk, who would have been astonished to learn he was a "servant" to the God of Israel; compare Isa. 45:1–6).

In addition, Israel (sometimes personified as Jacob) is spoken of by God as "my servant" in the same way: as a people God has commissioned to embody and carry out God's intention for human life (see Isa. 41:8–9; 44:1–3; Jer. 30:10; Ezek. 28:25).

Chapters 40—55 of Isaiah (sometimes called Second Isaiah) contain a remarkable concentration of instances when God speaks of "my servant" (eighteen times). Five of these references occur in the so-called Suffering Servant Songs of Isaiah 42:1–4; 49:1–6; 50:4–9; 52:13–53:12. In 49:3, this Servant is identified as Israel, although 49:6 indicates that the Servant has a mission to perform on behalf of Jacob/Israel.

A whole library of books and articles have been written, by Jews and Christians alike, trying to shed light on who this Suffering Servant is and how his mission is to be understood. Without getting into that enormously complex discussion, ordinary readers of Job should be aware of eight striking similarities that link "my servant Job" with the Suffering Servant of Second Isaiah:

1. In Isaiah 42:1, the Servant is described as one "in whom [God's] soul delights"; see Job 1:8.
2. In Isaiah 42:2–4, the Servant, though vulnerable (42:4a), is set an apparently overwhelming task; see Job 1:8–11; 2:4–6.
3. In Isaiah 49:4, the Servant encounters despair yet "persists in his integrity" toward God; see Job 2:3 and the many texts in Job that alternate between despair and a last-ditch confidence that God will yet vindicate Job.
4. In Isaiah 50:6, the Servant undergoes extreme humiliation and rejection from others; Job 30 summarizes the many instances in which Job laments such treatment.
5. Isaiah 52:14b and 53:3 suggest that the Servant is disfigured with suffering and sorrow "beyond human semblance," so that he is unrecognizable; see Job 2:12–13.
6. According to Isaiah 53:3–5, people turn away from the Servant and

reject him on religious grounds: He has been "struck down" and "afflicted" by God as "punishment" for his own "transgressions" and "iniquities"; Job's friends argue this against him repeatedly, perhaps most sharply in Job 22:5–11.

7. According to Isaiah 53:4–6, 8b, and 9b, the "great surprise" is that the Servant was innocent all along, and those who had judged him guilty are exposed in his presence as the ones whom God has judged guilty; see Job 42:7–8.

8. According to Isaiah 53:4–12, the innocent suffering of the Servant is somehow borne for the sake of the guilty, climaxing in intercession on their behalf; see Job 42:8–10.

A noted critical scholar of the 1930s and 1940s argued on different grounds (mostly linguistic and stylistic) that Isaiah 40—55 and Job were closely related, and that the author of Isaiah 40—55 borrowed language and stylistic elements from Job (Pfeiffer, *Introduction to the Old Testament*, 467–69). While this opinion was neither widely shared nor much discussed by later critical scholars, Robert H. Pfeiffer's evidence suggests that a comparison of Job with the Servant Songs of Second Isaiah is not altogether far-fetched.

It would be a mistake, in my view, to suppose that Job and the Servant Songs are merely saying the same thing. There are significant differences between them, and each bears witness to the God of Israel in its own distinctive way. For the purposes of this study, I propose only that there are profound resonances between the two, and that readers may be stimulated by putting these two magnificent sets of scripture in conversation with each other. Each illuminates the other.

1. The Prologue
Job 1:1–2:13

Job 1:1–5

1:1 **There was once a man in the land of Uz whose name was Job. That man was blameless and upright, one who feared God and turned away from evil.** [2] **There were born to him seven sons and three daughters.** [3] **He had seven thousand sheep, three thousand camels, five hundred yoke of oxen, five hundred donkeys, and very many servants; so that this man was the greatest of all the people of the east.** [4] **His sons used to go and hold feasts in one another's houses in turn; and they would send and invite their three sisters to eat and drink with them.** [5] **And when the feast days had run their course, Job would send and sanctify them, and he would rise early in the morning and offer burnt offerings according to the number of them all; for Job said, "It may be that my children have sinned, and cursed God in their hearts." This is what Job always did.**

The function of these verses is to present Job as a uniquely righteous and blessed human being. According to the conventional view presented in the book of Proverbs, such righteousness and blessedness also mark Job as exceptionally wise. Wisdom in the ways of the world produces prosperity; wisdom in the ways of God evokes God's blessing. This may be implied in the judgment that Job was "the greatest of all the people of the east," who, according to 1 Kings 4:30, were renowned for their wisdom.

Questions abound about these five verses. Are we to overhear the Hebrew word *enemy* or *adversary* in Job's name, which is made up of the same consonants (see Job 13:24)? Is the "land of Uz" to be identified with ancient Edom (see Lam. 4:21)? Does Ezekiel 14:14, 20 suggest that we are to think of Job as a figure who, like Noah, lived in the most ancient imaginable past (compare Job 1:1 with Gen. 6:9)? Is there special significance in the fact that Job possessed herds of sheep, camels, and asses (usually associated with nomadic and seminomadic lifestyles) as well as oxen (usually associated with settled farm life)?

What was the occasion of the regular feasts thrown by each of Job's sons in turn, to which the brothers and sisters were all invited? What was the religious basis for Job's rituals of purification and burnt offerings, apparently designed to ward off the evil consequences of any affront to God that may have occurred during the festivities?

We simply have no definitive answers for questions of this kind, or for many other questions of language and interpretation that crop up regularly in the study of the book of Job. We may take note of them from time to time, but the goal of this book is to concentrate on what is most clearly understandable in Job, rather than on unresolved scholarly questions.

On any reading of Job 1:1–5, we are invited to imagine an absolutely extraordinary human being, one who lives a flawless life before God; one who enjoys a completely blessed existence (the recurring numbers seven and three in verses 2 and 3 are almost surely to signal completeness, as they often do elsewhere in the Bible); and one whose concern for a right relation to God extends beyond his own to embrace that of his family as well. Yet we cannot escape the note of tension that intrudes in verse 5. Are we being warned that none of this blessing and prosperity is to be taken for granted, that all of it ultimately hinges on the favor of God?

Job 1:6–12

1:6 **One day the heavenly beings came to present themselves before the LORD, and Satan also came among them. 7 The LORD said to Satan, "Where have you come from?" Satan answered the LORD, "From going to and fro on the earth, and from walking up and down on it." 8 The LORD said to Satan, "Have you considered my servant Job? There is no one like him on the earth, a blameless and upright man who fears God and turns away from evil." 9 Then Satan answered the LORD, "Does Job fear God for nothing? 10 Have you not put a fence around him and his house and all that he has, on every side? You have blessed the work of his hands, and his possessions have increased in the land. 11 But stretch out your hand now, and touch all that he has, and he will curse you to your face." 12 The LORD said to Satan, "Very well, all that he has is in your power; only do not stretch out your hand against him!" So Satan went out from the presence of the LORD.**

If it is difficult to imagine a human being as righteous, wise, and wealthy as Job, what comes next stretches human imagination to the breaking point. Now we are invited to imagine what it might be like to be present in the very council chamber of God, to overhear conversations between God and one of the special members of God's royal assembly, to hear decisions being taken that have enormous consequences for people on earth.

Human language is clearly inadequate to describe the decision-making process of God. Yet the Bible regularly uses very human, even crude language to point to the unimaginable reality of God. It is an article of faith, in my theological tradition, to believe that God is able to use our wholly inadequate human language to bear faithful witness to God's own truth. As John Calvin once suggested, God talks "baby talk" to us in scripture, since it is the only talk we can possibly understand. The true indicator that we have heard and understood rightly is to be found not in theological statements but in faithful praise and faithful service to God.

The human language in which Job 1:6–12 is cast is not difficult to trace. People in the ancient Near East had a readily available human model for an awesome decision-making process, one that could have serious consequences for ordinary people living far away from the center of power. It was the royal court of an imperial despot who exercised absolute power over the realm. While few people ever saw the imperial court in action, there were those who could describe its grandeur and its power: the throne, the emperor, the ranks of officials and counselors who were assembled at the emperor's command. Agents of the emperor might offer advice, make reports on the state of the realm, suggest alternative plans, perhaps even register points of disagreement (*very* carefully). But the final decision belonged to the sovereign, and once made, it was put into action with the awesome power at the empire's disposal.

As a democrat, I find any such political system reprehensible. The question for me, then, as I read Job 1:6–12, is whether I can accept the ancient author's invitation to see through this terribly flawed human imagery to the unimaginable wonder of God's own decision making. (Note how 1 Kings 22:19–23 and Isaiah 6 place a very similar demand on the imagination. It has been suggested, rightly I think, that Isaiah 40:1–11, Jeremiah 23:18, Zechariah 3, and perhaps even Genesis 1:26, among other biblical texts, owe at least something to this vision of the divine council chamber.)

Two dangers confront us in this extreme exercise of the imagination. One is that we will take this scene as a direct revelation of who God is and how God acts toward human beings. If we do this, then we must conclude that God is like an ancient Near Eastern tyrant inflated to cosmic proportions. On biblical grounds, I am forced to reject any such notion of God out of hand.

The other danger, of course, is that we will dismiss Job 1:6–12 as the outmoded relic of an ancient culture, as if it had nothing to do with the God who confronts us in the pages of the Bible. Yet we have already noted that biblical faith will not let us dismiss Job's God so cheaply.

In what follows I attempt to listen to Job 1:6–12 in a third way, without taking it literally but also without patronizing it as beneath our theological dignity.

On the analogy of an ancient imperial court, the "sons of God" in verse 6 (translated "heavenly beings" in the NRSV) correspond generally to the kinds of people entitled by rank or quality to stand in attendance on the emperor. The word *God* in this phrase is *Elohim*, which is frequently used in the Bible as a designation for the God of Israel. The Bible also occasionally uses *Elohim* in the plural sense, referring to beings that are somehow quite different from God but also distinct from ordinary human beings (see Gen. 6:1–4; Psalms 8:5; 82:1, 6). The term *sons of* in the Bible does not always refer to lineal descendants. It may also refer to the type or category to which these "sons" belong. "The sons [or 'children'] of Israel," when it refers to the people as a whole, is a familiar biblical example of this usage. The Hebrew text of Job 1:3 offers a parallel example: The phrase "people of the east" is literally "sons of the East," that is, "Easterners," those who belong to this category. The attendants of God in the divine council, then, are best understood as beings of the "*Elohim* category"—neither equal to God nor offspring of God and yet of a different order from human beings.

Texts such as Psalm 89:1–7, Deuteronomy 32:8 (in the earliest Greek translation), Isaiah 6:2–7, and Psalm 82 suggest that a much more vivid lore than the Bible sets forth once existed about these *Elohim* types. The wonder is that the resolute monotheism of those who preserved the ancient Hebrew texts did not lead them to eradicate all references to "heavenly beings" at God's side, even in the extravagant language of praise. At best, Judaism and Christianity came to understand such heavenly beings as "angels," "ministering spirits" whose sole dignity it is to reflect God's glory and stand in God's service. It may be appropriate that neither Judaism nor Christianity has ever succeeded in working out a satisfactory "doctrine" of angels. This would require us to pay inordinate attention to the angels in their own right (their origins, their qualities, their rank, their functions). To do so would do no honor to the angels, since their vocation is to glorify and serve God alone.

For people of faith, however, the most disturbing aspect of this heavenly council scene in Job is the presence of Satan and God's interaction with him. Is Satan the evil one, the supernatural embodiment of all antigodly power, God's ultimate enemy? Is God somehow in league with Satan as they agree to subject Job to hideous and wholly undeserved suffering? If so, who is the greater villain, God or Satan?

I can still remember the shock of this question when I first read Job as a committed member of the Christian church. I can also remember the joyous discovery, at the beginning of my formal Hebrew studies, that Job's Satan is by no means to be understood as that archenemy of God identified in the New Testament as "Satan," "the devil," "the evil one," "the father of lies," "that old dragon," and so forth. For one thing, the Hebrew text of Job places a definite article (*ha-*) before the word *satan* (Hebrew, *hassatan*), indicating that Satan is not a proper name of a known individual. Rather, *hassatan* describes a function or an office. *Satan* appears in the Hebrew Bible as both a verb and a noun, and this allows us to determine with some precision what kind of function or office Job's *hassatan* might have in God's heavenly court. The range of meanings associated with the word *satan* in Hebrew includes "accusing," "withstanding," "playing the adversary," "denouncing."

The analogy of an ancient imperial court strongly suggests what kind of special office *hassatan* may have had among the *Elohim* types (NRSV "heavenly beings") who attend on God when the divine council is in session. Every emperor in the ancient world required agents who moved throughout the empire looking for signs of treason or malfeasance that required the emperor's attention. The bizarre vision related in Zechariah 6:1–7 (see also 4:2, 10b) suggests something like this kind of activity.

If *hassatan* in the prologue of Job is understood to be this kind of functionary, it makes sense that he should be present among the heavenly beings on council day. God's initial question to *hassatan* is entirely appropriate to the special function of this official: "Where have you come from [that is, on your journeys in my behalf]?" *Hassatan*'s reply indicates the diligence and the completeness of his investigation: "From going to and fro on the earth, and from walking up and down on it."

I find it both surprising and significant, however, that God does not wait to hear what the royal investigator/accuser has to say. Instead, God asks whether *hassatan* has had occasion to investigate God's "servant Job" (see the Introduction, pp. 9–11). Before the accuser can answer, God gives Job an astonishing accolade: "There is no one like him on the earth, a blameless and upright man who fears God and turns away from evil."

The Bible has few heroes without blemish, and accolades such as those paid to Noah (Gen. 6:9), Moses (Num. 12:6–8; Deut. 34:10–12), and the Servant of Isaiah 42:1 are extremely rare. But perhaps nowhere in scripture do we find a comprehensive endorsement of human life that matches what God here says of Job. The language may strike us as somewhat antiquated, but the inference is that nothing separates Job from the quality of human life God desires for us. As we shall see, it may be essential for our understanding of the entire book of Job not to forget or underestimate this unique accolade as God's first (and final) estimate of Job's character.

In that light, God's judgment about Job can be heard as a direct challenge to *hassatan*. With all his inquisitorial skills, has the professional accuser found anything in Job's life to refute God's judgment of the man?

Apparently *hassatan* has discovered no such evidence, but *hassatan* is a clever and conscientious prosecutor. There is one potential flaw in Job's admittedly spectacular faithfulness and integrity, one that has never been put to the test: the question of Job's motive for living the life approved by God.

We have already learned from Job 1:1–5 that Job's righteous life has been rewarded thus far with every conceivable blessing from God. When *hassatan* wonders out loud, "Does Job fear God for nothing?" all the extravagant things we have heard about Job (including God's own accolade) are suddenly tarnished with doubt. Maybe Job's deepest motive is no nobler than raw self-interest. Maybe he pretends at faithfulness and integrity only because he believes God's richest blessings are reserved only for those who act out this pious charade.

"Have you not put a [protective] fence around him and his house and all that he has, on every side?" asks *hassatan*. "You have blessed the work of his hands, and his possessions have increased in the land." Are God's motives being questioned here, as well as Job's? Has God blessed Job so richly in order to win such flawless devotion from a human being? It's worth a thought.

As we have said, *hassatan* is not Satan. Neither is the serpent in Genesis 3. (See verse 1; the serpent is only the most "crafty" among the animals God created.) Yet there is surely something "satanic" in the questions and assertions of each figure. Both call into question the intactness of a relationship between God and people that had appeared serene until now. The breaking of relationship, the shattering of trust between people and people, between people and God, not from inside but from outside these relationships, by a "third party"—may this not rightly be called "satanic"?

A strange twist on this theme occurs in Zechariah 3:1–5, where *hassatan* accuses Joshua, the high priest, who has returned from exile. Verses 2–5 suggest the content of this accusation: Joshua has been rendered "unclean," and therefore unfit to serve as high priest, because of the defilement of exile in Babylon. The angel of the Lord invokes the Lord's rebuke against *hassatan*, but apparently not because the accusation isn't true. What is amiss in *hassatan*'s accusation is that it reckons without God's intention to cleanse and restore Joshua, as a "brand plucked from the fire." The intactness of God's intended relationship with Joshua, beyond all past breaches of it, is therefore called into question in a "satanic" way by the otherwise true "accusation" of *hassatan*. (Does Peter's challenge to Jesus in Matthew 16:22, presumably made in the "best interests" of Jesus, share this satanic characteristic by calling into question the covenanted relationship between Jesus and God?)

In Job 1:11, *hassatan* proposes a means of testing Job's motives for maintaining his side of this outwardly flawless relationship with God: "But stretch out your hand now, and touch all that he has, and he will curse you to your face." Is this an experiment God can undertake in a "scientific" (that is, objective, neutral, unbiased) way, as a matter of curiosity? God's extravagant affirmation of Job in Job 1:8 suggests otherwise. Whatever is now to befall Job will happen to a human being in whom God delights, one whose life reflects God's own character as does no one else on earth. Are we to assume that it will cost God nothing to look on while Job is plunged into the depths of human wretchedness?

The only clue to God's possible reluctance about the proposed test comes in God's response to *hassatan* in verse 12: "Very well, all that he has is in *your* power; only do not stretch out *your* hand against him!" God here rejects *hassatan*'s proposal that God's power should be used directly against Job. This test was proposed by *hassatan*, not God. It is to be by the hand of *hassatan*, not by God's hand, that Job's suffering is to be inflicted. God's final word sets a protective limit beyond which *hassatan*'s assault on Job may not go.

This interchange with *hassatan* by no means exempts God from responsibility for what is about to happen to Job. By analogy with an ancient imperial court, *hassatan* is at most an emissary of God. Without any dignity or power in his own right, *hassatan* can act only within the framework of God's absolute authority. Yet the narrator of Job 1:6–12 has planted a fascinating suggestion in the reader's mind. Even though God is ultimately responsible for what is about to happen, Job's suffering will not reflect God's estimate of Job's worth (v. 8); nor will it reflect the kind of existence God desires for such a person (suggested in vv. 1–5?). If there is anything "right" about this "alien" test, it is God's astonishing confidence in a fragile human being, confidence that not even the worst imaginable and least comprehensible suffering can alter Job's inmost character. True, God is willing to risk everything Job has, without Job's knowledge or consent, to demonstrate that this confidence is well founded. But the narrator also allows us to ponder what *God* may be risking in this "alien" test of God's relationship with Job, at what exquisite cost to God this test takes place. In any case, it is clear that God's reputation, as well as Job's, hinges on the outcome. If Job should buckle under pressure, if Job should "curse God to God's face" as *hassatan* predicts he will, then both Job and God will have been proven false. What ancient emperor (to return to the analogy of the vision) would have staked his imperial reputation, in so utterly vulnerable a way, on the unaided performance of one of his subjects under the most extreme duress?

The question posed by Job 1:1–12, then, is not the one that usually comes to mind when people talk about Joblike suffering: namely, "Why do bad things happen to good people?" The question is rather: "Can there be a human being of such incorruptible integrity toward God and people that not even the worst imaginable experiences of life are capable of shattering it?" *Hassatan* is confident that, even for the best of us (and Job is surely presented as "the best" in Job 1:1–8), the ultimate motivation is "What's in it for me?" God's confidence is that Job's heart is not for sale at any price.

Agonized questions about why innocent people suffer are surely raised by Job in the course of the book. But I will keep coming back to this less familiar question of whether Job's integrity is corruptible as we read all the speeches of Job and his friends, as well as the chilling speeches of God. This may open the way to some fresh insights into the always unfinished and tentative interpretation of this mighty work.

JOB'S FIRST TEST AND ITS OUTCOME
Job 1:13–22

Job 1:13–19

> 1:13 **One day when his sons and daughters were eating and drinking wine in the eldest brother's house,** [14] **a messenger came to Job and said, "The oxen were plowing and the donkeys were feeding beside them,** [15] **and the Sabeans fell on them and carried them off, and killed the servants with the edge of the sword; I alone have escaped to tell you."** [16] **While he was still speaking, another came and said, "The fire of God fell from heaven and burned up the sheep and the servants, and consumed them; I alone have escaped to tell you."** [17] **While he was still speaking, another came and said, "The Chaldeans formed three columns, made a raid on the camels and carried them off, and killed the servants with the edge of the sword; I alone have escaped to tell you."** [18] **While he was still speaking, another came and said, "Your sons and daughters were eating and drinking wine in their eldest brother's house,** [19] **and suddenly a great wind came across the desert, struck the four corners of the house, and it fell on the young people, and they are dead; I alone have escaped to tell you."**

It is unnecessary to pause long over the details of Job 1:13–19. In four swift episodes we see what happens as a result of God's concession to *hassatan* in verse 12: "All that he has is in your power." Verse 13 allows us to wonder whether Job's worst fears for his children may have come true (see v. 5)—an ungodly prelude to the trip-hammer blows that destroy in one day all the blessings enumerated in verses 1–3. In any event, the narrator's intention is clear: If verses 1–3 confront us with an extreme caricature of human blessedness, verses 13–19 confront us with an extreme caricature of human loss. All the details conspire to set up the dramatic question posed by the conversation between God and *hassatan:* If such unparalleled loss befell a person of such unparalleled blessedness, what would become of his renowned faithfulness and integrity?

Job 1:20–22

1:20 **Then Job arose, tore his robe, shaved his head, and fell on the ground and worshiped.** 21 **He said, "Naked I came from my mother's womb, and naked shall I return there; the LORD gave, and the LORD has taken away; blessed be the name of the LORD."**
        22 **In all this Job did not sin or charge God with wrongdoing.**

The answer to the question posed above comes in verses 20–22, which may strike us as a third extreme caricature: unswerving affirmation of God, out of the depths, without asking, "What's in it for me?" Job never had any claim on God's blessings ("Naked I came from my mother's womb"), nor was it ever possible that he should retain them ("and naked shall I return there," that is, to "mother earth" or the grave). In that light, neither God's "giving" nor God's "taking away" can alter Job's trusting affirmation of God. Verse 22 comes as an explicit refutation of *hassatan*'s confident prediction in verse 11.

JOB'S SECOND TEST AND ITS OUTCOME
Job 2:1–10

Job 2:1–8

2:1 **One day the heavenly beings came to present themselves before the LORD, and Satan also came among them to present himself before the LORD.** 2 **The LORD said to Satan, "Where have you come from?" Satan answered the LORD, "From going to and fro on the earth, and from walking up and down on it."** 3 **The LORD said to Satan, "Have you considered my servant Job? There is no one like him on the earth, a blameless and upright man who fears**

God and turns away from evil. He still persists in his integrity, although you incited me against him, to destroy him for no reason." ⁴ Then Satan answered the LORD, "Skin for skin! All that people have they will give to save their lives. ⁵ But stretch out your hand now and touch his bone and his flesh, and he will curse you to your face." ⁶ The LORD said to Satan, "Very well, he is in your power; only spare his life."

⁷ So Satan went out from the presence of the LORD, and inflicted loathsome sores on Job from the sole of his foot to the crown of his head. ⁸ Job took a potsherd with which to scrape himself, and sat among the ashes.

Using almost the same words, the narrator now invites us to envision a second encounter between God and *hassatan* in the divine council chamber. As we might have anticipated, this is the occasion for God to say, "I told you so!" in at least a mildly gloating tone of voice: "He still persists in his integrity, although you incited me against him, to destroy him for no reason." (Note how the narrator here enshrouds God's responsibility for Job's suffering in another fold of ambiguity. Again, it is on the alien initiative of a "third party," not as a result of God's own attitude toward Job, that Job's testing has come.)

It comes as a well-designed shock to the reader to discover that *hassatan* still refuses to concede defeat. The crude phrase "Skin for skin!" is now thrown into God's face with an unmistakable tone of defiance. Again, I do not believe the story presents *hassatan* to us as the personal embodiment of all evil, but the "satanic" aspect of his accusations against Job here takes on an anti-godly dimension. The phrase "skin for skin" remains somewhat obscure (was it used in marketplace haggling to indicate something like "value given for value received" ?), but its meaning becomes clear enough in what follows. As long as Job's own physical well-being is intact, he has something worth bargaining for. Take that away, says *hassatan*, and the test will yield the predicted results. Once again, God acquiesces in the "satanic" plan; once again, God assigns its execution to *hassatan*; and once again, God sets a limit beyond which the test may not go: "Only spare his life."

One can argue (as Job does in chapter 3) that mere existence is no blessing, not for one who lives in a state of total wretchedness. But like the limit set by God in 1:12, this ultimate limit suggests that God is not willing to let Job's suffering have the last word about Job's superb life or about the mutual relationship between Job and God on which that life is based. When Job has passed this ultimate test, as God is confident he will, the way still lies open for a "blessed" relationship between them, one that can no longer be slandered as a conspiracy of mutual self-interest.

Job 2:9–10

2:9 Then his wife said to him, "Do you still persist in your integrity? Curse God, and die." 10 But he said to her, "You speak as any foolish woman would speak. Shall we receive the good at the hand of God, and not receive the bad?" In all this Job did not sin with his lips.

Once again, Job vindicates both his own selfless integrity and God's confidence in him. One can think that Job's wife is motivated by sheer compassion when she urges him to "curse God and die." Suicide in the modern sense never emerges as an option in Job, but the deliberate and public cursing of God was apparently understood to be a sure means of summoning death. If Job's wife is pleading with Job to end it all, even for compassionate reasons, she is nevertheless planting in Job's mind a delicious seduction to take the course predicted by *hassatan:* When relationship with God no longer pays off, *end it!*

Job rejects this exquisite temptation as foolish: Relationship with God must not and cannot hinge on whether one receives good things or bad things in the course of God's providence (v. 10). Once again, the narrator drives home the point that Job has passed the test to perfection. Job has refused to rebel against God by thought, deed, or word as a result of this wholly undeserved and incomprehensible suffering. Everything else in Job's world has been altered beyond recognition, but his "integrity" (that is, his heart toward God and people) remains constant.

On hearing the story for the first time, the listener is ready now for a third scene in the heavenly council chamber. Surely, now *hassatan* must concede defeat. Surely, now God may celebrate Job's breathtaking vindication of God's own estimate of his character. And surely, now it is time to end the deadly charade of Job's suffering, to let Job hear the good news that, through it all, God had always taken Job's side and trusted him to win through.

Instead, the story takes a wholly unexpected turn. For reasons we cannot fathom Job's suffering continues, as if no victory had been won, as if *hassatan* had lost a skirmish or two in the divine council but the war is still on. The narrator apparently is not content to leave us with so simple and idyllic a picture of Job the innocent sufferer, whose legendary patience is "an example for us all." If there ever was a widespread folktale that carried such a moral, the narrator of Job now demands that we plunge beneath its surface—that we face the titanic human struggles, in real life, by which alone such human integrity might be accomplished.

JOB AND HIS FRIENDS
Job 2:11–13

Job 2:11–13

> 2:11 **Now when Job's three friends heard of all these troubles that had come upon him, each of them set out from his home—Eliphaz the Temanite, Bildad the Shuhite, and Zophar the Naamathite. They met together to go and console and comfort him.** [12] **When they saw him from a distance, they did not recognize him, and they raised their voices and wept aloud; they tore their robes and threw dust in the air upon their heads.** [13] **They sat with him on the ground seven days and seven nights, and no one spoke a word to him, for they saw that his suffering was very great.**

To delve beneath the surface of the moral tale, the narrator leads us not into a third heavenly council scene but into a "council chamber on earth," where Job's decision-making process is attended by three very human friends. (I am indebted to Professor Norman G. Habel's commentary on Job in the Westminster Press Old Testament Library series for this provocative insight.) For the next thirty-six chapters, we hear nothing but human voices ringing the changes on the reality of human suffering and the reality of God, and passionate human thoughts about how these realities relate to each other.

Job's three friends do not turn out well as the story unfolds, but at the beginning they are models of compassion. Each hears independently about Job's distress, and each cares enough to drop other affairs and hasten to his side. Like God's servant in Isaiah 52:14, Job is so ravaged by suffering that he is "marred . . . beyond human semblance," so that his friends cannot recognize in him the Job they had known before. Rather than turning away from this horror, however, they join Job in the signs of ritual mourning (compare Job 1:20 and Job 2:12), indicating that Job's distress is their distress, to be lamented before God. The high-water mark of their compassion comes during these seven days when they found grace just to *be* there with Job—and to keep their mouths *shut*, "for they saw that his suffering was very great." Consoling words rarely improve on the silent comfort of a friend's presence. In the case of Job's friends, the words destroy the comfort altogether, especially when they "plead the case for God," as Job puts it in 13:8.

2. The First Round of Discourses between Job and His Friends
Job 3—11

JOB'S CRY OF PAIN
Job 3

Job 3

3:1 After this Job opened his mouth and cursed the day of his birth. ² Job said:

> ³ "Let the day perish in which I was born,
>   and the night that said,
>   'A man-child is conceived.'
> ⁴ Let that day be darkness!
>   May God above not seek it,
>   or light shine on it.
> ⁵ Let gloom and deep darkness claim it.
>   Let clouds settle upon it;
>   let the blackness of the day terrify it.
> ⁶ That night—let thick darkness seize it!
>   let it not rejoice among the days of the year;
>   let it not come into the number of the months.
> ⁷ Yes, let that night be barren;
>   let no joyful cry be heard in it.
> ⁸ Let those curse it who curse the Sea,
>   those who are skilled to rouse up Leviathan.
> ⁹ Let the stars of its dawn be dark;
>   let it hope for light, but have none;
>   may it not see the eyelids of the morning—
> ¹⁰ because it did not shut the doors of my mother's womb,
>   and hide trouble from my eyes.
>
> ¹¹ "Why did I not die at birth,
>   come forth from the womb and expire?
> ¹² Why were there knees to receive me,

or breasts for me to suck?
13 Now I would be lying down and quiet;
    I would be asleep; then I would be at rest
14 with kings and counselors of the earth
    who rebuild ruins for themselves,
15 or with princes who have gold,
    who fill their houses with silver.
16 Or why was I not buried like a stillborn child,
    like an infant that never sees the light?
17 There the wicked cease from troubling,
    and there the weary are at rest.
18 There the prisoners are at ease together;
    they do not hear the voice of the taskmaster.
19 The small and the great are there,
    and the slaves are free from their masters.

20 "Why is light given to one in misery,
    and life to the bitter in soul,
21 who long for death, but it does not come,
    and dig for it more than for hidden treasures;
22 who rejoice exceedingly,
    and are glad when they find the grave?
23 Why is light given to one who cannot see the way,
    whom God has fenced in?
24 For my sighing comes like my bread,
    and my groanings are poured out like water.
25 Truly the thing that I fear comes upon me,
    and what I dread befalls me.
26 I am not at ease, nor am I quiet;
    I have no rest; but trouble comes."

Nothing in chapters 1 and 2 prepares us for Job's "primal scream" in chapter 3. It begins with a mighty curse against the day of Job's birth (Job 3:1–10). Both the form and the language of this curse are exceptionally difficult for modern readers to grasp, although the point is clear enough: Job's pain is so intolerable that he cries out against the very fact that he exists at all. As we have noted, suicide never appears as an option in the book of Job, but this curse brings us to the very brink. Not being at all is here declared preferable to existing in Job's present wretchedness. Job's pain is total.

Cursing one's birthday would not occur to contemporary people as the way to express suffering of this magnitude. Yet we should not let this strangeness blind us to two powerful claims the curse makes on our imaginations. First, we are challenged to remember the response *hassatan* predicted when Job's unprecedented blessings are suddenly exchanged for unprecedented wretchedness. Job does not "curse you [God] to your face," but he comes to the very brink. Does this undercut Job's pious reactions described in 1:20–22 and 2:10, or does it take us beneath the surface to disclose the exquisite cost such breathtaking faithfulness demands? In either case, we are being asked to face the reality of Job's suffering at utter depth: *Almost*, Job has been brought to the point of cursing God and choosing death.

The second claim the curse places on our imagination is to sense something of the horror ancient people would have registered on hearing this mighty curse. The words of such a curse were understood to have a supranatural power in their own right. Once uttered they could not be recalled, and they set powerful forces in motion, forces that lay beyond all human control. At various points in this passage (most obviously in v. 8), scholars have traced references to tales of monsters who represented to ancient minds chaotic powers that would threaten the created order. At the very least, Job's outcry may generate in our minds the question of whether human suffering of this intensity does not threaten the very order of the universe. Job seems to think it does, and that's scary.

At verse 11, Job's outcry shifts from rage to lament. The "Why?" questions in verses 11–23 remind us of several Psalms (see, e.g., Psalms 10:1; 22:1–21; 44:20–26), but with a difference. In the Psalm texts, the "Why?" question is both passionate and intimate, addressed directly to God. In Job 3:11–26, by contrast, there is no indication that the questions are addressed to anyone in particular. (Note that God is spoken of in the third person in verse 23.) The matter of Job's guilt or innocence (that is, whether his suffering is deserved or undeserved) is also missing here. Later on, Job will indeed address God directly and maintain his innocence of any crime deserving such "punishment"—but not now. This cry of pain expresses only that Job's suffering is both intolerable (vv. 1–10) and incomprehensible (vv. 11–26). In different ways, the curse and the lament affirm that it would be better not to have lived at all than to live in the depths of this distress. Chapter 3 is not an "argument," whether theological or philosophical, but an elemental cry of pain. Yet the fleeting references to God in verses 4 and 23 inevitably pose the question of how God relates to all this—not just to Job's suffering but to all who share Joblike misery. (Note how verses 20–23 reach out to include all such others.)

THE ENTIRE CASE OF ELIPHAZ AGAINST JOB
Job 4—5, 15, and 22

It is the function of Eliphaz, Bildad, Zophar, and Elihu in the book of Job to challenge Job's right to cry out as he does in the face of his suffering. In the case of these "friends," as in the case of Job, it is necessary to remember that we know something they don't. Having eavesdropped on the deliberations between God and *hassatan* in the heavenly council chamber, we know that Job enjoys God's unequaled approbation. We also know that there is something alien to God in this ungodly "test" to which Job is being put. Job and his friends must therefore wrestle in the dark with Job's suffering and the questions it raises, using only the fragile resources of mind and heart available to each one. This gives the reader a double perspective on all the speeches that follow. We need to listen to each speech first of all in its own right, but then ask how it sounds from the perspective of the heavenly council.

Eliphaz is the first to respond to Job's outcry in chapter 3. For the purposes of this study, I consider all three speeches of Eliphaz together, without interruption (chaps. 4—5, 15, and 22). His case against Job is remarkably comprehensive, including most, if not all, of the themes that recur in the speeches of Bildad, Zophar, and Elihu. Taken together, these discourses set out to instruct Job in the mysterious but just ways of God's providence in human affairs and to warn him of the consequences of calling God's justice into question. By giving Eliphaz a sympathetic hearing at the outset, we may be able to judge more clearly what Job is up against as he tries to make the case for his integrity.

Eliphaz's First Speech
(Job 4—5)

Job 4

4:1 **Then Eliphaz the Temanite answered:**
    2 **"If one ventures a word with you, will you be offended?**
       But who can keep from speaking?
    3 **See, you have instructed many;**
       you have strengthened the weak hands.
    4 **Your words have supported those who were stumbling,**
       and you have made firm the feeble knees.
    5 **But now it has come to you, and you are impatient;**
       it touches you, and you are dismayed.
    6 **Is not your fear of God your confidence,**
       and the integrity of your ways your hope?

7 "Think now, who that was innocent ever perished?
   Or where were the upright cut off?
8 As I have seen, those who plow iniquity
   and sow trouble reap the same.
9 By the breath of God they perish,
   and by the blast of his anger they are consumed.
10 The roar of the lion, the voice of the fierce lion,
   and the teeth of the young lions are broken.
11 The strong lion perishes for lack of prey,
   and the whelps of the lioness are scattered.

12 "Now a word came stealing to me,
   my ear received the whisper of it.
13 Amid thoughts from visions of the night,
   when deep sleep falls on mortals,
14 dread came upon me, and trembling,
   which made all my bones shake.
15 A spirit glided past my face;
   the hair of my flesh bristled.
16 It stood still,
   but I could not discern its appearance.
   A form was before my eyes;
   there was silence, then I heard a voice:
17 'Can mortals be righteous before God?
   Can human beings be pure before their Maker?
18 Even in his servants he puts no trust,
   and his angels he charges with error;
19 how much more those who live in houses of clay,
   whose foundation is in the dust,
   who are crushed like a moth.
20 Between morning and evening they are destroyed;
   they perish forever without any regarding it.
21 Their tent-cord is plucked up within them,
   and they die devoid of wisdom.'

The beginning of Eliphaz's response to Job reflects the quality of pastoral concern already evident in the compassionate silence reported in 2:13. Eliphaz does not wish to "offend" Job, but the outcry of chapter 3 must not be allowed to go unanswered (4:2). Job needs to be reminded of the serene days when Job's renowned goodness included exemplary words and deeds designed to comfort and strengthen others (4:3–4; is 1:4–5 to be understood as an example of such solicitude?). The implication is that Job has no right to be "impatient" or dismayed now that he finds himself in need of strengthening from others (v. 5).

If we recall the deliberations in the heavenly council, 4:6 is loaded with double meaning: "Is not your fear of God your confidence, and the integrity of your ways your hope?" It becomes increasingly clear in the speeches of Eliphaz what is meant by the "fear of God" and the "integrity of your ways": affirmation of God's ultimate justice in punishing the wicked and rewarding the righteous, together with unswerving commitment to the righteous life, no matter what happens. On that basis, Job's outcry in chapter 3 strikes Eliphaz as coming dangerously near a rejection of the "fear of the Lord." Implicitly, at least, Job's cry of pain affirms that something is terribly wrong about the descent into wretchedness that he has experienced. Job has conceded God's power in these events, in passing (3:23), but not God's justice or God's compassion. For Eliphaz, there can be no integrity of one's ways that does not affirm God's sovereign justice in all that occurs. From the perspective of the heavenly council, however, the reader knows that God and *hassatan* have set Job precisely this test: Can Job maintain the integrity of his ways (see 2:3) in the contrived absence of any external signs of God's approbation, any tokens of God's justice and compassion?

When Eliphaz asks Job, "Who that was innocent ever perished, or where were the upright cut off?" the question about Job's integrity is slyly insinuated. Eliphaz is not ready to accuse Job directly, but he does challenge him to place his suffering in the context of widespread experience that people get what they deserve in life (Job 4:7–11; even the fiercest predators ultimately become God's prey). Later on, Eliphaz has occasion to deal with what appear to be exceptions to the rule.

The key to Eliphaz's insights into these matters is not derived from ordinary experience, however. In 4:12–21 he describes a literally "hair-raising" experience (v. 15) in which a fundamental truth about all human life was conveyed to him by an other-than-human "voice" (v. 16) while he was in the grip of an unexpected and eerie, trancelike state. (The word for "deep sleep" in Hebrew is the same one used to describe Abraham's visionary trance in Genesis 15:12.) Eliphaz is careful not to claim that he has seen or heard God directly, but he leaves no doubt that what he has experienced is nothing less than God's own truth, a divine revelation.

What the voice actually says to Eliphaz may strike us as ridiculously anticlimactic. We hardly require a visionary experience to arrive at the conclusion that "nobody's perfect"! But we should not overlook the weight this "revealed doctrine" has for Eliphaz's case against Job. If it is true that no human being, not even the best of us, can claim to be "righteous" or "pure" before God, then innocent suffering is ruled out by definition. As this doctrine is spelled out in verses 18–21, it has nothing in common with traditional Christian notions of "original sin" or "total depravity." No willful act of rebellion against God has placed us in this state of chronic imperfection. Rather, it is our fragile status as God's creatures that makes us incapable by nature of approximating the righteousness and purity that belong only to God. *None* of God's creatures, not even those who stand in attendance in the divine council, shares God's perfection. If God "charges [them] with error . . . how much more those who live in houses of clay"— that is, we fragile earthlings who live so briefly and die "devoid of wisdom"?

As we shall see, Eliphaz has strong convictions about the *relative* righteousness that we mortals can achieve and for which we are accountable to God. But this doctrine of universal human fallibility sets an absolute limit to any human claim to innocence. The implication for Job is that neither he nor any other human being has any right to cry out, as Job has in chapter 3, no matter how severe the distress may be. Not even a member of God's heavenly court can be expected to hear and vindicate Job's protest, since even such "holy ones" are subject to error (5:1; see 4:18).

We readers know, of course (as Job and Eliphaz do not), that in this particular case God has not "charged [Job] with error." What has happened to Job is not a punishment for any fault God has discovered in Job (1:8; 2:3). It is God's confidence in Job's integrity, not God's disdain for Job's mortal fallibility, that has provoked God to this alien test. But in the absence of this knowledge, Job might have found Eliphaz's doctrine devastating. Perhaps, in some hidden way, he has "deserved" this suffering after all. Perhaps his interior sense of integrity toward God and people is no more than an arrogant illusion. Will Job still "persist in his integrity" (2:3) under the pressure of this apparently unassailable doctrine?

Job 5

5:1 **"Call now; is there anyone who will answer you?**
   To which of the holy ones will you turn?
    2 **Surely vexation kills the fool,**
      and jealousy slays the simple.
    3 **I have seen fools taking root,**
      but suddenly I cursed their dwelling.
    4 **Their children are far from safety,**
      they are crushed in the gate,
      and there is no one to deliver them.
    5 **The hungry eat their harvest,**
      and they take it even out of the thorns;
      and the thirsty pant after their wealth.
    6 **For misery does not come from the earth,**

nor does trouble sprout from the ground;
⁷ but human beings are born to trouble
    just as sparks fly upward.

⁸ "As for me, I would seek God,
    and to God I would commit my cause.
⁹ He does great things and unsearchable,
    marvelous things without number.
¹⁰ He gives rain on the earth
    and sends waters on the fields;
¹¹ he sets on high those who are lowly,
    and those who mourn are lifted to safety.
¹² He frustrates the devices of the crafty,
    so that their hands achieve no success.
¹³ He takes the wise in their own craftiness;
    and the schemes of the wily are brought to a quick end.
¹⁴ They meet with darkness in the daytime,
    and grope at noonday as in the night.
¹⁵ But he saves the needy from the sword of their mouth,
    from the hand of the mighty.
¹⁶ So the poor have hope,
    and injustice shuts its mouth.

¹⁷ "How happy is the one whom God reproves;
    therefore do not despise the discipline of the Almighty.
¹⁸ For he wounds, but he binds up;
    he strikes, but his hands heal.
¹⁹ He will deliver you from six troubles;
    in seven no harm shall touch you.
²⁰ In famine he will redeem you from death,
    and in war from the power of the sword.
²¹ You shall be hidden from the scourge of the tongue,
    and shall not fear destruction when it comes.
²² At destruction and famine you shall laugh,
    and shall not fear the wild animals of the earth.
²³ For you shall be in league with the stones of the field,
    and the wild animals shall be at peace with you.
²⁴ You shall know that your tent is safe,
    you shall inspect your fold and miss nothing.
²⁵ You shall know that your descendants will be many,
    and your offspring like the grass of the earth.
²⁶ You shall come to your grave in ripe old age,
    as a shock of grain comes up to the threshing floor in its season.

²⁷ **See, we have searched this out; it is true.**
Hear, and know it for yourself."

In Job 5:2–7, Eliphaz recites ancient proverbial wisdom about what happens to "fools," that is, people who forsake the "fear of God" and reject the ways of relative righteousness. Stated in this rhythmic form, these sentences would sound familiar if we found them in the book of Proverbs, for example, or in the wisdom literature of a variety of ancient Near Eastern cultures. If we hear them as words addressed directly to Job, however, these well-worn adages produce sinister overtones. If "vexation kills the fool, and jealousy [that is, jealous anger] slays the simple" (5:2), what does Eliphaz think of Job's passionate outcry in chapter 3? If Eliphaz is not saying to Job, "You fool!" he is coming close. If we think of the catastrophes Job has undergone, verses 3–5 are transformed into a gross accusation: Job has suffered a worse fate than this, yet this is the well-deserved fate of "fools."

In 5:8–27, however, Eliphaz indicates that there is still hope for Job. Apparently, Eliphaz presumes to think he is able to put himself in Job's shoes (v. 8). If it is true that no mortal can be righteous or pure before God (4:17–21), Eliphaz cannot be certain that Joblike catastrophe may not also happen to him, just as suddenly and just as unexpectedly. "If I were in your place," says Eliphaz, "I would seek God, rather than cry out in anger. I would entrust my cause to God—rather than ask 'Why?' as Job has done."

In 1:20–21 and 2:10, Job appears to have made exactly the kind of response Eliphaz here recommends. Can Job's outburst in chapter 3 be reconciled with what it means to "seek God" and entrust one's cause to God? Many readers of Job have concluded that it cannot. Perhaps the passionate speeches of Job are intended as a direct attack against the facile and submissive piety contained in an ancient tale about Job the patient sufferer.

From the perspective of the divine council, however, it is possible to measure a significant difference between Job's faithfulness, as described in chapters 1 and 2, and the kind of faithfulness Eliphaz is now holding out before Job as an example. Eliphaz has powerful theological reasons for the piety he recommends. The first is his confidence in the transcendent wisdom and power of God, who "does great things and unsearchable, marvelous things without number" (5:9). God is God and we're not! Our wisdom can never match God's, and it is not up to us to question God's providence simply because we do not understand it. As God's fragile creatures (remember 4:17–21), it is blasphemous to suppose that we are ever blameless when the blast of God's anger devastates us. What we can be sure of (5:11–12) is that God's power, whether we understand it or not, is always working toward the vindication of the righteous (in Eliphaz's vocabulary, the "lowly," "those who mourn," the "needy," and the "poor" are all synonyms for "the righteous") and the ultimate defeat of the wicked (the "crafty," the "wise" in their own eyes, the "wily," the "mighty"). In the face of God's wisdom, justice, and power, injustice cannot and will not have the last word about us (v. 16).

Countless millions of God's "poor" (v. 16) throughout the centuries have sustained a magnificent hope for themselves and for the world based on something very like this simple trust, so Eliphaz's advice to Job can't be *all* bad! Why can't Job simply take it to heart and have done with all the wrangling that follows?

From the perspective of the divine council, only one thing stands in the way: Job really is "blameless and upright" (God says so in 1:8 and 2:3), and this suffering really has come on him "for no reason" (2:3). If Job takes Eliphaz's advice, he will have to concede that he is somehow at fault, that his suffering fits into the scheme of God's justice. No longer will he be able to "persist in his integrity" (2:3), as God is confident he will. Eliphaz's advice may serve well for all of us who are not like Job, but in Job 1:8 and 2:3, God declares Job to be one of a kind. The question raised in the prologue was not whether the general run of people can muster the spiritual resources to sustain hope in the face of adversity. The question posed there was whether any human being, even the best of us (even Job!), is capable of what Samuel Terrien once called "exquisite" faithfulness—faithfulness that is not based on "what's in it for me," faithfulness that stands fast no matter what happens, for good or ill. If, under the double pressure of his own suffering and Eliphaz's argument, Job were to relinquish confidence in his own integrity, then *hassatan* would win victory: not as predicted, with Job "cursing you [God] to your face," but with a whimper, conceding that his sense of integrity was hollow from the beginning.

In 5:17–18, Eliphaz makes the temptation more delectable by suggesting that God is motivated by something like "tough love" in sending this wretchedness on Job. The point of Job's pain is to "reprove" or chastise him (v. 17), that is, to make him face the limits of his mortality and to warn him of the consequences of anti-godly pride in his own wisdom and worth. People who take this to heart and amend their ways accordingly may count themselves "happy" or blessed when they experience chastisement, because the hand that wounds them (out of tough love) is also the hand that can and will heal them (v. 18). From the perspective of the divine council, this notion is simply wrong—at least, in the unique case of Job. God has not sent this suffering on Job in order to shock him into greater faithfulness. If God expresses "love" toward Job at all in these events, it is only in a way that Job cannot possibly know: in God's limitless confidence that Job will pass this alien test, which precisely does *not* express God's idea of what Job "deserves."

Like offering water to one who is dying of thirst, Eliphaz now holds out before Job's suffering eyes a glorious vision of future blessedness—provided, of course, he lives by the advice Eliphaz has given. For the righteous, suffering is temporary. By accepting it from God's hand as just (whether as punishment for past error, as a warning designed to discipline and instruct, or as an inscrutable expression of God's transcendent, but always just, wisdom), the righteous may look forward to a blessed life to come. The picture of the blessed life that is dangled before Job in 5:19–26 has much in common with the description of Job's blessedness in Job 1:1–3. In each text we are invited to see a direct link between the righteous life and the "good life" (that is, the peaceful enjoyment of economic and social prosperity, culminating in a "good death"). From the depths of Job's suffering, this promise of release makes the temptation overwhelming: Where do I sign up? What do you have to *do* or *say* or *be* to escape such misery and find such happiness? In verse 24, Eliphaz offers Job the golden key: My friends and I have searched these things out and found this counsel to be true. All you have to do is listen, act accordingly, and discover for yourself the truth that we have discovered.

Will Job embrace a religious attitude that his heart cannot affirm (that is, that his suffering is somehow "just," that he is somehow to blame for it) in order to secure his own future blessedness? To the grave disappointment of Eliphaz (*hassatan* too, if he is watching), Job's resolute answer, beginning in chapter 6, is no! So far, at least, Job "still persists in his integrity" (Job 2:3), as God said he would.

Eliphaz's Second Speech (Job 15)

Job 15

15:1 **Then Eliphaz the Temanite answered:**
  2 **"Should the wise answer with windy knowledge,**
      and fill themselves with the east wind?
  3 **Should they argue in unprofitable talk,**
      or in words with which they can do no good?
  4 **But you are doing away with the fear of God,**
      and hindering meditation before God.
  5 **For your iniquity teaches your mouth,**
      and you choose the tongue of the crafty.
  6 **Your own mouth condemns you, and not I;**
      your own lips testify against you.

⁷ "Are you the firstborn of the human race?
     Were you brought forth before the hills?
⁸ Have you listened in the council of God?
     And do you limit wisdom to yourself?
⁹ What do you know that we do not know?
     What do you understand that is not clear to us?
¹⁰ The gray-haired and the aged are on our side,
     those older than your father.
¹¹ Are the consolations of God too small for you,
     or the word that deals gently with you?
¹² Why does your heart carry you away,
     and why do your eyes flash,
¹³ so that you turn your spirit against God,
     and let such words go out of your mouth?
¹⁴ What are mortals, that they can be clean?
     Or those born of woman, that they can be righteous?
¹⁵ God puts no trust even in his holy ones,
     and the heavens are not clean in his sight;
¹⁶ how much less one who is abominable and corrupt,
     one who drinks iniquity like water!

¹⁷ "I will show you; listen to me;
     what I have seen I will declare—
¹⁸ what sages have told,
     and their ancestors have not hidden,
¹⁹ to whom alone the land was given,
     and no stranger passed among them.
²⁰ The wicked writhe in pain all their days,
     through all the years that are laid up for the ruthless.
²¹ Terrifying sounds are in their ears;
     in prosperity the destroyer will come upon them.
²² They despair of returning from darkness,
     and they are destined for the sword.
²³ They wander abroad for bread, saying, 'Where is it?'
     They know that a day of darkness is ready at hand;
²⁴ distress and anguish terrify them;
     they prevail against them, like a king prepared for battle.
²⁵ Because they stretched out their hands against God,
     and bid defiance to the Almighty,
²⁶ running stubbornly against him
     with a thick-bossed shield;
²⁷ because they have covered their faces with their fat,
     and gathered fat upon their loins,

^{28} they will live in desolate cities,
      in houses that no one should inhabit,
      houses destined to become heaps of ruins;
^{29} they will not be rich, and their wealth will not endure,
      nor will they strike root in the earth;
^{30} they will not escape from darkness;
      the flame will dry up their shoots,
      and their blossom will be swept away by the wind.
^{31} Let them not trust in emptiness, deceiving themselves;
      for emptiness will be their recompense.
^{32} It will be paid in full before their time,
      and their branch will not be green.
^{33} They will shake off their unripe grape, like the vine,
      and cast off their blossoms, like the olive tree.
^{34} For the company of the godless is barren,
      and fire consumes the tents of bribery.
^{35} They conceive mischief and bring forth evil
      and their heart prepares deceit."

We shall return to Job's reply to all this in Job 6—7. For now, let us continue with the speeches of Eliphaz in chapters 15 and 22, in order to grasp his argument as a whole.

Compare the opening lines of Eliphaz in chapter 4 (vv. 1–6) with the opening lines of his second speech (15:1–5). Pastoral sensitivity to Job's suffering has now vanished altogether. The presumably well and happy Eliphaz is clearly threatened by this wretched creature sitting on his ash heap (2:8). It is not just that Job has rejected his sage advice. As we shall see, Job's words in chapters 6—7, as well as his replies to the first speeches of Bildad and Zophar in chapters 8—14, have attacked the fundamental grounds on which Eliphaz's wisdom (and with it, his self-esteem) is based. Job is no longer a friend to be consoled but an adversary to be defeated.

What is at stake between them is expressed most directly in verse 4: "But you are doing away with the fear of God, and hindering meditation before God." For the biblical sages, the term *fear of God* combines the range of meaning we assign to "religion" and "piety." It has to do with a sense of awestruck wonder, tinged with terror, in the presence of God the Maker and Ordainer of all things. To acknowledge God's transcendent wisdom, power, and rightness in all that God does and to submit to it without murmur—that is the fear of God. Human wisdom is the art of discerning God's ways, insofar as we are able, and so to "think the thoughts of God." The limits of human wisdom, however, are the limits of our fragile and transient humanity.

For that reason, as the sages loved to say, "The fear of the LORD is the beginning of [human] wisdom" (see Job 28:28; Psalm 111:10; Prov. 15:33).

In a world that has virtually lost the capacity for authentic wonder, this quaint notion of the "fear of the Lord" is a refreshing alternative to the cynical cocksureness that dominates contemporary attitudes. For Eliphaz, Job's outburst in chapter 3, together with his subsequent protestations that he has suffered unjustly, are sufficient evidence (vv. 4–5) that he has attacked the justice of God, and with it the cornerstone of the fear of God. Only anti-godly human arrogance could produce such tirades against God's providential order (vv. 7–13). Verse 7 apparently refers to a prototypical human figure who came into being before creation itself. Proverbs 8:22–31 personifies God's wisdom in a similar way. While the Bible contains only puzzling hints of such a "primeval human" myth, the sarcastic meaning of Eliphaz's questions in 15:7–9 is crystal clear: Who do you think you are? Do you have privileged access to a wisdom that exceeds our wisdom and the wisdom of ancient sages as well?

Eliphaz is incensed that Job has rejected "the consolations of God" and "the word that deals gently with you" (v. 11; that is, Eliphaz's wise pastoral counsel). Instead, Job has turned his "spirit against God" (v. 13) with continued angry outbursts. But apparently Eliphaz thinks Job still has time to accept "the consolations of God" already spelled out for him in chapters 4 and 5. In 15:14–35, Eliphaz reiterates two unfailing truths on which Job may rely in his present distress: (1) Since no mortal can be righteous before God, it is never "right" to call God's justice in question (15:14–16; see 4:17–21); (2) the "wicked," that is, those who have "stretched out their hands against God and bid defiance to the Almighty" (v. 25), face nothing but utter wretchedness and disaster at God's hands. Note, however, that Eliphaz drops any reference to the blessing Job may expect by accepting his suffering without question (see 5:17–26). This speech ends on the note of sheer terror, detailed at length and with a certain relish, as if this were the only motivation that might break through the "thick-bossed shield" (v. 26) of Job's arrogant defiance.

The statements in verses 20–35 clearly belong to the kind of proverbial instruction about the wicked and their destiny that would have been at home in any traditional teaching situation. In the special context of an argument with Job, however, these generally accepted proverbs take on a sinister meaning. If Job is already existing in a state of absolute wretchedness (2:8), the old proverbs have lost their capacity to terrify and warn. All they can do now is identify Job as the embodiment of the fate that befalls the wicked. Has Eliphaz taken the step from "advice" to "accusation" that is implied here?

Eliphaz's Third Speech (Job 22)

Job 22

22:1 Then Eliphaz the Temanite answered:
² "Can a mortal be of use to God?
    Can even the wisest be of service to him?
³ Is it any pleasure to the Almighty if you are righteous,
    or is it gain to him if you make your ways blameless?
⁴ Is it for your piety that he reproves you,
    and enters into judgment with you?
⁵ Is not your wickedness great?
    There is no end to your iniquities.
⁶ For you have exacted pledges from your family for no reason,
    and stripped the naked of their clothing.
⁷ You have given no water to the weary to drink,
    and you have withheld bread from the hungry.
⁸ The powerful possess the land,
    and the favored live in it.
⁹ You have sent widows away empty-handed,
    and the arms of the orphans you have crushed.
¹⁰ Therefore snares are around you,
    and sudden terror overwhelms you,
¹¹ or darkness so that you cannot see;
    a flood of water covers you.

¹² "Is not God high in the heavens?
    See the highest stars, how lofty they are!
¹³ Therefore you say, 'What does God know?
    Can he judge through the deep darkness?
¹⁴ Thick clouds enwrap him, so that he does not see,
    and he walks on the dome of heaven.'
¹⁵ Will you keep to the old way
    that the wicked have trod?
¹⁶ They were snatched away before their time;
    their foundation was washed away by a flood.
¹⁷ They said to God, 'Leave us alone,'
    and 'What can the Almighty do to us?'
¹⁸ Yet he filled their houses with good things—
    but the plans of the wicked are repugnant to me.
¹⁹ The righteous see it and are glad;
    the innocent laugh them to scorn,
²⁰ saying, 'Surely our adversaries are cut off,
    and what they left, the fire has consumed.'

21 "Agree with God, and be at peace;
   in this way good will come to you.
22 Receive instruction from his mouth,
   and lay up his words in your heart.
23 If you return to the Almighty, you will be restored,
   if you remove unrighteousness from your tents,
24 if you treat gold like dust,
   and gold of Ophir like the stones of the torrent-bed,
25 and if the Almighty is your gold
   and your precious silver,
26 then you will delight yourself in the Almighty,
   and lift up your face to God.
27 You will pray to him, and he will hear you,
   and you will pay your vows.
28 You will decide on a matter, and it will be established for you,
   and light will shine on your ways.
29 When others are humiliated, you say it is pride;
   for he saves the humble.
30 He will deliver even those who are guilty;
   they will escape because of the cleanness of your hands."

Once again, we jump ahead in order to give Eliphaz a complete hearing. In his final speech, Eliphaz is driven beyond insinuation to direct accusation: Job is a prodigiously wicked human being (vv. 5–9), and this is why God has brought suffering on him (vv. 10–11). The indictment begins with a variation on the theme "God is God and we are not" (vv. 2–4; see 4:17–21 and 15:14–16). Here the question is not whether a mere mortal can be "pure" in the eyes of the transcendent God. Now Eliphaz asks whether God the Almighty has anything to gain from any human being, even the wisest, the most blameless. The implication is that God does not play favorites, that God's judgment cannot be swayed by any human performance or any pleasure God may derive from merely human righteousness. Does Job suppose, asks Eliphaz, that God "enters into judgment" with him because of his self-proclaimed "piety"? From the perspective of Eliphaz, such a notion is slander against the disinterested and evenhanded justice of God. No, the reason Job is being punished is because "there is no end to [his] iniquities" (v. 5).

From the perspective of the divine council, of course, all these rhetorical questions are open to answers that are shockingly different from the ones Eliphaz assumes. God does seem to take personal delight in the matchless integrity of "my servant Job" (1:8; 2:3). At least a hint appears in

1:9–10 that God may have purchased Job's delightful response by showering him with unparalleled blessings. God's reputation, as well as Job's, is riding on whether Job can "still persist in his integrity" after God has been incited to move "against him without cause" (2:3). In this bizarre sense, it can even be said that God "enters into judgment" with Job *because* of his "piety" (22:4). What Eliphaz takes to be clear evidence of Job's wickedness—his suffering at the hands of God—is in fact God's supreme accolade: Not even these appalling losses can sway the course of Job's selfless integrity.

How has Eliphaz arrived at his estimate of Job, diametrically opposed to that of God? Eliphaz clearly did not regard Job as an exceptionally wicked person from the beginning (see 4:2–6). If there had been any evidence of the crimes listed in 22:6–9, Eliphaz would hardly have commiserated with Job for seven days and seven nights, in silence, because he "saw that his suffering was very great" (2:13). Are we to think that Eliphaz has now invented a whole series of groundless charges against Job out of his own overheated imagination?

Possibly not. In his first and second speeches Eliphaz warned Job, with increasing intensity, that his protests called into question the justice of God, to the point of blasphemy. For Eliphaz, the ultimate sin is "doing away with the fear of God" (15:4) and "bid[ding] defiance to the Almighty" (15:25).

By his persistent rejection of these warnings, Job has now convinced Eliphaz that he has committed just this cardinal sin, identifying himself as the wicked man *par excellence* (22:5). The ungodly crimes enumerated in verses 6–9 can then be seen as the indelible symptoms of the godless heart. To characterize Job by this traditional portrait of "the wicked" drives home Eliphaz's accusation: "You are the man!" (see 2 Sam. 12:7).

If we reverse all the characteristics of "the wicked" in 22:6–9, we gain a corresponding picture of "the righteous." For instance, to exact "pledges from your family for no reason" connotes the worst possible case of usury and extortion: using one's status and economic power to exploit the socially and economically powerless. It derives from the practice of taking something in pawn from a debtor, a pledge of a value greater than the amount of the debt. If the debtor cannot repay the entire debt, on the agreed terms, the lender retains the pawn at a nice profit. Abuses of this practice are condemned in the Law and the Prophets of Israel (see Exod. 22:25–27; Amos 2:6–8). To perpetrate such extortion against members of one's own family, "without cause" (on the basis of fraudulently contrived debt?), exemplifies the extreme case of ruthless avarice.

Reverse this image and you discern the corresponding characteristic of the righteous: generosity and compassion toward those in need, even at cost to oneself. Reversing the other images in 22:6–9 projects a portrait of the righteous as people who willingly provide shelter for the shelterless, water for the thirsty, bread for the starving, and intervention on behalf of those without social or legal standing (epitomized in the Bible by the phrase "widows and orphans").

Interestingly enough, God, *hassatan*, Job, and Eliphaz all agree on these characterizations of "the righteous" and "the wicked." In God's judgment, Job qualifies as righteous (1:8; 2:3). *Hassatan* suspects that Job's apparent righteousness is motivated by raw self-interest (1:9–12; 2:4–5). Job struggles to affirm that his righteousness is genuine, in spite of overwhelming loss and rejection (most vividly, as we shall see, in chaps. 29—31). Eliphaz counts Job as "wicked" on the grounds that his outcries betray a godless heart, the root of all the "symptoms" listed in 22:6–9.

On this point, the book of Job echoes one of the central themes of the Law and the Prophets of Israel, as well as the New Testament: Devotion to God simply cannot be separated from just and compassionate action on behalf of others in everyday life. Jesus was never more Jewish than when he combined Deuteronomy 6:5 with Leviticus 19:18 to express the whole claim of God on human life. (See Matt. 22:35–40; note that the student of Old Testament law in Luke 10:25 already knows this, without prompting from Jesus.) According to the criteria that separate the "sheep" from the "goats" in Matthew 25:31–46, Eliphaz clearly identifies Job as a "goat" in Job 22:5–9. In this connection, it is worth noting that on the judgment day, the "sheep" are unaware that their simple acts of justice and compassion have qualified them to "inherit the kingdom" (Matt. 25:34; note their astonished questions in vv. 37–39). Their righteousness is clearly not motivated by self-interest. In *hassatan*'s judgment, such selfless devotion is impossible even for the best of us—even for Job.

The nearest biblical parallel to Eliphaz's wholesale indictment of Job in 22:5–9 is probably the verdict God renders against the entire human race in the prologue to the story of the Flood: "The LORD saw that the wickedness of humankind was great in the earth, and that every inclination of the thoughts of their hearts was only evil continually" (Gen. 6:5). According to Genesis 6, the Deluge was the catastrophic sign of God's total rejection of such wickedness. According to Eliphaz, God's rejection of Job is signaled by Job's suffering in a comparable way: "Therefore . . . sudden terror overwhelms you, or darkness so that you cannot see; a flood of water covers you" (Job 22:10–11).

After this ultimate and comprehensive verdict against Job, it is surprising to hear Eliphaz pressing on with the argument, as if there were still time for Job to repent. It is the folly of the wicked to suppose that God is so exalted above the earth, so hidden from human eyes, that God knows and cares nothing about human affairs (vv. 12–14). Eliphaz accuses Job of this folly (v. 13), but the whole argument of 22:12–30 evokes the "stick-and-carrot" method that Eliphaz has used from the beginning to force Job into submission. The stick (vv. 13–20) is the threat of God's inexorable destruction of the wicked in all ages (vv. 15–16), to the utter delight of the "righteous" and the "innocent" (vv. 19–20). (In German, this is called *Schadenfreude*: gleeful satisfaction at the misfortune of others. As we shall see, Job rejects this peculiar delight as unworthy of him [31:29–30]. According to Job 42:7–9, Eliphaz turns out to be a direct beneficiary of this astonishing forbearance.)

The carrot is the promise of rich blessings for those who submit to the just will of God—that is, to the logic of Eliphaz. These blessings were first offered to Job in 5:17–26, where the emphasis lay on the restoration of the idyllic existence Job once enjoyed (according to Job 1:2–3 and 10). In the meantime, Eliphaz may have learned that Job is not tempted by the crassly material side of "blessedness." What Eliphaz now dangles before Job is the possibility that his once unbroken friendship with God can be restored: the capacity once again to "delight yourself in the Almighty, and lift up your face to God" (v. 26); to pray with serene confidence in being heard, to worship God without reserve, to know that your way is God's way, illuminated by God's light (vv. 27–28). As we follow the speeches of Job, longing for just this kind of relationship with God will emerge with increasing intensity. All Job must do to gain this superb peace of the soul, according to Eliphaz, is to "agree with God, and be at peace" (v. 21), to accept God's "instruction" and cherish God's "words" (v. 22), to "return to the Almighty" (that is, repent), to forsake "unrighteousness" (v. 23), and to value nothing more highly than God (vv. 24–26).

Will Job fake the piety Eliphaz prescribes in hope of gaining what is obviously, for him, the greatest imaginable personal blessing: unmarred communion with God? Here the question of *hassatan* ("Does Job fear God for nothing?") reemerges in its most satanic form. If Job concedes that Eliphaz is right, that his protest of innocence is blasphemy against God, that he has richly deserved all his suffering—if, in short, Job no longer "persists in his integrity" (2:3)—then *hassatan* will have won. Self-interest, even in this perfect disguise, will have proven to be the ultimate motivation for his attitudes and actions toward God and neighbor. *Hassatan* must have been severely disappointed when Job refused to take even this delectable bait.

The Hebrew text of 22:29–30 is notoriously difficult. This has led to a confusing variety of attempts at translation, each based on more or less educated guesses. (Compare these verses in the RSV and the NRSV.) As in the case of many texts in Job where the meaning can only be conjectured, so here we must place large question marks before and after any attempt at translation or interpretation. If the NRSV translation of verse 30 is on the right track, however, a fascinating theme emerges: "They [the wicked] will escape because of the cleanness of your hands." Would a restored and therefore righteous Job be able to secure the deliverance even of "wicked" people? This recalls Isaiah 53:11, where it is said of God's Suffering Servant that he "shall make many righteous, and he shall bear their iniquities." In Ezekiel 14:14 and 20, Job is apparently remembered as one who in former times proved able to save others by his righteousness (see also Gen. 6:8–10, 18; 7:1; 18:22–32). In Job 42:7–9, Eliphaz himself appears to be a beneficiary of just such righteous intercession.

In any case, Eliphaz concludes his argument against Job on a note of grace that can only be called amazing. None of the bitter things he has said to Job, not even the horrendous indictment in 22:5–9, is to be taken as God's last word about him. Eliphaz turns out to be wrong about Job, and in that respect at least, wrong about God. But even in this wrongheaded way, he here bears witness to a God who does not give up on the worst of sinners (of whom Eliphaz thinks Job is chief) and whose ultimate goal for Job, and for us, is friendship and peace.

Before turning to the speeches of Job and the other friends, it is well to keep in mind the basic elements of Eliphaz's case against Job:

1. God's governance of the universe is supremely wise, just, and compassionate.
2. Human wisdom cannot comprehend all the ways of God, who "does great things and unsearchable, marvelous things without number" (5:9).
3. Yet we may have supreme confidence, borne out by experience, that God punishes the wicked and rewards the righteous in this life.
4. By our very nature as God's fragile creatures, none of us may claim to be altogether innocent in God's eyes.
5. Nevertheless, God distinguishes between the righteous and the wicked among us in ways we can understand and for which we are held accountable.
6. The righteous are above all those who "fear God," that is, who accept whatever comes to us in this life as the expression of God's just

and righteous will. This is to be mirrored in attitudes and actions toward others marked by justice and compassion.

7. The wicked are above all those who "bid defiance to the Almighty" (15:25) in thought, word, and deed, from angry complaints against one's lot in life to the foolish supposition that God neither knows nor cares about what we do on earth, to acts of greed and oppression against the powerless. In all these ways, the wicked defy the justice, righteousness, and compassion of God.

8. While no suffering is ever "innocent" (see point 4, above), even relatively righteous people may undergo periods of intense suffering that are not related to any specific unrighteousness of which they are aware. In such cases, the righteous turn to God with renewed repentance, accepting the suffering as God's just and benevolent act of "reproving" them or "disciplining" them toward greater faithfulness.

9. While the wicked may flourish for a time, and the righteous may undergo temporary "chastisement," the ultimate victory of God over the wicked and on behalf of the righteous is absolutely assured.

If this sounds very like the religious instruction you have heard all your life, don't be surprised. In one form or another, all these convictions are deeply rooted in the piety of Judaism and Christianity, as well as the piety of other religions. It is probably not the point of the book of Job to demonstrate that all these notions are equally wrong. What we are about to hear from Job, however, leaves none of these classic religious truisms unchallenged, at least in their conventional form. Job will be moving against a very deep and very powerful religious stream.

JOB'S RESPONSE TO ELIPHAZ'S FIRST SPEECH
Job 6—7

It is natural to assume that Job's words in chapters 6 and 7 are his counterarguments to what Eliphaz has just said in chapters 4 and 5. Yet a quick glance at 7:8–19 shows that Job's ultimate quarrel is with God, not with his so-called friends. Most of what Job has to say is intended for God's ears, even when his thoughts are triggered, as they sometimes are, by the theological arguments of Eliphaz and the others. Readers must be ready, at any time, for Job to shift from the language of debate to the language of prayer (that is, direct discourse with God).

Job 6

6:1 Then Job answered:
²"O that my vexation were weighed,
    and all my calamity laid in the balances!
³ For then it would be heavier than the sand of the sea;
    therefore my words have been rash.
⁴ For the arrows of the Almighty are in me;
    my spirit drinks their poison;
    the terrors of God are arrayed against me.
⁵ Does the wild ass bray over its grass,
    or the ox low over its fodder?
⁶ Can that which is tasteless be eaten without salt,
    or is there any flavor in the juice of mallows?
⁷ My appetite refuses to touch them;
    they are like food that is loathsome to me.

⁸ "O that I might have my request,
    and that God would grant my desire;
⁹ that it would please God to crush me,
    that he would let loose his hand and cut me off!
¹⁰ This would be my consolation;
    I would even exult in unrelenting pain;
    for I have not denied the words of the Holy One.
¹¹ What is my strength, that I should wait?
    And what is my end, that I should be patient?
¹² Is my strength the strength of stones,
    or is my flesh bronze?
¹³ In truth I have no help in me,
    and any resource is driven from me.

¹⁴ "Those who withhold kindness from a friend
    forsake the fear of the Almighty.
¹⁵ My companions are treacherous like a torrent-bed,
    like freshets that pass away,
¹⁶ that run dark with ice,
    turbid with melting snow.
¹⁷ In time of heat they disappear;
    when it is hot, they vanish from their place.
¹⁸ The caravans turn aside from their course;
    they go up into the waste, and perish.
¹⁹ The caravans of Tema look,
    the travelers of Sheba hope.

²⁰ They are disappointed because they were confident;
   they come there and are confounded.
²¹ Such you have now become to me;
   you see my calamity, and are afraid.
²² Have I said, 'Make me a gift'?
   Or, 'From your wealth offer a bribe for me'?
²³ Or, 'Save me from an opponent's hand'?
   Or, 'Ransom me from the hand of oppressors'?

²⁴ "Teach me, and I will be silent;
   make me understand how I have gone wrong.
²⁵ How forceful are honest words!
   But your reproof, what does it reprove?
²⁶ Do you think that you can reprove words,
   as if the speech of the desperate were wind?
²⁷ You would even cast lots over the orphan,
   and bargain over your friend.

²⁸ "But now, be pleased to look at me;
   for I will not lie to your face.
²⁹ Turn, I pray, let no wrong be done.
   Turn now, my vindication is at stake.
³⁰ Is there any wrong on my tongue?
   Cannot my taste discern calamity?

Eliphaz warned Job in 5:2 that "vexation kills the fool, and jealousy slays the simple." By that he implies it is a deadly error to cry out, as Job has done, against the rightness of God's judgment in any affliction we may be asked to bear. In 6:2–7, Job responds by confessing that his "vexation" is indeed immeasurable, but the root cause of it lies with God. The homely proverbs in verses 5–6 make the point that his outcry is altogether justified, and he cannot be content with the theological pabulum that has been placed before him.

The language of 6:8–10, however, echoes the agonized rejection of life under these wretched circumstances heard in chapter 3. Why does God not at least honor Job's innocence (v. 10) by the gracious act of snuffing out Job's wretched existence? It is not as though Job had some superhuman strength to endure all this or some distant goal to make it all worthwhile (vv. 11–12). All his fragile human resources are spent (v. 13). Only God, of course—surely not Eliphaz—can respond to a cry such as this.

Job's complaint against his friends (6:14–30) has less to do with theology than with compassion. At such a time as this, the "fear of the Almighty"

(v. 14) requires loyal compassion for a friend in need, not a panic-ridden anxiety about one's own precious theological maxims (v. 21). It is just here, however, that Job's friends have proven as unreliable as a desert gulch whose desperately needed water runs dry at the most critical time (vv. 15–20; see Jer. 15:18, where the "traitor" is God). Job senses that he has become for them a burden to be borne, rather than a friend to be consoled (vv. 21–23).

From verses 24–26 it is obvious that Job has not received the counsel of Eliphaz as "honest words" appropriate to their friendship and adequate to Job's wretched condition. The fundamental issue between them, of course, is whether Job has "deserved" his suffering. The whole argument of Eliphaz aims at making Job confess his guilt. From Job's standpoint, this means Eliphaz has neither comprehended the depth of Job's suffering nor entertained the possibility that Job is innocent (vv. 26, 29–30). What Job needs is to be heard, friend to friend (v. 28), not haggled over as a theological case to be resolved in Eliphaz's favor (v. 27). On this point, Job calls his friends to repentance ("Turn . . . turn now," v. 29) as if they were the guilty ones, not he.

Job 7

7:1 **"Do not human beings have a hard service on earth,**
    and are not their days like the days of a laborer?
2 **Like a slave who longs for the shadow,**
    and like laborers who look for their wages,
3 **so I am allotted months of emptiness,**
    and nights of misery are apportioned to me.
4 **When I lie down I say, 'When shall I rise?'**
    But the night is long,
    and I am full of tossing until dawn.
5 **My flesh is clothed with worms and dirt;**
    my skin hardens, then breaks out again.
6 **My days are swifter than a weaver's shuttle,**
    and come to their end without hope.

7 **"Remember that my life is a breath;**
    my eye will never again see good.
8 **The eye that beholds me will see me no more;**
    while your eyes are upon me, I shall be gone.
9 **As the cloud fades and vanishes,**
    so those who go down to Sheol do not come up;
10 **they return no more to their houses,**
    nor do their places know them any more.

¹¹ "Therefore I will not restrain my mouth;
     I will speak in the anguish of my spirit;
     I will complain in the bitterness of my soul.
¹² Am I the Sea, or the Dragon,
     that you set a guard over me?
¹³ When I say, 'My bed will comfort me,
     my couch will ease my complaint,'
¹⁴ then you scare me with dreams
     and terrify me with visions,
¹⁵ so that I would choose strangling
     and death rather than this body.
¹⁶ I loathe my life; I would not live forever.
     Let me alone, for my days are a breath.
¹⁷ What are human beings, that you make so much of them,
     that you set your mind on them,
¹⁸ visit them every morning,
     test them every moment?
¹⁹ Will you not look away from me for a while,
     let me alone until I swallow my spittle?
²⁰ If I sin, what do I do to you, you watcher of humanity?
     Why have you made me your target?
     Why have I become a burden to you?
²¹ Why do you not pardon my transgression
     and take away my iniquity?
     For now I shall lie in the earth;
     you will seek me, but I shall not be."

Job now tries again, as in chapter 3 and in 6:2–4, 8–13, to express the cry of his heart, out of the depths of a suffering Eliphaz cannot or will not understand (7:1–6). For the first time so explicitly, Job sets his personal suffering in the context of the "hard service" that human beings in general must endure throughout their lives (7:1). The prologue (chaps. 1 and 2) invites us to see Job as one who suffered at the hand of God "for no reason" (2:3), as a unique test of his extraordinary righteousness. Job knows, however, that he is not alone in the experience that life is "solitary, poor, nasty, brutish and short" (Thomas Hobbes, *Leviathan*, part 1, chap. 13). If this is so, then the question of God's justice in relation to human suffering becomes global. No individual or "private" answer Job may receive to this question will be adequate unless it includes the whole human family of innocent sufferers with whom Job here claims kinship. We shall follow this theme with special interest as Job develops it later on.

In 5:19–26, Eliphaz described the blessed life as a crescendo of positive experiences coming to its proper climax in the "harvest" of a good death, "in ripe old age," surrounded by heirs to whom the future may be entrusted. In 7:1–6, Job describes his existence in opposite terms. It is a life of longing for a good that never comes, of suffering without hope. Days of longing for the night are replaced by restless nights of longing for the dawn (7:2, 4). It is a life too long and hard to bear (7:1, 4) and yet too short to offer any sign of hope (7:6).

This is surely "the speech of the desperate," which Job has accused Eliphaz of dismissing as "wind" (6:26) in his eagerness to set Job theologically straight. Are the words of 7:1–6 designed to gain from Eliphaz a fresh and honest hearing (see 6:28)? Perhaps. In 7:7–21, however, it is clear that Job is appealing his case to a higher court. Whether or not his friends are eavesdropping, Job now addresses his words to God in a prayer of shocking intimacy. God is being held accountable for a mutual relationship with Job, even though Job's fragile humanity is as nothing by comparison with God's transcendent power. Job is aware that God's eye "watches" him (7:8, 20), implying that God has an investment of some kind in Job's attitudes and actions as a mere human. But if that is so, says Job in 7:7–10, God must "remember" (v. 7) that Job will not be able to sustain his side of this ludicrously unequal but somehow mutual relationship indefinitely. One of these days God will come looking for Job, and there won't be any Job left to "watch" (7:8–10)!

For that reason, Job is prepared to tell God straight out exactly how things stand between them as Job experiences it, from the depth of his suffering (v. 11). Is this the proper language and attitude of prayer? The notes of joyous adoration and thanksgiving are surely missing here, along with the tone of simple trust, contrition, intercession, and humble supplication—in short, all the characteristics of "prayer" as we usually understand it. Yet the Bible records a number of instances when people risk telling God how things are from the human side with unsparing candor, when the hard experiences of life call God's side of the relationship in question. Moses took such a risk, according to Numbers 11:10–15, 21–22, as did Jeremiah (see Jer. 15:15–18; 20:7, 14–18) and Habakkuk (see Hab. 1:2–4, 13–17). Page after page of the Psalms resound with wounded outcries to God out of the depths of incomprehensible suffering, the so-called Psalms of Lament. (Psalm 88 is perhaps the most Joblike, although Christians remember Psalm 22:1–21 most vividly because its opening cry is echoed by Jesus on Good Friday's cross.) The book of Lamentations gets its name from its appalling cries of anguish over the destruction of Jerusalem, the utter ruin of its people, and the apparent end of the bright promises of God on which it was founded. Can it be that God is "angry with us beyond measure" (Lam. 5:22)?

The aim of such reckless prayers was never to break off relationship with God from the human side, by some Promethean "declaration of independence." By holding God accountable for God's side of an obviously broken relationship, prayers of lamentation express a kind of "upside-down trust": trust that God can handle anything and everything we have to say, trust that God alone can answer our cries of the heart, if any answer is possible at all. This is what separates an authentic crisis of faith from a relatively cheap and self-glorifying atheism.

In such a hate-love encounter with God, Job sees himself as hopelessly overmatched. According to ancient legend, God had to overcome ferocious chaos dragons to establish God's order in heaven and on earth (the "Sea" and the "Dragon" of 7:12). Does God suppose Job to be an enemy of this magnitude, a threat to be kept under constant guard? In 7:13–20, Job wonders aloud, to God, why God should care one way or the other about the quality of merely human life, fragile and transient as it obviously is. The apparent reference to Psalm 8:4 in Job 7:17–18 requires reflection on the momentous claim Psalm 8 makes about human life. People have always been driven to wonder by the starry universe visible to the naked eye on clear nights (Psalm 8:1–3), especially in this century, when cosmic magnitudes have gone off the scale of human imagination. As one physicist put it, "The universe is not only stranger than we think, it is stranger than we can think." People may surely be forgiven if they regard this incomprehensible hugeness and strangeness as the wonder beyond all wonders and therefore somehow akin to God. The greater wonder for the psalmist, however, lies in the fact that the God of all creation pays inordinate attention to fragile earthlings such as we. (The two words for "human being" in Psalm 8:4 stress this transience and lowliness.) Yet God has granted almost "*elohim*-like" capacities to human beings, empowering us to function as God's stewards of life on earth (for the *Elohim*, see above, p. 15).

In his desolate suffering, however, Job has experienced God's "inordinate attention" as a nightmarish terror that makes death preferable to such a "life." God's unaccountable claim on Job has become a burden he would gladly be spared for the last, brief days of his life (7:13–16). The glad hymn of Psalm 8:4 is here transformed into a cry of lamentation: "What are human beings, that you make so much of them, that you set your mind on them, visit them every morning, test them every moment?" (vv. 17–18). The Hebrew word translated "visit" here and "care for" in Psalm 8:4 has nothing to do with "dropping by." Rather, it indicates what God "metes out" to human beings whether for good (Psalm 8:4) or for ill (Job 7:17). Is Job somehow dimly aware that God is putting him to some inscrutable "test" in these catastrophic events? If so, the test is beyond his strength as well as his understanding. Why doesn't God simply let Job alone, cancel whatever wrongs the test was designed to expose, give Job time to "swallow his spittle," for heaven's sake, and go quietly to his grave (vv. 19–21). Yet the final line of chapter 7 carries a poignant suggestion: If God is "seeking" Job in all this (Job apparently thinks so), time is running short. Will God be hurt (or frustrated, or angry, or sad) to discover that Job is no longer there to be dealt with? However we choose to read this forlorn little warning, it highlights the basic character of chapter 7: Like a wounded child, Job cries out against a relationship with God so broken that he can't bear it yet so intense that he cannot be rid of it. A child may cry out to a parent, "I hate you!" when the underlying message is "I hurt! I don't understand! I can't take it! I need you! I want you!" Is this anything like the message of Job to God here? The boldest reading of verse 21b suggests Job's awareness that God somehow "needs" and "wants" Job too! By holding God accountable, by wrestling with God so passionately, by this "upside down" expression of longing for an intact relation with God—in all these ways Job is "persisting in his integrity" (2:3) toward God. If so, perhaps we can sense something of the cost *to God* of this "ungodly" test to which God's servant Job is being subjected.

BILDAD'S FIRST SPEECH
Job 8

Job 8

8:1 **Then Bildad the Shuhite answered:**
2 **"How long will you say these things,**
   and the words of your mouth be a great wind?
3 **Does God pervert justice?**
   Or does the Almighty pervert the right?
4 **If your children sinned against him,**
   he delivered them into the power of their transgression.
5 **If you will seek God**
   and make supplication to the Almighty,
6 **if you are pure and upright,**
   surely then he will rouse himself for you
   and restore to you your rightful place.

⁷ Though your beginning was small,
    your latter days will be very great.

⁸ "For inquire now of bygone generations,
    and consider what their ancestors have found;
⁹ for we are but of yesterday, and we know nothing,
    for our days on earth are but a shadow.
¹⁰ Will they not teach you and tell you
    and utter words out of their understanding?
¹¹ "Can papyrus grow where there is no marsh?
    Can reeds flourish where there is no water?
¹² While yet in flower and not cut down,
    they wither before any other plant.
¹³ Such are the paths of all who forget God;
    the hope of the godless shall perish.
¹⁴ Their confidence is gossamer,
    a spider's house their trust.
¹⁵ If one leans against its house, it will not stand;
    if one lays hold of it, it will not endure.
¹⁶ The wicked thrive before the sun,
    and their shoots spread over the garden.
¹⁷ Their roots twine around the stoneheap;
    they live among the rocks.
¹⁸ If they are destroyed from their place,
    then it will deny them, saying, 'I have never seen you.'
¹⁹ See, these are their happy ways,
    and out of the earth still others will spring.

²⁰ "See, God will not reject a blameless person,
    nor take the hand of evildoers.
²¹ He will yet fill your mouth with laughter,
    and your lips with shouts of joy.
²² Those who hate you will be clothed with shame,
    and the tent of the wicked will be no more."

Like a vulture descending on a lion's kill, Bildad now tears away at Job
with accusations and seductions familiar to us from Eliphaz. Job's "windy"
words (see Job 6:26b) constitute a direct assault on the justice of God
(8:1–3). Job's dead children got exactly what they deserved (v. 4)—an interestingly cruel way to convince a bereaved father of the doctrine of God's
unimpeachable justice. Fortunately for Job, however, Bildad is in a position to offer Job a deal. God will intervene on Job's side and restore his
fortunes (a regular "rags-to-riches" story; v. 7), if—but *only* if—Job will

stop crying out against the catastrophes that have befallen him, accept his suffering as God's just punishment, throw himself on God's mercy, and live the upright life. All this is implied, I think, in the terse words of verses 5–6a, as if Eliphaz had already spelled out the details.

Whereas Eliphaz based his insights on the authority of an extraordinary revelation (4:12–21), Bildad claims the authority of an ancient wisdom passed on from the "ancestors" to succeeding generations (8:8–10; Eliphaz hints at this in 5:27 and 15:7–10). The mixed figures of speech in 8:11–19 pose significant problems for scholarly translation and interpretation. Fortunately, the point of all the allusions appears to be made clear in verse 20: "See, God will not reject a blameless person, nor take the hand of evildoers." With this theme in mind, verses 11–15 clearly depict the hopeless and insubstantial "paths of all those who forget God," the "godless" (v. 13). There is no clear consensus as to whether verses 16–21 portray the contrasting paths of the righteous (as I tend to suppose), or whether these verses extend the negative images begun in verses 11–15. (The NRSV notes that the word *wicked* in verse 16 has been added by the translators, presumably to clarify the unstated subject of the verb *thrive*. This suggests the images of verses 16–21 are to be read negatively.)

In any case, this ancient doctrine of the two ways—the way of wisdom/righteousness, which leads to life, versus the way of folly/wickedness, which leads to ruin—is introduced by Bildad as the clincher in his case against Job. The blithe assurances of verses 21–22 appear to be based on the assumption that Job, having now been set on the right path by Bildad, will take the recommended steps and so enter upon the twofold delights of the righteous: the joy of sharing the victories of God on behalf of the righteous and the joy of watching wicked enemies get their comeuppance (see Job 31:29–30).

JOB'S RESPONSE TO BILDAD
Job 9—10

Job 9

9:1 **Then Job answered:**
   2 **"Indeed I know that this is so;**
      but how can a mortal be just before God?
   3 **If one wished to contend with him,**
      one could not answer him once in a thousand.
   4 **He is wise in heart, and mighty in strength**

—who has resisted him, and succeeded?—
⁵ he who removes mountains, and they do not know it,
    when he overturns them in his anger;
⁶ who shakes the earth out of its place,
    and its pillars tremble;
⁷ who commands the sun, and it does not rise;
    who seals up the stars;
⁸ who alone stretched out the heavens
    and trampled the waves of the Sea;
⁹ who made the Bear and Orion,
    the Pleiades and the chambers of the south;
¹⁰ who does great things beyond understanding,
    and marvelous things without number.
¹¹ Look, he passes by me, and I do not see him;
    he moves on, but I do not perceive him.
¹² He snatches away; who can stop him?
    Who will say to him, 'What are you doing?'

¹³ "God will not turn back his anger;
    the helpers of Rahab bowed beneath him.
¹⁴ How then can I answer him,
    choosing my words with him?
¹⁵ Though I am innocent, I cannot answer him;
    I must appeal for mercy to my accuser.
¹⁶ If I summoned him and he answered me,
    I do not believe that he would listen to my voice.
¹⁷ For he crushes me with a tempest,
    and multiplies my wounds without cause;
¹⁸ he will not let me get my breath,
    but fills me with bitterness
¹⁹ If it is a contest of strength, he is the strong one!
    If it is a matter of justice, who can summon him?
²⁰ Though I am innocent, my own mouth would condemn me;
    though I am blameless, he would prove me perverse.
²¹ I am blameless; I do not know myself;
    I loathe my life.
²² It is all one; therefore I say,
    he destroys both the blameless and the wicked.
²³ When disaster brings sudden death,
    he mocks at the calamity of the innocent.
²⁴ The earth is given into the hand of the wicked;
    he covers the eyes of its judges—
    if it is not he, who then is it?

25 "My days are swifter than a runner;
    they flee away, they see no good.
26 They go by like skiffs of reed,
    like an eagle swooping on the prey.
27 If I say, 'I will forget my complaint;
    I will put off my sad countenance and be of good cheer,'
28 I become afraid of all my suffering,
    for I know you will not hold me innocent.
29 I shall be condemned;
    why then do I labor in vain?
30 If I wash myself with soap
    and cleanse my hands with lye,
31 yet you will plunge me into filth,
    and my own clothes will abhor me.
32 For he is not a mortal, as I am, that I might answer him,
    that we should come to trial together.
33 There is no umpire between us,
    who might lay his hand on us both.
34 If he would take his rod away from me,
    and not let dread of him terrify me,
35 then I would speak without fear of him,
    for I know I am not what I am thought to be.

In 8:3, Bildad stated the issue of God's justice in courtroom language, implying that Job's outbursts have placed God on trial. Job picks up this legal theme in chapter 9 and describes what it's like for a mere "mortal" to go to court against Almighty God. The transcendent wisdom and power of God are so awesome that no human being can expect to get a fair trial in God's presence (9:2–20). Eliphaz must have been appalled to hear Job take his great insight, received by supernatural revelation (see 4:12–21), and draw this blasphemous conclusion from it. The huge imbalance of wisdom and power between God and any human being means for Eliphaz that not even Job can claim to be "righteous" or "pure" before God. For Job it means that no human being, however just the cause, can receive a legitimate hearing in a courtroom dominated by such cosmic opposition (9:2–3).

The images used to describe God's power are drawn from the rich lore of ancient Near Eastern cultures. Creation was understood to be the result of God's mighty victories over the monsters of chaos (*Yam*, "the Sea," in 9:8; Rahab and company in 9:13; though defeated, these monsters must continually be restrained lest they challenge God's order anew; see 7:12). When God's wrath is kindled, however, God's own created order may come under attack (9:5–7). (See Psalm 18:7–15; Hab. 3:3–15. There are indications in Genesis 6 and 7 that the Deluge was a kind of "unmaking" of creation because of God's wrath against it.) The implication for Job in all this is that his lawsuit with God is lost from the beginning: "Who has resisted [God], and succeeded?" (9:4). Job agrees with Eliphaz that God "does great things beyond understanding, and marvelous things without number" (9:10; see 5:9), but here also, he draws opposite conclusions. The upshot for Job is that he can never come face to face with God or comprehend God's ways or hold God accountable (9:11–12).

But what would it be like if Job somehow could take his case to court against such an opponent? Job 9:14–20 invites readers to envision such a scene in all its absurdity. Job's case for his innocence could never be put into words adequate to God's overwhelming presence (v. 14). How could Job expect to be heard by an opponent at law who "crushes me with a tempest, and multiplies my wounds without cause" (vv. 15–17)? According to Job 2:3, Job's assessment of this absurd situation is altogether accurate. In his ignorance of the "test" contrived by *hassatan* and God in the divine council chamber, Job can perceive his suffering only as an unaccountable outburst of God's raw power. If, as Job's friends suppose, this attack represents God's judgment against Job, then Job's powerless claim to innocence is irrelevant. "If it is a contest of strength" (rather than justice?), says Job, "he is the strong one! If it is a matter of justice, who can summon him?" (vv. 18–19). Such intimidating power is capable of reversing the meaning of words. The outcries of the innocent are perverted into self-condemnation, so that victims become co-conspirators in their own humiliation and oppression (v. 20).

If this is how things stand between Job and God, the obvious course of action is to "curse God, and die" (see 2:9). When Job's friends hear what he says next, they may conclude that Job has issued this "curse" in the form of a sweeping accusation against God: God "destroys both the blameless and the wicked" (v. 22). Job is already suffering the consequences of such blasphemy, and his death is close at hand. For Job, however, there is an important distinction between cursing and telling the truth. On the basis of what Job has already said, absolutely nothing is to be gained by "persisting in his integrity": No heavenly court will hear his case, and even his best friends count him guilty. If Job's friends "did not recognize him" because of the ravages of his suffering (see 2:12), Job has the same problem: "I do not know myself" (9:21). Nothing remains of the familiar fabric of relationships and experiences that once gave him his sense of self. The tortured face in the mirror is that of a stranger. "Life" on these terms holds no promise, and nothing matters one way or the other. Nevertheless, Job can still tell the one truth of which he is sure, whether anybody out there is listening or not: He is *blameless* (v. 21), and if that means God is unfair, so be it (vv. 22–24). Once again, Job identifies himself with the whole family of human beings who suffer for no reason (vv. 22–23): "The earth is given into the hand of the wicked." God covers the eyes of its judges. If God is not responsible for the human condition, here portrayed with devastating accuracy, then who is (v. 24)? As a rhetorical device, this final question demands the answer: "No one but God!"

In the context of the bizarre story of God with Job, however, the obvious rhetorical question and its equally obvious answer are charged with double meanings. Yes, Job has suffered at the hands of God "for no reason" (2:3), but no, this suffering neither demonstrates God's attitude toward Job nor reflects the kind of existence God wants for Job. Yes, Job has experienced God as a terrifyingly unjust enemy, but no, Job is not prepared (yet) to cut off his tenacious quest for a relationship with God that honors Job's innocence. It is just this agonizing quest that takes center stage in Job 9:25–35 and 10:1–22.

The urgency of Job's quest is intensified by his awareness that time is running short, with no evidence that the goal is in sight (9:25–26). Shall he "put on a happy face" and pretend that all is well (v. 27)? Both the intensity of his suffering and the authenticity of his sense of rejection by God forbid any such Pollyanna denial (vv. 28–29). The relationship Job seeks with God is not to be won so cheaply.

Shall Job subject himself to a rigorous discipline of self-purification in order to improve his chances of being accepted by God (v. 30)? Job already knows that his innocence cannot be improved upon by such cleansing, in the face of God's ruthless power to twist his best defense into an argument for the prosecution (v. 31; see 9:20).

What Job longs for, even though it is obviously quite impossible, is to have it out with God on a level playing field, where the imbalance of wisdom and power would not obscure the simple issues of fairness between them. But God "is not a mortal, as I am" (v. 32); and where could Job hope to find an "umpire" capable of holding Almighty God accountable to the same rules of fair play as Job (v. 33)? Yet Job longs for nothing less than to meet God face to face, in a setting where the terror of God's presence does not destroy Job's case before it is heard. On the point of his integrity, Job would then face God without fear. But this could happen only on God's initiative, only if God withdrew the cosmic anger and terror that now intimidate Job beyond measure (vv. 34–35; the second half of v. 35 in the Hebrew text remains puzzling, as a comparison of modern translations indicates).

Job 10

10:1 "I loathe my life;
  I will give free utterance to my complaint;
  I will speak in the bitterness of my soul.
 2 I will say to God, Do not condemn me;
   let me know why you contend against me.
 3 Does it seem good to you to oppress,
   to despise the work of your hands
   and favor the schemes of the wicked?
 4 Do you have eyes of flesh?
   Do you see as humans see?
 5 Are your days like the days of mortals,
   or your years like human years,
 6 that you seek out my iniquity
   and search for my sin,
 7 although you know that I am not guilty,
   and there is no one to deliver out of your hand?
 8 Your hands fashioned and made me;
   and now you turn and destroy me.
 9 Remember that you fashioned me like clay;
   and will you turn me to dust again?
 10 Did you not pour me out like milk
   and curdle me like cheese?
 11 You clothed me with skin and flesh,
   and knit me together with bones and sinews.
 12 You have granted me life and steadfast love,
   and your care has preserved my spirit.
 13 Yet these things you hid in your heart;
   I know that this was your purpose.
 14 If I sin, you watch me,
   and do not acquit me of my iniquity.
 15 If I am wicked, woe to me!
   If I am righteous, I cannot lift up my head,
 for I am filled with disgrace
   and look upon my affliction.
 16 Bold as a lion you hunt me;
   you repeat your exploits against me.
 17 You renew your witnesses against me,
   and increase your vexation toward me;
   you bring fresh troops against me.

 18 "Why did you bring me forth from the womb?
   Would that I had died before any eye had seen me,
 19 and were as though I had not been,

> carried from the womb to the grave.
> ^{20} Are not the days of my life few?
>> Let me alone, that I may find a little comfort
> ^{21} before I go, never to return,
>> to the land of gloom and deep darkness,
> ^{22} the land of gloom and chaos,
>> where light is like darkness."

In 9:21–24, the reckless freedom of having nothing else to lose (and no hope of gain) led Job to a sweeping accusation that God's providence is unjust. In 10:1–22, the same freedom now empowers Job to speak to God with surprising intimacy, as if the impossible longing expressed in 9:34–35 had somehow been fulfilled. Like a wounded lover, Job asks God to explain why their relationship has been shattered from God's side (10:2). How could God do this to "the work of your hands" (vv. 3, 8; see Gen. 2:7), whose marvelous formation bears testimony to God's exquisite artistry and craftsmanship (vv. 9–12; see Psalm 139:13–16) and whose very life and sustenance bear witness to God's continuing care (v. 12)? Even though these mysteries are hidden in God's heart, Job knows that he is "fearfully and wonderfully made" (Psalm 139:14), that God created him on purpose.

This makes his present rejection and abandonment by God all the more incomprehensible and intolerable. Does it seem "good" to God to "oppress" this wonderful creature with a life of servitude (see 7:1–6), to "favor the schemes of the wicked," that is, subject this creature to injustice (10:3; see 9:22–24)? Does God know what it's like to be human? Can God see things from the human point of view (10:4)? Does God share the transience of human life (v. 5)? It might befit a human adversary to dog the trail of other human beings, seeking out some grounds of complaint against them—but God? God *knows* Job is not guilty and that there is no one to rescue him from God's hand (vv. 6–7).

It matters not whether Job is wicked or righteous. Either way, God makes Job the victim and renews the angry attack against him (vv. 14–17). Here the accusation of injustice made in 9:22–24 becomes acutely personal: There is no justice in God's victimization of Job. Readers of Job 2:3, of course, know a startling fact that Job doesn't: God *agrees* with Job on this point! It isn't fair!

No wonder Job returns now to the agonizing cry first expressed in 3:11–26. But this time the despairing question is put directly to God, in the language of prayer: "Why did you bring me forth from the womb?" (v. 18; see vv. 9–13). Would it not be more just, or at least more humane, for God to leave Job alone during this last, brief interval before he enters the final darkness of death (vv. 20–22; see 7:16, 19)? In 3:11–22, death was described as a place of restful sleep, a place of freedom from oppression and inequity, a place the wretched search for as if it were hidden treasure, rejoicing when it is found at last. Here death is a land of impenetrable darkness from which there is no return. In 10:18, Job wishes he had "died before any eye had seen me." Is this is a veiled reference to the ruthless scrutiny of God, which Job regards as the reason God has singled him out as a target (see 7:19–20)? If so, the darkness of death will at last shield him from God's sight (see 7:8, 21b).

It is perhaps fair to ask how Job's lot would improve if God were to grant this repeated request to be "left alone" (7:16, 19; 10:20). Job clearly longs for relationship with God, one that is fair, open, and free from intimidation (9:34–35). For reasons Job cannot comprehend, God persists in seeking him out as well, but only as a relentless "watcher" (7:20; 10:6) bent on exposing and punishing Job's "guilt," even though Job is confident God knows Job is not guilty (10:7). Why on earth would it be of interest to Almighty God to maintain a relationship with a fragile human being—a relationship that is so unfair and so destructive? For God to "leave Job alone" would mean to break off the relationship with Job from God's side, as a fruitless enterprise for both parties. Job could then approach death without agonizing further about his innocence or about God's justice in the ordering of human affairs. Does God have some mysterious investment in Job that is *not* reflected in the inquisitorial terror Job has experienced at God's hands? In 10:12–13, Job intimates that there must be. But if there is, then 10:20–22 may contain a gentle note of warning to God, in the vein of 7:7–8 and 7:21b: The day is coming soon when the "deep darkness" of death will blot me out of your sight. (It is perhaps worth noting that, according to Psalm 139:11–12, not even this ultimate darkness can thwart God's relentless will to relationship.)

The opening scenes in the divine council chamber disclose two highly relevant facts about all of this, which Job cannot possibly know: (1) God does indeed have an investment in Job that is not reflected in the terror he is experiencing (1:8; 2:3); and (2) God has no intention of breaking off the relationship with Job from God's side, for any reason. God's integrity is also at stake here.

ZOPHAR'S FIRST SPEECH
Job 11

Job 11

11:1 **Then Zophar the Naamathite answered:**
² **"Should a multitude of words go unanswered,
and should one full of talk be vindicated?**

³ Should your babble put others to silence,
    and when you mock, shall no one shame you?
⁴ For you say, 'My conduct is pure,
    and I am clean in God's sight.'
⁵ But oh, that God would speak,
    and open his lips to you,
⁶ and that he would tell you the secrets of wisdom!
    For wisdom is many-sided.
Know then that God exacts of you less than your guilt deserves.

⁷ "Can you find out the deep things of God?
    Can you find out the limit of the Almighty?
⁸ It is higher than heaven—what can you do?
    Deeper than Sheol—what can you know?
⁹ Its measure is longer than the earth,
    and broader than the sea.
¹⁰ If he passes through, and imprisons,
    and assembles for judgment, who can hinder him?
¹¹ For he knows those who are worthless;
    when he sees iniquity, will he not consider it?
¹² But a stupid person will get understanding,
    when a wild ass is born human.

¹³ "If you direct your heart rightly,
    you will stretch out your hands toward him.
¹⁴ If iniquity is in your hand, put it far away,
    and do not let wickedness reside in your tents.
¹⁵ Surely then you will lift up your face without blemish;
    you will be secure, and will not fear.
¹⁶ You will forget your misery;
    you will remember it as waters that have passed away.
¹⁷ And your life will be brighter than the noonday;
    its darkness will be like the morning.
¹⁸ And you will have confidence, because there is hope;
    you will be protected and take your rest in safety.
¹⁹ You will lie down, and no one will make you afraid;
    many will entreat your favor.
²⁰ But the eyes of the wicked will fail;
    all way of escape will be lost to them,
    and their hope is to breathe their last."

Zophar is perhaps the most schoolmasterly of Job's friends in the sense that all the maxims of traditional wisdom are textbook clear and final for him. What Job has said interests him only as material for classroom debate and instruction. After making the customary rhetorical comments designed to expose one's opponent as an arrogant windbag (11:2–3; see 8:2), Zophar zeros in on his blockbuster argument: God's wisdom is qualitatively greater than and different from any wisdom to which human beings may aspire (vv. 6–12). Job is obviously ignorant of this, since he claims that his "conduct is pure" and he is "clean in God's sight" (v. 4; the NRSV notes that the Hebrew text reads "teaching" for "conduct," a translation I regard as preferable. Zophar thinks Job is a teacher of doctrine rather than a suffering servant of God. The difference is vast). Zophar wishes God would speak directly to Job (Job does too; 10:2) and reveal to him the secrets of wisdom (vv. 5–6). That is because Zophar is confident God would tell Job what Zophar already knows: that "wisdom is many-sided" (or "two-sided"), that is, there is a level (or levels) of wisdom beyond direct human understanding. (Eliphaz touches on this in 5:9.) According to God's transcendent wisdom, not only does Job deserve everything that has happened to him but God has actually let him off lightly (v. 6)!

To clinch the point, Zophar challenges Job to test his human wisdom against the wisdom of God. Job will find himself beyond his depth in every direction (vv. 7–9). Yet God's inscrutable and irresistible wisdom always issues in just condemnation of iniquity and those who practice it (vv. 10–11). But the case is hardly worth arguing with a "wild ass" such as Job (v. 12; according to 39:5–8, it is characteristic of the wild ass that it scorns all efforts at domestication). The implication is that Job lacks not only wisdom but the ordinary human capacity to acquire it.

If Job can perceive it, however, a way out of his present dilemma does exist. If Job will change his mind ("direct your heart rightly," v. 13; that is, accept Zophar's assessment of the situation), throw himself on God's mercy as a repentant sinner, "stretch out your hands toward [God]" (v. 13; see 5:8; 8:5), and renounce all wickedness (v. 14; see 4:6; 8:6), the way to the blessed life still lies open (11:15–19; see 5:19–26; 8:20–21). For Job, of course, this enormous personal gain can be purchased only at the price of his integrity, that is, by accepting blame for crimes against God that he has not committed. Zophar follows this "carrot" with the inevitable "stick" of verse 20. The alternative to admission of sinfulness is a well-deserved and utterly hopeless ruin, in the company of all the rest of "the wicked."

3. The Second Round of Discourses between Job and His Friends
Job 12—20

JOB'S RESPONSE TO ZOPHAR'S FIRST SPEECH
Job 12—14

Job has now heard from each of his friends in turn. The "wisdom" they all offer him is clear in its broad outlines. The justice of all God's dealings with human beings is unfailing, even though God's transcendent wisdom often eludes mere human understanding. Human beings are incapable by nature of being blameless before God. It is a blasphemous affront to God to claim that one's suffering is undeserved, thereby calling God's justice into question. Joblike suffering is to be received as punishment in a spirit of abject repentance or welcomed as discipline at God's hand in a spirit of renewed determination to live the just and pious life. To do this opens the way to the blessed existence of the righteous. To do otherwise is to suffer the inevitable torment and destruction God has prepared for the wicked.

In chapters 12—14, Job mounts a wholesale attack against this conventional theological "wisdom." Here also, however, Job's most passionate words are addressed to God, in the language of outraged and heartbroken prayer. Predictably, Job does not win the argument with his friends. He succeeds only in triggering a second round of argument from Eliphaz, Bildad, and Zophar. God remains silent.

Job 12
12:1 **Then Job answered:**
2 **"No doubt you are the people,**
and wisdom will die with you.
3 **But I have understanding as well as you;**
I am not inferior to you.
Who does not know such things as these?
4 **I am a laughingstock to my friends;**
I, who called upon God and he answered me,
a just and blameless man, I am a laughingstock.

⁵ Those at ease have contempt for misfortune,
  but it is ready for those whose feet are unstable.
⁶ The tents of robbers are at peace,
  and those who provoke God are secure,
  who bring their god in their hands.

⁷ "But ask the animals, and they will teach you;
  the birds of the air, and they will tell you;
⁸ ask the plants of the earth, and they will teach you;
  and the fish of the sea will declare to you.
⁹ Who among all these does not know
  that the hand of the LORD has done this?
¹⁰ In his hand is the life of every living thing
  and the breath of every human being.
¹¹ Does not the ear test words
  as the palate tastes food?
¹² Is wisdom with the aged,
  and understanding in length of days?

¹³ "With God are wisdom and strength;
  he has counsel and understanding.
¹⁴ If he tears down, no one can rebuild;
  if he shuts someone in, no one can open up.
¹⁵ If he withholds the waters, they dry up;
  if he sends them out, they overwhelm the land.
¹⁶ With him are strength and wisdom;
  the deceived and the deceiver are his.
¹⁷ He leads counselors away stripped,
  and makes fools of judges.
¹⁸ He looses the sash of kings,
  and binds a waistcloth on their loins.
¹⁹ He leads priests away stripped,
  and overthrows the mighty.
²⁰ He deprives of speech those who are trusted,
  and takes away the discernment of the elders.
²¹ He pours contempt on princes,
  and looses the belt of the strong.
²² He uncovers the deeps out of darkness,
  and brings deep darkness to light.
²³ He makes nations great, then destroys them;
  he enlarges nations, then leads them away.
²⁴ He strips understanding from the leaders of the earth,
  and makes them wander in a pathless waste.
²⁵ They grope in the dark without light;
  he makes them stagger like a drunkard.

The whole of chapter 12 is taken up with Job's claim that he knows all the tired maxims of conventional wisdom as well as any of his friends. The opening sentences indicate that he, too, can use the debater's technique of ridiculing one's opponent before the argument begins (see 8:2; 11:2–3). Job's friends have spoken as if they were the sole repository of all wisdom, yet Job knows everything they do, and so does everyone else (12:2–3). Difficulties in translation and interpretation make verses 4–6 somewhat unclear, but the wording of the NRSV opens the possibility that Job is making an extremely serious charge against his friends at this point. If Job is indeed a "just and blameless man" who has become a "laughingstock" to his friends, what does this reveal about the character of such "friends"? Are they the ones who "have contempt for [Job's] misfortune" while they themselves remain "at ease"? Job has argued that "the earth is given into the hand of the wicked" (9:24). Such injustice is epitomized in 12:6: "The tents of the robbers are at peace, and those who provoke God are secure, who bring their god in their hands" (that is, "control God"). Is Job identifying his friends as such "robbers," living proof of Job's claim that the wicked are not punished and the righteous are not rewarded in this life? We cannot be certain of this interpretation, but it is consistent with the charge Job makes more explicitly in 13:7–11, as we shall see.

Both Eliphaz (see 5:8–16) and Zophar (11:7–10) have stressed God's wisdom and power that rule over all and determine all outcomes. Job responds to this wise counsel with a sarcastic lesson that sounds like an introductory lecture in Wisdom 101. Each animal and bird and plant and fish shares with the others the profound insight that "the hand of the LORD has done this." "In God's hand is the life of every living thing and the breath of every human being" (vv. 7–10). The little aside in verse 11 may convey the notion that high-sounding words can be tested for content as easily as the tongue can distinguish between edible and inedible food. Do you have to be a wise old elder to figure these things out (see 8:8–10)?

It is striking that Job and his friends agree on this critical point. Nowhere in the book of Job is the opinion expressed that things may happen "accidentally," that is, outside the scope of God's transcendent wisdom and power. This forces Job's friends to construct theological arguments that affirm God's justice in everything that occurs, even when the meager resources of human wisdom cannot perceive it. Job, in contrast, must hold *God* accountable when he meets with injustice in human affairs, whether in his own experience or that of others. His integrity demands it. The God we encounter in the heavenly council is this same absolute sovereign, who ordains "whatsoever comes to pass" as the Westminster Confession of Faith puts it. Yet the scenes in the heavenly council also disclose a scandalous possibility that lies beyond the ken of Job or his friends: This sovereign God may be "incited" to act in ways that surely demonstrate God's power but do not demonstrate either God's justice or God's estimate of the person against whom this power is exercised.

Confronted with these three simplistic alternatives, contemporary hearts of faith may well cry out, "None of the above!" If we are to continue reading Job, however, we need to remember that it has never been the proper function of this book to provide answers for the questions it raises (see above, pp. 2–3). If Job drives us to use all the resources of biblical faith to find some alternative ways of relating the reality of God to the realities of human experience, the book has done its work well.

We have not yet heard Job through to the end, however, if we simply reject the basic premise of the book that God is totally in charge of human destinies, whether as Job sees it or as Job's friends see it or as the heavenly council sees it. If we can accept this premise, by a deliberate "suspension of disbelief," we may discover that Job probes far beyond the limits of these three simplistic "solutions" to the question of divine-human relationships.

Job is well acquainted with the grand old hymns to God's transcendent wisdom and power. In 12:13–25 he composes one of his own, but with a twist calculated to drive Eliphaz, Bildad, and Zophar straight up the wall. God is surely as wise and powerful as everybody says, sings Job in verse 13, but just look at the ways in which this sovereign wisdom and power are demonstrated. God is the one who destroys and walls in (v. 14). God is the one who orders up drought or floods at will (v. 15). God owns equally the deceived and the deceivers (v. 16). God rids the community of its intellectual and judicial leadership (v. 17). God humiliates kings, clergy, and VIPs (vv. 18–21). God shuts the mouths of respected leaders and drives the learned elders mad (v. 20). God unleashes chaos from the primeval depths and lets its darkness dominate the scene (v. 22). God sets up nations and then knocks them over, expands their empires and then leads them to oblivion (v. 23). God makes world leaders mindless and puts them in a maze with no exit (v. 24). They grope in the dark without a flashlight and crash into things as drunks do (v. 25).

As a hymn, this poem has its limitations; but as a portrayal of the way things are in human life and history, it corresponds all too closely to reality. Job might well have asked here the question he asked in 9:24: If the all-wise and all-powerful God is not responsible for these chaotic conditions, who is?

If we compare 12:13–25 with the doxologies sung by Eliphaz (5:9–16) and Zophar (11:7–11), the issue between them and Job is exposed dramatically. For these friends, the chaotic conditions Job describes are indeed caused by God, but in everything that occurs, God is working toward the destruction of the wicked and the vindication of the righteous. (Note, for example, that those who "grope in the dark" according to Job in 12:25 are identified by Eliphaz with "the crafty," those who are "wise in their own craftiness," and "the wily" in 5:12–14.) If the justice of God's work is not always transparent to human eyes, Eliphaz and Zophar are covered by the doctrine that God's ultimate wisdom surpasses all human understanding (see 5:9; 11:7–9). This leaves the friends with no alternative except to take Job's suffering as evidence of God's just punishment for sin (11:6) or, at best, God's gracious disciplinary action (5:17).

Job 13

13:1   **"Look, my eye has seen all this,**
     my ear has heard and understood it.
  2 **What you know, I also know;**
     I am not inferior to you.
  3 **But I would speak to the Almighty,**
     and I desire to argue my case with God.
  4 **As for you, you whitewash with lies;**
     all of you are worthless physicians.
  5 **If you would only keep silent,**
     that would be your wisdom!
  6 **Hear now my reasoning,**
     and listen to the pleadings of my lips.
  7 **Will you speak falsely for God,**
     and speak deceitfully for him?
  8 **Will you show partiality toward him,**
     will you plead the case for God?
  9 **Will it be well with you when he searches you out?**
     Or can you deceive him, as one person deceives another?
  10 **He will surely rebuke you**
     if in secret you show partiality.
  11 **Will not his majesty terrify you,**
     and the dread of him fall upon you?
  12 **Your maxims are proverbs of ashes,**
     your defenses are defenses of clay.

  13 **"Let me have silence, and I will speak,**
     and let come on me what may.
  14 **I will take my flesh in my teeth,**

and put my life in my hand.
¹⁵ See, he will kill me; I have no hope;
    but I will defend my ways to his face.
¹⁶ This will be my salvation,
    that the godless shall not come before him.
¹⁷ Listen carefully to my words,
    and let my declaration be in your ears.
¹⁸ I have indeed prepared my case;
    I know that I shall be vindicated.
¹⁹ Who is there that will contend with me?
    For then I would be silent and die.
²⁰ Only grant two things to me,
    then I will not hide myself from your face:
²¹ withdraw your hand far from me,
    and do not let dread of you terrify me.
²² Then call, and I will answer;
    or let me speak, and you reply to me.
²³ How many are my iniquities and my sins?
    Make me know my transgression and my sin.
²⁴ Why do you hide your face,
    and count me as your enemy?
²⁵ Will you frighten a windblown leaf
    and pursue dry chaff?
²⁶ For you write bitter things against me,
    and make me reap the iniquities of my youth.
²⁷ You put my feet in the stocks,
    and watch all my paths;
    you set a bound to the soles of my feet.
²⁸ One wastes away like a rotten thing,
    like a garment that is moth-eaten.

The theological wisdom that God works for the destruction of the wicked and upholds the righteous is as familiar to Job as it is to any of his friends (13:1–2). The problem for Job is that the doctrine simply does not fit his case. He may be suffering the "fate of the wicked," but Job knows he has done nothing to deserve it. That is an issue that Job longs to take up with God (v. 3), not with a theological discussion group. In 13:4–12, Job develops the countercharge he may have hinted at in 12:4–6. His theological mentors are engaged in a lying cover-up, as plasterers might disguise a rotting wall. As "healers," they are quacks guilty of malpractice. They are at their best when they have wisdom enough to keep silent and listen (vv. 4–6; see 2:13).

In a sudden reversal of roles, Job now warns his friends of the consequences of their deceitful attitudes, when God calls them to account and
they stand before God's majesty in fear and trembling (13:7–11). The
charge is a startling one. Job does not accuse them of having committed
sins of the kind Eliphaz lists in 22:5–9. Rather, the charge is that they are
bearing false witness on God's behalf (13:7). They have appointed themselves attorneys for God's defense, prepared to commit perjury in God's
name in order to win the case. To "show partiality" (vv. 8, 10) means to
slant one's judgment in favor of people who have status, wealth, or power,
perhaps in exchange for a bribe or some anticipated personal benefit (see
Exod. 23:6–8; Deut. 1:16–17). Job's accusation is that his friends have declared him guilty, not on the grounds of any evidence but in order to pro-
tect the reputation of God "from whom all blessings flow." Job, in
contrast, appears to affirm the incorruptibility of God's justice, even if the
present case puts God in the wrong rather than Job. Apparently, Job believes God would rather hear Job's honest words than listen to the lying
testimony of these theologians who try to curry divine favor by "plead[ing]
the case for God" (13:8; Job 42:7–8 bears out Job's shocking confidence on
this point). On this basis, Job dismisses the tired old "maxims" and "de-
fenses" of his friends as altogether worthless (13:12).

In 13:3, Job indicated that his argument was not with these friends but
with God. In a culture where words are cheap and mindless "blasphemies"
abound, it is difficult to recapture the high drama of Job's formal declaration of intent to argue his case directly before God (13:13–16). For Job, as
well as for his pious friends, addressing defiant words to God was an invitation to swift and terrible retribution. Actors portraying Eliphaz, Bildad,
and Zophar in this scene would not only fall silent at Job's command (v.
13). They would also shut their eyes, clap their hands over their ears, and
turn away in terror lest they be consumed by the cataclysm Job's words
might provoke. Job himself would wear the face of a condemned man prepared to defy his executioners with his last breath, at the cost of his life (vv.
13b–15).

One of the most famous lines in the book of Job is found in 13:15a.
Readers of the King James Version (KJV) in every generation since 1611
have heard Job make this heroic declaration of faith: "Though he slay me,
yet will I trust in him." The possibility of this translation is rooted in an
ancient marginal note provided by Jewish scholars who began copying and
annotating the sacred Hebrew text as early as the first century A.D. These
scholars preserved the written text in a form that suggests a translation
such as the one we find in the NRSV: "See, [God] will kill me; I have no

hope." In the margin, however, the ancient copyists suggested a different spelling of the written text, one that could be read: "Though he slay me, yet will I trust [or 'wait' or 'hope'] in him." Modern biblical scholars tend to follow the written Hebrew text rather than the ancient marginal note, for three reasons: (1) The written text is almost certainly more ancient than the marginal notes; (2) the written text is more appropriate to the context, in which Job states that he knows he takes his life in his hands by saying these things; and (3) the marginal note can be explained as a pious interpretation that avoids the harshest implications of the written text. I find these reasons convincing. It seems unlikely to me that Job here breaks through to a heroic level of unqualified trust, only to fall back into the same kind of heartbroken lament and protest that dominate his speeches from beginning to end. Perhaps after the story of Job is over, after Job has emerged from his ordeal vindicated by God, after Job has become a symbol of indomitable fidelity for the community of faith—perhaps then we can hear this iconic Job challenging us to faith with the words "Though God slay me, yet will I trust in God" (see Hab. 3:17–19).

Without any prospect of personal gain, without any "happy ending" in sight, Job proposes to do the unthinkable: "I will defend my ways to [God's] face. This will be my salvation, that the godless shall not come before [God]" (vv. 15b–16). The term *salvation* can be misleading here—perhaps especially to Christian readers, for whom this word connotes God's gracious victory on behalf of sinners, opening the way to eternal life with God. The basic meaning of the Hebrew word is simply "help," although the Hebrew Bible often uses the word to describe a gracious intervention of God on behalf of God's people. What I hear Job saying in 13:15–16 is this: When I come face to face with God, the only help I have to rely on is the integrity of "my ways," the confidence that I shall not come before God as a "godless" person (that is, a wicked, arrogant lawbreaker; see 8:13). For the impending trial, Job has prepared his case well. He is confident that when all the facts are in and all the evidence has been examined, he will be "vindicated" (that is, found not guilty; 13:18). On this point, Job is prepared to challenge all comers. I see this as an indication that Job "still persists in his integrity," as God puts it in 2:3.

What follows might be described in lawyer's jargon as a "motion *in limine*": an appeal to the court to set certain limits within which the argument may be pursued. Job pleads with God to withhold God's "hand" (God's overwhelming power to destroy any opponent) and to spare Job the terrifying dread of God that would reduce Job to jelly before his case could be heard. Under these conditions, says Job, "I will not hide myself from your face: . . . Then call, and I will answer; or let me speak, and you reply to me" (vv. 20–22; see 9:32–35, where we can also discern Job's most urgent longing: a face-to-face encounter with God in which the issue of Job's innocence could be fairly resolved).

There is no indication, of course, that Job's motion *in limine* has been granted. Nothing has happened to change the chaotic circumstances that have driven Job to the outer limits of despair. The shocking thing is that Job now proceeds (in 13:23–14:22) to pour out his heart to God "as if"— as if God were to grant him that privileged place and time to make his case, as if one could speak with God face to face, as one speaks to a friend (see Exod. 33:11; Deut. 34:10).

The first thing Job wants to hear from God is a clear indication of what grievances God nurses against him that have triggered the "punishment" he is enduring (v. 23). Why has God broken their relationship from God's side, so that Job is now counted as God's enemy? (See p. 12, where we noted a possible wordplay involving Job's name: '*Iyyob*/'*oyeb*, Hebrew for "Job" and "enemy," respectively. For God to "hide God's face" is an idiom for God's disfavor; see Psalms 13:1; 44:24; 88:14.) Why should God mount a major assault against so fragile a target (v. 25), or make a federal case out of long-forgotten sins (v. 26), or hound such a "guilty" person as if he were a public enemy (v. 27)?

Job 14

14:1 "A mortal, born of woman,
　　few of days and full of trouble,
  2 comes up like a flower and withers,
　　flees like a shadow and does not last.
  3 Do you fix your eyes on such a one?
　　Do you bring me into judgment with you?
  4 Who can bring a clean thing out of an unclean?
　　No one can.
  5 Since their days are determined,
　　and the number of their months is known to you,
　　and you have appointed the bounds that they cannot pass,
  6 look away from them, and desist,
　　that they may enjoy, like laborers, their days.

  7 "For there is hope for a tree,
　　if it is cut down, that it will sprout again,
　　and that its shoots will not cease.
  8 Though its root grows old in the earth,

and its stump dies in the ground,
⁹ yet at the scent of water it will bud
    and put forth branches like a young plant.
¹⁰ But mortals die, and are laid low;
    humans expire, and where are they?
¹¹ As waters fail from a lake,
    and a river wastes away and dries up,
¹² so mortals lie down and do not rise again;
    until the heavens are no more, they will not awake
    or be roused out of their sleep.
¹³ Oh that you would hide me in Sheol,
    that you would conceal me until your wrath is past,
    that you would appoint me a set time, and remember me!
¹⁴ If mortals die, will they live again?
    All the days of my service I would wait
    until my release should come.
¹⁵ You would call, and I would answer you;
    you would long for the work of your hands.
¹⁶ For then you would not number my steps,
    you would not keep watch over my sin;
¹⁷ my transgression would be sealed up in a bag,
    and you would cover over my iniquity.

¹⁸ "But the mountain falls and crumbles away,
    and the rock is removed from its place;
¹⁹ the waters wear away the stones;
    the torrents wash away the soil of the earth;
    so you destroy the hope of mortals.
²⁰ You prevail forever against them, and they pass away;
    you change their countenance, and send them away.
²¹ Their children come to honor, and they do not know it;
    they are brought low, and it goes unnoticed.
²² They feel only the pain of their own bodies,
    and mourn only for themselves."

God's seeming zealousness in punishing Job leads Job to muse out loud (at length) about the absurdity of the human situation, given the fact that God appears to have such an inordinate concern with the details of human behavior (13:28–14:22; scholars have noted, perhaps rightly, that 13:28 would fit beautifully between 14:2 and 14:3). That these musings are intended for God's ears is clear from verses 5–6 and 13–17, yet they are broadly philosophical in their import, embracing all human experience as well as Job's particular relationship with God. It is a fundamental reality of human existence, says Job, that people have a remarkably brief life span, on a par with unrefrigerated meat or garments exposed to moths (13:28). What is to be expected of a race "born of woman" whose life span is so brief and trouble ridden (14:1)? (Attempts have been made to render this verse politically correct, but I suspect a pandemic sexism is at work here, according to which the fact that every "man" is born of woman is taken to be a peculiar embarrassment.) Whatever seems lively or impressive in human life is actually no more substantial than a spring flower that quickly withers in the desert winds of summer (see Isa. 40:6–7); or than a long shadow that disappears with the setting sun (Job 14:2). For the life of him, Job fails to understand why God bothers to haul such an insignificant creature before the bar of God's judgment (v. 3). The next verse appears to echo the argument of Eliphaz in 4:17–21 (see 9:2). Is Job reciting this bit of conventional wisdom, perhaps sarcastically, to underscore the futility of God's insistence on probing human behavior with inscrutable acts of "punishment"? If so, verse 5 carries the sarcasm a step further by citing the conventional doctrine of God's foreknowledge and predestination. Since God determines human life spans, knows the details in advance, and sets the limits by which every human being is bound, God should get off their backs. Let them slave away their remaining days without being troubled by God (vv. 5–6; see 7:16–20; 10:20–22). While thoughts such as these may express Job's sense of helplessness and despair, that they are poured out to God implies both a longing and a challenge. The longing is for a relationship with God that is very different from the miserable and pointless one Job has just described. The challenge is for God to give Job an alternative way of reading the hard facts of human experience, to demonstrate that God's relationship with Job is not as it seems to be (see 7:21; 9:34–35; 10:9–13; 13:20–22, where this longing and this challenge are expressed directly).

Having eavesdropped on deliberations in the divine council, we know that God's relationship with Job is not as it seems to be. The suffering Job endures does not reflect either God's attitude toward Job or God's proper intention for Job's life. Job's urgent longing for a face-to-face encounter with God indicates that Job somehow knows this too. A person of Job's integrity would hardly seek audience with a God he knows to be inherently tyrannical, inscrutable, and unjust.

In 14:7–22, Job expresses both the apparent hopelessness of such a longing for relationship with God (vv. 7–12; 18–22) and the deep passion with which he longs for it (vv. 13–17). Job envies the trees their resurgent vitality. A fresh young shoot emerges from an apparently dead stump in token of the well-grounded "hope" (v. 7) that life prevails over the worst that can happen (vv. 7–9). It is more than a little surprising that Job sees no comparable hope for human beings (vv. 10–12). It is a rare culture, throughout all human history, that lacks some form of belief in life after death, from "happy hunting grounds" to reincarnation, together with all their variations. The fertility cults that dominated so much of the ancient Near East saw a particularly strong link between resurgent vitality in nature and human participation in that process. Yet Job is startlingly confident that the entire human drama is played out between birth and death. Everything decisive for human life, whether for good or for ill, happens within our lifetimes. The notion of survival after death is simply not available to Job as a means of "answering" the urgent questions of God's righteousness and ours in *this* life or of making those questions irrelevant.

This remarkable skepticism about life after death appears characteristic of what is sometimes called an "international wisdom tradition" that can be documented from Egyptian and Babylonian literature, as well as from a variety of biblical texts (see Psalm 90:9–12; Eccl. 3:19–22; 9:4–6). Yet this kind of life-weary skepticism cannot account for the fact that the Hebrew scriptures as a whole place no emphasis on life after death as a significant element of the faith of Israel. Absolutely central, in contrast, is the relationship between God and Israel as this is worked out on the plane of this-worldly life and history. At the outer limits of Israel's confidence in God's faithfulness, we find isolated affirmations that not even death will have the last word about the promises of God (e.g., Isa. 26:16–19; Dan. 12:1–3; see also Psalm 139:7–12). Even these texts, however, are better understood as witnesses to the ultimate vindication of God's purposes on earth than as intimations of some future blessedness that will trivialize the meaning of this life. "Pie in the sky by and by" has no place in the intensely relational understanding of God and people that characterizes biblical faith.

If this is so, it is critical for the understanding of Job 14:13–17. Do these poignant words disclose Job's longing for a blessed existence far removed from the "slings and arrows of outrageous fortune" that make life on earth so intolerable? Or do they express again Job's single-minded longing for a face-to-face encounter with God, one in which Job's case could be fairly heard and their mutual relationship could be restored (see 9:32–35; 10:8–13; 13:20–22)? Job must accept the inevitability of death as the ultimate end of all human life (14:7–12). What he cannot accept is the notion that he will go to his grave without ever having been heard by God, without having had the opportunity of setting things straight once and for all. It is this longing that drives him to imagine the impossible: Suppose God were to hide Job in the grave until God's unaccountable anger against Job had spent itself. Suppose, then (impossible!), God would set a time (at last) for Job's hearing and "remember" Job's case. Is it possible for a dead person to live again? Obviously not; yet if Job could look forward to that post-mortem hearing, he would gladly put up with the worst life has to offer in the meanwhile. There is literally nothing he wants more. For then "you would call, and I would answer you [that is, give an account of my innocence]; you would long for the work of your hands" (14:13–15; see 10:8–13). Somehow, beyond all evidence, Job is convinced that God also has a stake in a restored relationship between them. I suspect it is this unsubstantiated hunch, as well as confidence in his own innocence, that drives Job's relentless quest for a fair hearing.

Verses 16 and 17 appear to present a problem for this interpretation. Is Job confessing that he bears a heavy burden of "sin," "transgression," and "iniquity" that God would somehow need to "cover over" in order to make this idyllic reconciliation complete? If so, I'm sure Eliphaz, Bildad, and Zophar would love to hear Job make such a confession. For pages now, they have been urging him to do so. In 10:5–7, however, Job has provided us with a different way of understanding 14:16–17. From the beginning Job has understood the suffering he endures to be a direct sign that God has found fault with him, is angry with him, and is punishing him for nameless "sins" of which Job knows he is innocent. What's more, Job is confident that God knows it too (10:7). It is for this unaccountable reason that Job experiences God as a relentless "watcher" who continually dogs his steps and deals with him as if he were guilty of the worst (7:12, 20–21; 9:20, 28–31). Job has no way of knowing, as we do, that God's "assault" on Job has nothing to do with God's estimation of Job's guilt. In that light, 14:16–17 corresponds to Job's plea for God to "withdraw your hand far from me, and do not let dread of you terrify me" (13:21; see 7:20–21; 9:34–35). The relationship between God and Job cannot be reconciled until God desists from this inquisitorial behavior and does away with whatever "sins" are supposed to have occasioned it.

Job quickly returns to earth from this brief flight into fantasy. The only thing real about it has been the moving testimony it bears to the deepest longing of Job's heart. This longing has nothing to do with the common lust for personal survival after death. It has everything to do with a quite extraordinary passion for a just and mutual relationship with God. The fact is, however, that God destroys any such hope for mortals as surely as the forces of nature reduce mountains to rubble and wash the good earth into the sea (vv. 18–19). God always wins out against people, sending them to their deaths without so much as a clue as to how their children turn out.

All they know for sure is their own pain and grief (vv. 20–22). It takes great pain indeed to evoke such an accusation against one as greatly loved and longed for as 14:15 suggests.

JOB'S RESPONSE TO ELIPHAZ'S SECOND SPEECH
Job 16—17

Job 16

16:1 **Then Job answered:**

² **"I have heard many such things;**
   miserable comforters are you all.
³ **Have windy words no limit?**
   Or what provokes you that you keep on talking?
⁴ **I also could talk as you do,**
   if you were in my place;
 I could join words together against you,
   and shake my head at you.
⁵ **I could encourage you with my mouth,**
   and the solace of my lips would assuage your pain.

⁶ **"If I speak, my pain is not assuaged,**
   and if I forbear, how much of it leaves me?
⁷ **Surely now God has worn me out;**
   he has made desolate all my company.
⁸ **And he has shriveled me up,**
   which is a witness against me;
 my leanness has risen up against me,
   and it testifies to my face.
⁹ **He has torn me in his wrath, and hated me;**
   he has gnashed his teeth at me;
   my adversary sharpens his eyes against me.
¹⁰ **They have gaped at me with their mouths;**
   they have struck me insolently on the cheek;
   they mass themselves together against me.
¹¹ **God gives me up to the ungodly,**
   and casts me into the hands of the wicked.
¹² **I was at ease, and he broke me in two;**
   he seized me by the neck and dashed me to pieces;
 he set me up as his target;
¹³ **   his archers surround me.**
 He slashes open my kidneys, and shows no mercy;
   he pours out my gall on the ground.

¹⁴ He bursts upon me again and again;
   he rushes at me like a warrior.
¹⁵ I have sewed sackcloth upon my skin,
   and have laid my strength in the dust.
¹⁶ My face is red with weeping,
   and deep darkness is on my eyelids,
¹⁷ though there is no violence in my hands,
   and my prayer is pure.

¹⁸ "O earth, do not cover my blood;
   let my outcry find no resting place.
¹⁹ Even now, in fact, my witness is in heaven,
   and he that vouches for me is on high.
²⁰ My friends scorn me;
   my eye pours out tears to God,
²¹ that he would maintain the right of a mortal with God,
   as one does for a neighbor.
²² For when a few years have come,
   I shall go the way from which I shall not return.

After Eliphaz's second, far less pastoral piece of advice to Job (Job 15; see above, pages 30–37), Job quickly brushes all such conventional theological wisdom aside (vv. 1–5). Describing the words of one's adversary in debate as "windy" appears to be a common rhetorical device (16:3; see 8:2; 15:2), but verses 2–5 put this summary rejection in the context of the profound failure of Job's "friends" to meet the demands of true friendship. If their intent was to comfort Job (2:11), they have turned out to be the sort of "comforters" who only compound Job's misery with their pious maxims (16:2). Suppose their roles were reversed, with Job at ease and his friends in despair. Would they be helped if Job followed their example, piling up arguments against them and holding them to blame (v. 4)? Or would it be the part of a true friend to stand by them and with them and for them, with words of encouragement and solace (v. 5)? (This verse can also be read as a sarcastic characterization of the friend's hateful words as "encouragement" or "solace" when, in fact, they are the opposite. In either case, the empathy and support required of true friendship emerge clearly in verse 5.) If you have already peeked at the ending of the story, you are aware that just this kind of role reversal does take place (see 42:7). We shall see then how well Job is able to handle the costly demands of friendship hinted at in 16:5. Those who read Job 16:4–5 from a New Testament perspective can overhear in these verses something rather like Matthew 7:12.

For Job, however, neither his own outcries nor his own silences assuage his pain any better than his friends can manage (16:6). This is because of a depth of undeserved suffering that Job now describes in harsher and more disheartening terms than any we have yet heard him use (16:6–17). Job has met the enemy, and the enemy is God. If Job is now utterly "worn out," utterly alone, shriveled and lean beyond recognition (vv. 6–8; see 2:12; compare Isa. 52:14), the sole cause is God. The implication of verse 8 is the conventional theological notion that God alone is the cause of such suffering. The external symptoms of suffering therefore bear witness that God has weighed Job in some inscrutable balance, found him guilty, and meted out just this horrific judgment against him.

In a series of devastating images, Job portrays "God the enemy" as a vicious predator (v. 9), a personal assailant (v. 12), an archer in command of a company of archers (vv. 12c–13), an attacking swordsman (v. 13b), a siege commander battering through protective walls (v. 14a), and a warrior intent on the destruction of the enemy (v. 14b).

Often in the Psalms the suffering of the righteous is described in terms of attacks by unnamed enemies, the "wicked" (see Psalms 3:1; 31:11–13; 38:12; see also Isa. 50:6), most often with the plea that God deliver the innocent from their depredations. Occasionally, these enemies are characterized as wild animals (Psalms 22:12–16; 57:4; 59:6–15). The injustice of God's attack on Job is compounded by the accusation that instead of coming to the rescue, God has delivered Job into the clutches of these predatory enemies (Job 16:11).

As a result of this betrayal and God's own ungodly attacks, the "sackcloth" of inconsolable mourning has become for Job like a second skin, weeping a way of life (see Psalm 6:6), the dust of death the repository of his strength, and "deep darkness" (or the "shadow of death"; see Psalm 23:4) the cast of his eyes. All of this, says Job, in spite of the fact that his hands are guiltless and his appeal to God, on the grounds of his innocence, is spotless (vv. 15–17).

How else is Job to interpret what has happened to him, given the fact that God is indeed the one who has caused (or permitted) this suffering to befall him, according to Job 1:12; 2:6? How is Job to know that God's confidence in Job's unshakable integrity, not God's anger against him, underlies the ungodly test to which Job is being put? Yet even here, in the very face of what appears to be God the enemy, Job will not knuckle under. Still he maintains that "there is no violence in my hands, and my prayer is pure."

But has Job "cursed God" with the reckless accusations of 16:7–17, as *hassatan* predicted he would? Job 16:18–21 suggests otherwise. At the very least, this remarkable passage still holds out the possibility that somehow, in some apparently impossible way, Job will yet break through to a hearing before God—a hearing whose only outcome must be the vindication of Job's integrity before God. Verse 18 calls to mind Genesis 4:10, where God says to Cain, "Listen; your brother's blood is crying out to me from the ground!" Mother earth has been forced to drink brother's blood, and she may not be expected to keep silence. In some such way Job now appeals to mother earth not to hold her tongue. If Job should indeed perish, let the word of this injustice not be silenced. Let the cry "Job is innocent yet suffers beyond measure" continue to reverberate after he is gone.

What follows in verse 19 has often been interpreted, perhaps especially among Christians, as a statement of Job's confidence that some third party in heaven will take Job's part and make things right between Job and God. The special temptation of Christians is to find here a veiled allusion to Christ, the "witness in heaven," the one who "vouches" for frail humanity in the presence of God (see Rom. 8:34). But if indeed Job were placing supreme confidence in some "third party" here, rather than in his own integrity, then the book of Job might well end at this point, with this astonishing breakthrough of faith. If we read on, however, it is clear that Job has achieved no such decisive breakthrough. Job 16:22 through 17:16 continue with a litany of hopelessness as profound as any we have heard thus far.

What shall we make, then, of 16:18–19? In 9:33, Job laments the fact that there is no "umpire," no third party, who might bring about a fair hearing for a mere human being in the presence of Almighty God. In 13:20–22, Job longs for a setting in which he could make his case before God in the absence of overwhelming divine terror. In 14:13–17, Job allows himself to speculate on the possibility that God might "hide [Job] in Sheol" and thus provide an opportunity even beyond death, when God's "wrath is past," for a tranquil resolution of the issues between them. Job 14:18–22 makes it clear, however, that he regards this "possibility" as quite impossible.

The common thread that runs through these passages, different as they are from one another, is simply this: If, by any imaginable means, he could finally make his case fairly before God, Job is supremely confident that God would vindicate Job's integrity. From the standpoint of Job 2:3, then, each of these texts demonstrates that Job "still persists in his integrity," in spite of the special agony of not being granted such a hearing.

Perhaps for this reason some interpreters have thought Job's "witness in heaven" is none other than God, even though verse 21 seems to point in the direction of a third party to the controversy (very like the "umpire" of 9:33). Such an interpretation might appear entirely inconsistent with all

Job's previous accusations against God and his frightful description of God as "the enemy" in 16:7–17. Yet Job's longing for a hearing before God (expressed, e.g., in 9:33–35; 13:20–22; and 14:13–17) suggests that he has a last-ditch confidence that God is just, even in the face of his experience of injustice at God's hands. The moral and spiritual depth of Job's protest evaporates if we suppose that Job longs to bring his case before a God who is inherently unjust. There is no doubt that Job continually cries out *against* God. The wonder, however, is that these outcries are addressed *to* God, on the grounds of God's *own* justice. Like the wounded prayers of Moses, Jeremiah, Lamentations, and the Psalms of Lament, Job's outbursts against God are carried upon what may be called a kind of upside-down trust: In spite of everything, God must be a God of justice and compassion as well as a God of power. *Therefore* one may cry out to God "out of the depths" (Psalm 130:1), even when there is no evidence that God knows or cares or is fair in the governance of human affairs. It is in just this astonishing, upside-down way that Job "persists in his integrity" toward God, not merely with respect to his own human behavior. Whether Job 16:19 refers to God or to some heavenly third party capable of securing Job's longed-for fair hearing before God, Job's twofold trust emerges clearly: trust in his own integrity and this curious, upside-down trust that an inherently just God must ultimately vindicate him. As in 7:7–8 and 10:18–21, Job 16:22–17:1 may contain a forlorn "warning" to God that time is running out. If this vindication is to occur, it must happen soon, before Job goes "the way from which I shall not return."

Job 17

17:1 **My spirit is broken, my days are extinct,**
    the grave is ready for me.
2 **Surely there are mockers around me,**
    and my eye dwells on their provocation.

3 **"Lay down a pledge for me with yourself;**
    who is there that will give surety for me?
4 **Since you have closed their minds to understanding,**
    therefore you will not let them triumph.
5 **Those who denounce friends for reward—**
    the eyes of their children will fail.

6 **"He has made me a byword of the peoples,**
    and I am one before whom people spit.
7 **My eye has grown dim from grief,**

and all my members are like a shadow.
⁸ The upright are appalled at this,
      and the innocent stir themselves up against the godless.
⁹ Yet the righteous hold to their way,
      and they that have clean hands grow stronger and stronger.
¹⁰ But you, come back now, all of you,
      and I shall not find a sensible person among you.
¹¹ My days are past, my plans are broken off,
      the desires of my heart.
¹² They make night into day;
      'The light,' they say, 'is near to the darkness.'
¹³ If I look for Sheol as my house,
      if I spread my couch in darkness,
¹⁴ if I say to the Pit, 'You are my father,'
      and to the worm, 'My mother,' or 'My sister,'
¹⁵ where then is my hope?
      Who will see my hope?
¹⁶ Will it go down to the bars of Sheol?
      Shall we descend together into the dust?"

At 17:2, Job apparently turns his attention back to the "friends" whose "provocation" he has described as the very opposite of the encouragement a true friend owes to one who is in distress such as his own (16:1–5). If so, however, it is clear from 17:2–12 that Job's three friends symbolize a whole class of people who typically harass the innocent sufferer (see Psalms 22:6–8; 69:9–12; 89:50–51; see also Isa. 50:6).

Scholars differ as to whether Job is demanding a "pledge" from his friends or offering a fresh pledge of his own integrity in 17:3. (The NRSV translation is obviously based on the former possibility.) In either case, the notion of the pledge indicates a willingness to back up one's convictions by risking the loss of much—or everything—in the event one is proven wrong ("Cross my heart and hope to die!"). In 13:13–16, Job has already staked his life on the authenticity of his claim to innocence. According to the translation offered in the NRSV, he now challenges his friends to stand behind their counterclaim in an equally costly way. Job's opinion of the friends' behavior is expressed in a fascinating aside addressed to God (17:4). God is the one who has blinded their eyes to the justice of Job's cause; it is therefore unthinkable that God (here again acknowledged to be just?) will allow their false words to prevail against Job. According to 42:7–8, Job turns out to be right about this. In 17:5, Job underscores his point in the form of a universally valid proverb, implying that his friends are motivated to denounce him solely for the "reward" they hope to gain, presumably from God, on the grounds that they have taken God's side in the argument with Job (see 13:7–11). By so doing, the friends invite ruin not only on themselves but also on their own families.

Job 17:6 lumps Job's friends together with the multitudes who characteristically taunt and insult the innocent sufferer, according to the Psalms of Lament. Genuinely upright people, in contrast, are appalled by Joblike suffering and take their stand on the side of the sufferer, against the "godless" (17:7–8).

Job 17:9 sounds contradictory on Job's lips, yet it reinforces Job's claim to innocence and possibly his upside-down trust in his ultimate vindication. Taken by itself, this verse appears to echo proverbial confidence in the ultimate success of "the righteous" (see Psalm 1). The diatribe against Job's "mockers" (17:2) ends in 17:10, with a challenge to the friends to give Job their best shot, since there is not a wise person among them!

If we prefer to think that Job achieved some sort of spiritual breakthrough in 16:18–19, it clearly did not last long. Job 17:11–16 confronts us with a Job who is on his way to "Sheol," to "darkness," to "the Pit," to the "worm" that symbolizes his total destruction. Indeed, the Pit and the worm are the only "family" he has left. Most poignantly, however, verses 15–16 raise the question of what is to become of Job's hope. On the basis of what Job has said so far, perhaps we may describe this hope in terms of an encounter with God free from all coercion and terror (9:34–35); a time of untroubled converse with God (13:20–22); a time beyond wrath for God to call, for Job to answer, for God to "long for the work of your hands" (14:13–15; see 10:8–13); a time when all God's (unjust?) charges against Job would be dropped (14:16–17), a time when "the right of a mortal with God" could be maintained (16:21). Taken together, these texts indicate that Job's hope goes beyond merely being proven innocent in some heavenly courtroom. Job looks forward to his vindication as the God-given earnest of a restored relationship with God, in all its remembered height and depth. The question of 17:15–16 is whether the magnificent hope of a tranquil relationship between a human being and God, based on mutual integrity and affirmation, can survive when Job is gone, or whether hope itself will "descend . . . into the dust" with him. In its most agonizing form, for contemporary communities based on biblical faith, this becomes the question as to whether hope in the God of whom the Bible speaks, hope for human beings, hope for the human future, is anything more than a transient illusion. Like Job before us, we must press on toward the end of a story that is not yet over.

BILDAD'S SECOND SPEECH
Job 18

Job 18

18:1 Then Bildad the Shuhite answered:
  ² "How long will you hunt for words?
      Consider, and then we shall speak.
  ³ Why are we counted as cattle?
      Why are we stupid in your sight?
  ⁴ You who tear yourself in your anger—
      shall the earth be forsaken because of you,
      or the rock be removed out of its place?

  ⁵ "Surely the light of the wicked is put out,
      and the flame of their fire does not shine.
  ⁶ The light is dark in their tent,
      and the lamp above them is put out.
  ⁷ Their strong steps are shortened,
      and their own schemes throw them down.
  ⁸ For they are thrust into a net by their own feet,
      and they walk into a pitfall.
  ⁹ A trap seizes them by the heel;
      a snare lays hold of them.
  ¹⁰ A rope is hid for them in the ground,
      a trap for them in the path.
  ¹¹ Terrors frighten them on every side,
      and chase them at their heels.
  ¹² Their strength is consumed by hunger,
      and calamity is ready for their stumbling.
  ¹³ By disease their skin is consumed,
      the firstborn of Death consumes their limbs.
  ¹⁴ They are torn from the tent in which they trusted,
      and are brought to the king of terrors.
  ¹⁵ In their tents nothing remains;
      sulfur is scattered upon their habitations.
  ¹⁶ Their roots dry up beneath,
      and their branches wither above.
  ¹⁷ Their memory perishes from the earth,
      and they have no name in the street.
  ¹⁸ They are thrust from light into darkness,
      and driven out of the world.
  ¹⁹ They have no offspring or descendant among their people,
      and no survivor where they used to live.

²⁰ **They of the west are appalled at their fate,**
   and horror seizes those of the east.
²¹ **Surely such are the dwellings of the ungodly,**
   such is the place of those who do not know God."

With a question of the magnitude of that expressed in Job 17:15–16 hanging in the balance, the harsh certitudes of Bildad may provide a kind of comic relief, if not a sure comfort. From Bildad's point of view, Job's ramblings are nothing more than playing with words, at a time when he ought to be listening to his betters (18:2). It is pure arrogance for Job to treat wise friends as dumb oxen, to make his own petty case the end of the world (vv. 3–4). Interestingly, Bildad addresses Job in the second-person plural here, according to the Hebrew text, as if he were saying "all you guys" or "your kind of people." We can understand why early Greek translations reverted to the singular in verse 2, but it is at least possible that Bildad deliberately dehumanizes Job here by speaking to him as a member of a well-known and rightly despised type of people.

What follows is a stereotypical description of what happens to "those who do not know God" (v. 21), a group in which Bildad is now certain Job is prominent. (See Job 8:5–7, 20–22, where Bildad apparently held out hope that Job might yet be brought into the orthodox fold.) The terrible irony of 18:5–22, of course, is that all the disasters Bildad describes as falling on "the wicked" have already befallen Job. What might otherwise be understood as a terror campaign designed to frighten people away from their wicked ways here becomes an indictment: Since all these things (and worse) have already happened to Job, his sufferings clearly identify him as one who richly deserves the wrath of God.

While Bildad's "fate of the wicked" speech in 18:5–21 clearly draws on proverbial wisdom of a very general sort, some of the details become especially accusatory if we apply them to Job's case. Job's misery is the result of his own pernicious scheming (v. 7), and the death of his children bears testimony to his wickedness (v. 19).

Fascinating questions and possibilities abound in 18:5–21 for students of ancient Near Eastern religion and conceptuality. Yet the essential meaning of all these vivid expressions is available to the ordinary reader of any good English translation: We have met "the wicked," Job, and you are it. The perennial seduction of such a cocksure orthodoxy is its promise of instant answers to all the hard questions of life ("All you have to do is . . ."). Its great liability, as the story of Job indicates, is that simple answers to complex problems may be simply wrong.

JOB'S RESPONSE TO BILDAD'S SECOND SPEECH
Job 19

Job 19

19:1 Then Job answered:
 ² "How long will you torment me,
  and break me in pieces with words?
 ³ These ten times you have cast reproach upon me;
  are you not ashamed to wrong me?
 ⁴ And even if it is true that I have erred,
  my error remains with me.
 ⁵ If indeed you magnify yourselves against me,
  and make my humiliation an argument against me,
 ⁶ know then that God has put me in the wrong,
  and closed his net around me.
 ⁷ Even when I cry out, 'Violence!' I am not answered;
  I call aloud, but there is no justice.
 ⁸ He has walled up my way so that I cannot pass,
  and he has set darkness upon my paths.
 ⁹ He has stripped my glory from me,
  and taken the crown from my head.
 ¹⁰ He breaks me down on every side, and I am gone,
  he has uprooted my hope like a tree.
 ¹¹ He has kindled his wrath against me,
  and counts me as his adversary.
 ¹² His troops come on together;
  they have thrown up siegeworks against me,
  and encamp around my tent.

 ¹³ "He has put my family far from me,
  and my acquaintances are wholly estranged from me.
 ¹⁴ My relatives and my close friends have failed me;
  ¹⁵ the guests in my house have forgotten me;
 my serving girls count me as a stranger;
  I have become an alien in their eyes.
 ¹⁶ I call to my servant, but he gives me no answer;
  I must myself plead with him.
 ¹⁷ My breath is repulsive to my wife;
  I am loathsome to my own family.
 ¹⁸ Even young children despise me;
  when I rise, they talk against me.
 ¹⁹ All my intimate friends abhor me,
  and those whom I loved have turned against me.

^{20} My bones cling to my skin and to my flesh,
      and I have escaped by the skin of my teeth.
^{21} Have pity on me, have pity on me, O you my friends,
      for the hand of God has touched me!
^{22} Why do you, like God, pursue me,
      never satisfied with my flesh?

^{23} "O that my words were written down!
      O that they were inscribed in a book!
^{24} O that with an iron pen and with lead
      they were engraved on a rock forever!
^{25} For I know that my Redeemer lives,
      and that at the last he will stand upon the earth;
^{26} and after my skin has been thus destroyed,
      then in my flesh I shall see God,
^{27} whom I shall see on my side,
      and my eyes shall behold, and not another.
      My heart faints within me!
^{28} If you say, 'How we will persecute him!'
      and, 'The root of the matter is found in him';
^{29} be afraid of the sword,
      for wrath brings the punishment of the sword,
      so that you may know there is a judgment."

Job's reply to Bildad in 19:1–22 can be read as a direct response to the vindictive hostility that dominates this latest attack. He is being tormented, broken in pieces, reproached, and wronged shamelessly by "friends" who have betrayed the very meaning of friendship (19:1–3; see 6:14–29; 16:2–5; 17:5). The next verse (19:4) seems to suggest that even if Job were guilty of some error worthy of divine retribution (which Job does not concede), it would not be the part of a true friend to take sides in an issue that could be resolved only between God and Job. But these friends have used the occasion of Job's suffering not only to turn it into an argument against him but to vaunt their own moral and spiritual superiority over him (19:5).

The issue between Job and his friends, of course, was set up by the ungodly test contrived by God and *hassatan* in the heavenly council chamber: It will appear to Job and all who know him that he has been singled out as the special object of God's wrath. The question in heaven is whether Job will be able to "persist in his integrity" even under this groundless assault of suffering and loss (2:3). From the earthly standpoint of Job and his friends, the question is not so subtle. What is at stake between them is whether God has indeed attacked Job "without cause," as Job maintains, or whether Job has defied God so enormously that all his suffering and loss represent God's just judgment against him. The friends are no more able than we are to understand how a just God could allow such catastrophes to befall a genuinely innocent human being. From their standpoint, it is simply a blasphemy against God's justice for Job to persist in maintaining his innocence.

Job, in contrast, having lost everything else, has nothing to rely on except his own fragile human integrity. But following the demands of his integrity, Job is bound to tell the truth. God in fact has stretched out God's hand against him "without cause." In his second reply to Bildad, Job once again identifies God as the one who has "put me in the wrong" (19:6–20). Nothing new appears in Job's indictment of God in 19:6–20, particularly after what has been said in 16:7–17. God is a "hunter" (v. 6), a deaf judge (v. 7), an imprisoner and a sender of darkness (v. 8), a despoiler of all honor and dignity (v. 9), a ravager and an uprooter of hope (v. 10), an implacable enemy general who has laid Job under siege (vv. 11–12).

Perhaps more poignantly than elsewhere, 19:13–19 laments the unbearable social isolation, the dreadful loneliness into which God has placed Job. Family, acquaintances, relatives, close friends, houseguests, wife and children, intimates, loved ones, all the people whose presence can make even the intolerable somehow endurable—all have been stripped away, and not all by death. Most agonizing for Job is the deliberate abandonment: "All my intimate friends abhor me, and those whom I loved have turned against me" (19:19; see 6:14–21, and note the recurrence of this theme in Psalms 38:11; 55:12–14; 69:8).

It is the wholly unwarranted onslaught of God that has brought all this about, leaving Job an utterly lonely and skeletal ruin, having come through it "by [or perhaps 'with'] the skin of my teeth." Does this mean with nothing at all? Scholars have made a number of efforts to emend and interpret the rather obscure Hebrew text of verse 20 in order to arrive at a clearer meaning. The translators of the NRSV have chosen (wisely, I think) to render the verse, obscure as it may be, in the traditional way, perhaps in view of the fact that it has provided us with one of the most memorable (if still not quite clear) phrases in the English language.

The litany of abandonment in 19:13–19 is rendered even more poignant by Job's direct appeal to his friends (19:21–22), who must surely have recognized references to themselves in 19:14–15. Since God is the cause of Job's distress (and not Job's guilt), surely it is the part of a friend to show compassion to the innocent sufferer (v. 21). Instead, Job is appalled to discover that they have followed God's lead, pursuing him like prey and

tearing at his flesh like insatiable predators (v. 22). The power of this renewed accusation lies in its capacity to bring the crisis between God and Job
closer and closer to what may be called "critical mass," the point at which the
crisis must simply explode into an encounter with God in which Job is either
annihilated or vindicated. At the same time, 19:2–22 makes the gulf that separates Job from his friends even wider, if not altogether unbridgeable.

Apparently despairing of any human support for his cause, Job now cries
out longingly for some indestructible record to be made, one capable of
bearing witness to his innocence beyond all the ravages of time and human
mortality (vv. 23–24). Whether verse 24 refers to inscribing letters with a
metal stylus on a leaden tablet or another such practice, perhaps forcing
malleable lead into letters previously incised in stone, the intent is equally
clear. On the very brink of death (19:20), Job is not willing for the justice
of his cause to be "interred with his bones."

In my view, the interpretation we place on 19:23–24 may well provide
the key to understanding the notoriously difficult and perennially fascinating words of verses 25–27. In 16:18, Job expresses his longing for a
permanent witness to his innocence using very different but, I think, fully
comparable imagery. There, Job calls on "mother earth" herself to keep
his cause alive by refusing to "cover [Job's] blood," just as Abel's blood is
said to have cried out to God "from the ground," testifying that an innocent man was wrongfully slain. Stripped of its imagery, the intent of Job
16:18 is clear: Job is *innocent*, as innocent as Abel was, and the event of Job's
death must not be allowed to extinguish the fact that he died undeserving
of all the wretchedness he had been forced to endure. Earlier, we looked
at the possibility that Job's apparent confidence in his "witness in heaven"
(16:19) may not represent a spiritual breakthrough, as if he had been
granted some sort of visionary assurance of vindication through a heavenly
advocate, whether God or a third party. The alternative possibility is that
the extravagant language of 16:19–21, like the extravagant language of
16:18, is designed to convey Job's last-ditch confidence that his cause is just
and therefore must—somehow—be vindicated. (In my view, this accounts
best for the fact that Job immediately reverts to the language of bitter
lamentation in 16:22 through 17:16.)

Glancing ahead to 19:28–29, one can see that Job's mighty affirmation
in 19:25–27 similarily issues in renewed argument with his friends, not in
a cry of final triumph. Perhaps 19:25–27, like 19:23–24 and 16:18–19, is to
be understood, above all, as an extravagant way of expressing Job's confidence that he must be, and somehow will be, vindicated. If so, then this
confidence forms the basis for the not-so-veiled threat Job issues to his

friends in 19:28–29. If they continue to persecute Job on the grounds of his presumed guilt (v. 28), they are walking on dangerous ground indeed. When Job is vindicated, the tables will be turned. They, not Job, will be disclosed as having been in opposition to God and therefore justly deserving of "wrath," "punishment," "judgment" at God's hand (19:29; see 13:9–11).

With these thoughts in mind, one may turn to 19:25–27 with a somewhat less frantic urgency to solve all its riddles and comprehend all its details. For Christians who cherish Handel's *Messiah* in its faith dimensions, "I know that my Redeemer liveth" (19:25) can hardly be torn free from its connotation of Easter celebration. The words have simply achieved a life of their own in the heart-language of Christian faith, and that language is not finally subject to correction by technical exegesis of Job 19:25. It is important for Christians, however, to recognize that when we identify the "Redeemer" of Job 19:25 with the risen Christ of the Gospels, it is *our* faith we are expressing, not the faith of Job. This becomes unmistakably clear when we ask what Christians mean when they sing, "I know that my Redeemer liveth." Christians require the mediation of Christ the Redeemer because we are painfully aware that we have "sinned and fallen short of the glory of God." The function of Christ the Redeemer is to be "the atoning sacrifice for our sins, and not for ours only, but also for the sins of the whole world" (1 John 2:2).

But look at what happens to the whole story of Job if he suddenly becomes aware that his Redeemer, by this definition, is not only alive but prepared to intercede on his behalf. All the meanings in the book of Job are knocked into a cocked hat. Job is, after all, a sinner in need of redemption, just as Eliphaz said we all are, as early as Job 4:17–21. Job is quite wrong in affirming his innocence—and so is God, if we take 1:8 and 2:3 seriously. *Hassatan* would also be vindicated, along with Eliphaz, Bildad, and Zophar, if it turned out that Job was a sinner in need of a redeemer. From the beginning, *hassatan* questioned whether Job could possibly be the unique example of human integrity God thought he was. In short, the traditional Christian conception of Christ as the "Redeemer" of Job 19:25 simply won't do—not if we respect the book of Job as Holy Scripture and commit ourselves to listen carefully to what Job has to say.

If we rule out the risen Christ as Job's "Redeemer," what options are left open? By most accounts, the Hebrew word *go'el*, "redeemer," appears to be rooted in the very ancient notion of the "avenger of blood." According to the biblical story, the right of blood revenge was extended by God to Cain, as a peculiar gift of grace to an unrepentant murderer, in order to quell the anarchy of unrestrained violence, even against one who deserved no such protection (see Gen. 4:13–15). While the word *go'el* does not appear in the Genesis passage, the connotation of "avenger of blood" does crop up in texts such as Numbers 35:16–28; Deuteronomy 19:6–12; and 2 Samuel 14:5–11. The common denominator of all the Old Testament references to *go'el* seems to be the notion of "blood relationship," that is, someone who is so closely kin to another that the cause of the one becomes the cause of the other. In some contemporary Near Eastern cultures it is still the case that the cause of an individual clan member becomes instantly the cause of the whole clan, through its acknowledged leadership. Within that social structure, one who intervenes on behalf of a clan member, whatever the cause, may be said to fulfill the role of the biblical *go'el*.

According to the book of Ruth, Naomi had two just claims on Benjaminite tribal law when she returned as a widow from Moab. By right, the parcel of land that had once belonged to her dead husband should have remained in the family. It was the right of Elimelech's (male) next of kin (*go'el* in Hebrew) to claim this land for the family. Along with this right came the responsibility to incorporate the dead man's name in his inheritance (Ruth 4:1–6). In the entirely male-dominated society within which the story of Naomi and Ruth unfolds, these two widows appear to lack any means of bringing their just claims into "the gate" (4:1; that is, the "civil court" where matters of legal right were adjudicated). Even though he is not Elimelech's closest male relative, Boaz begins to function as *go'el* when he brings the case in the gate, to the attention of the man who is. As the story turns out, the closest kinsman declines his right to the land because of his unwillingness to accept responsibility for Naomi and Ruth, pleading that this would dilute his own inheritance (4:6). This opens the way for Boaz to function as *go'el* and thus secure for the two widows the legal rights they deserved but could not otherwise have enjoyed. (See Ruth 4:1–12. Genesis 38 and Deuteronomy 25:5–10 throw additional light on this issue of justice, even though the terms that governed it were obviously not identical at all times or in differing social situations.)

For the interpretation of Job 19:25, all this suggests that whoever Job's *go'el* may be, the function of such a figure is not to win forgiveness for Job or even to strengthen the case for his innocence. At most, he could bring Job's case into "the gate" of God, so that it might be fairly heard. If Job requires the intervention of a *go'el*, it is because Job has otherwise despaired of achieving such a fair hearing before God on his own (see Job 9:2–3,

11–20, 28–35; 13:13–16). Yet there is nothing Job longs for more (see 9:34–35; 10:2; 13:3, 20–24; 14:13–17), and his confidence in his innocence is such that he occasionally speaks as if he is certain the longed-for moment of his vindication before God must ultimately come (see 13:18; 16:18–19; 23:10).

Job 19:23–25 is best understood as yet another extravagant projection of this apparently contradictory certainty: Beyond all this agony and despair, beyond all the evidence that God has blocked off any access to a fair hearing, beyond Job's passionate denunciation of God's injustice in the ordering of human affairs, Job's vindicating moment can, and must, and *will* come. Somehow Job's "eyes shall behold, and not another" (19:27; that is, not the eyes of some later archaeologist of the spirit, who might conceivably read Job's testimony "engraved on a rock forever"; see 19:23–24). Unfortunately, the Hebrew text of 19:25–27 bristles with so many difficulties of grammar, syntax, and word meanings that no two scholars interpret these verses in precisely the same way. This is especially true of verse 26, where there is competent scholarly support for two diametrically opposed readings: Either Job is to behold God from within his own ruined but still living flesh or this vision will be accorded him only after his flesh has been destroyed. (The translators of the RSV and the NRSV appear to have differed on this point.) The notion of a postmortem vindication is perhaps especially appealing to Christians, for whom both the "resurrection of the body" and the coming of the risen Christ to "judge the quick and the dead" have been wrought into ecumenical creeds. But such notions fly in the face of what Job has said clearly about this possibility in 14:7–22. Perhaps more important, if Job 19:25–27 relates a kind of "Damascus road" experience that answers all Job's questions and assures him of victory, the book should surely end here. Yet the tired old quarrel with his friends is picked up immediately in 19:28, and the argument continues without letup until 27:23.

In short, the detailed meaning of 19:25–27 remains a riddle. All interpretations of these verses known to me appear to agree on two counts: (1) Whoever the *go'el* is taken to be, and whether Job expects to be alive or dead when it happens, Job expects to be ultimately vindicated; and (2) God is the one who will ultimately vindicate him. Each of these themes has become familiar to us throughout the speeches of Job. At the heart of each theme is Job's confidence in his innocence and his unwillingness to settle for anything less than a face-to-face vindication before God. This confidence forms the basis for the dire warning to Job's friends with which chapter 19 concludes (vv. 28–29).

ZOPHAR'S SECOND SPEECH
Job 20

Job 20

20:1 Then Zophar the Naamathite answered:
    ² "Pay attention! My thoughts urge me to answer,
        because of the agitation within me.
    ³ I hear censure that insults me,
        and a spirit beyond my understanding answers me.
    ⁴ Do you not know this from of old,
        ever since mortals were placed on earth,
    ⁵ that the exulting of the wicked is short,
        and the joy of the godless is but for a moment?
    ⁶ Even though they mount up high as the heavens,
        and their head reaches to the clouds,
    ⁷ they will perish forever like their own dung;
        those who have seen them will say, 'Where are they?'
    ⁸ They will fly away like a dream, and not be found;
        they will be chased away like a vision of the night.
    ⁹ The eye that saw them will see them no more,
        nor will their place behold them any longer.
    ¹⁰ Their children will seek the favor of the poor,
        and their hands will give back their wealth.
    ¹¹ Their bodies, once full of youth,
        will lie down in the dust with them.

    ¹² "Though wickedness is sweet in their mouth,
        though they hide it under their tongues,
    ¹³ though they are loath to let it go,
        and hold it in their mouths,
    ¹⁴ yet their food is turned in their stomachs;
        it is the venom of asps within them.
    ¹⁵ They swallow down riches and vomit them up again;
        God casts them out of their bellies.
    ¹⁶ They will suck the poison of asps;
        the tongue of a viper will kill them.
    ¹⁷ They will not look on the rivers,
        the streams flowing with honey and curds.
    ¹⁸ They will give back the fruit of their toil,
        and will not swallow it down;
        from the profit of their trading
        they will get no enjoyment.

¹⁹ For they have crushed and abandoned the poor,
    they have seized a house that they did not build.

²⁰ "They knew no quiet in their bellies;
    in their greed they let nothing escape.
²¹ There was nothing left after they had eaten;
    therefore their prosperity will not endure.
²² In full sufficiency they will be in distress;
    all the force of misery will come upon them.
²³ To fill their belly to the full
    God will send his fierce anger into them,
    and rain it upon them as their food.
²⁴ They will flee from an iron weapon;
    a bronze arrow will strike them through.
²⁵ It is drawn forth and comes out of their body,
    and the glittering point comes out of their gall;
    terrors come upon them.
²⁶ Utter darkness is laid up for their treasures;
    a fire fanned by no one will devour them;
    what is left in their tent will be consumed.
²⁷ The heavens will reveal their iniquity,
    and the earth will rise up against them.
²⁸ The possessions of their house will be carried away,
    dragged off in the day of God's wrath.
²⁹ This is the portion of the wicked from God,
    the heritage decreed for them by God."

In his second address, Zophar elaborates on a theme that might appear damaging to the friends' case that God punishes the wicked and blesses the righteous: the incontrovertible fact that good things sometimes happen to bad people. Convinced as they all are that Job is at fault before God, how can the friends account for the fact that he appeared to be so exceptionally "blessed" before the present catastrophes came suddenly upon him? The orthodox answer is that we may expect a delay in God's work of punishing the wicked. Hints of such a "delay" are scattered throughout the speeches of Eliphaz (see 5:3–16; 15:27–29; 22:18) and Bildad (see 8:12–19), but Zophar now uses it as a major weapon against Job. Job's initial blessedness is here accounted for as the momentary exulting and joy of the godless (20:5). The wicked may indeed "mount up as high as the heavens" for a time, but all such attempts to storm divine heights are as perishable as dung, soon to be forgotten (vv. 6–11; see Gen. 11:4; Isa. 14:13–14; Ezek.

28:2–10). The implication for Job is clear. His former wealth, status, and well-being (see 1:3) were never signs of God's favor. Rather, they resulted from his insatiable appetite, his ruthless greed for every good thing, for acquisition of property and power, regardless of the consequences to those who stood in his way (20:12–22). The wicked (that is, Job) will find such food to be poisonous (vv. 12–16). They will never enjoy its fruits (vv. 17–18). They will never be sated (vv. 20–22), because God will ultimately give them a bellyful of wrath and destruction (vv. 23–29). By the measure of verse 29, Zophar has accounted not only for Job's former blessedness but also for his descent into utter wretchedness: "This is the portion of the wicked from God."

4. The Third Round of Discourses between Job and His Friends
Job 21—27

JOB'S RESPONSE TO ZOPHAR'S SECOND SPEECH
Job 21

Job 21

21:1 **Then Job answered:**
² **"Listen carefully to my words,**
   and let this be your consolation.
³ **Bear with me, and I will speak;**
   then after I have spoken, mock on.
⁴ **As for me, is my complaint addressed to mortals?**
   Why should I not be impatient?
⁵ **Look at me, and be appalled,**
   and lay your hand upon your mouth.
⁶ **When I think of it I am dismayed,**
   and shuddering seizes my flesh.
⁷ **Why do the wicked live on,**
   reach old age, and grow mighty in power?
⁸ **Their children are established in their presence,**
   and their offspring before their eyes.
⁹ **Their houses are safe from fear,**
   and no rod of God is upon them.
¹⁰ **Their bull breeds without fail;**
   their cow calves and never miscarries.
¹¹ **They send out their little ones like a flock,**
   and their children dance around.
¹² **They sing to the tambourine and the lyre,**
   and rejoice to the sound of the pipe.
¹³ **They spend their days in prosperity,**
   and in peace they go down to Sheol.
¹⁴ **They say to God, 'Leave us alone!**
   We do not desire to know your ways.
¹⁵ **What is the Almighty, that we should serve him?**

And what profit do we get if we pray to him?'
¹⁶ Is not their prosperity indeed their own achievement?
　　The plans of the wicked are repugnant to me.

¹⁷ "How often is the lamp of the wicked put out?
　　How often does calamity come upon them?
　　How often does God distribute pains in his anger?
¹⁸ How often are they like straw before the wind,
　　and like chaff that the storm carries away?
¹⁹ You say, 'God stores up their iniquity for their children.'
　　Let it be paid back to them, so that they may know it.
²⁰ Let their own eyes see their destruction,
　　and let them drink of the wrath of the Almighty.
²¹ For what do they care for their household after them,
　　when the number of their months is cut off?
²² Will any teach God knowledge,
　　seeing that he judges those that are on high?
²³ One dies in full prosperity,
　　being wholly at ease and secure,
²⁴ his loins full of milk
　　and the marrow of his bones moist.
²⁵ Another dies in bitterness of soul,
　　never having tasted of good.
²⁶ They lie down alike in the dust,
　　and the worms cover them.

²⁷ "Oh, I know your thoughts,
　　and your schemes to wrong me.
²⁸ For you say, 'Where is the house of the prince?
　　Where is the tent in which the wicked lived?'
²⁹ Have you not asked those who travel the roads,
　　and do you not accept their testimony,
³⁰ that the wicked are spared in the day of calamity,
　　and are rescued in the day of wrath?
³¹ Who declares their way to their face,
　　and who repays them for what they have done?
³² When they are carried to the grave,
　　a watch is kept over their tomb.
³³ The clods of the valley are sweet to them;
　　everyone will follow after,
　　and those who went before are innumerable.
³⁴ How then will you comfort me with empty nothings?
　　There is nothing left of your answers but falsehood."

Once again, Job pleads for the minimum consolation due from a true friend to one in distress: a listening ear (21:2–3; 5; see 2:13; 13:5–6). And again Job affirms that his controversy is with God, not with the theological viewpoint of any human being (21:4; see 13:3; 19:2–6, 21–22). Yet Job and Zophar are in full agreement on one issue: Good things really do happen to bad people in this world, with appalling regularity. Unlike Zophar, however, Job sees no evidence of a divine justice operating in human affairs to bring the wicked to their well-deserved destruction. This is the counterpart of Job's conviction that his own suffering, as well as that of countless others, bears no relationship to the state of the heart toward God and neighbor.

It is probably a mistake to suppose that Job now simply turns Zophar's doctrine on its head, as if to say that the wicked invariably prosper and crime always pays. Even one case in which good things happened to bad people without retribution would be sufficient to demolish Zophar's defense of God's justice. But Job's experience of life is that such cases abound on every side, without any evidence of God's intervention against the wicked. It is interesting to compare Job 21:7–13 with the idyllic life Eliphaz describes as the reward of the righteous in 5:20–26 (see also Zophar in 11:15–19): long life, power, many children, freedom from fear, prosperity, a "good death." Yet Job affirms that just such an idyllic life may befall people who turn their backs on God, who reject God's ways, who see no "profit" in piety toward an inconsequential God (21:14–15). (Is there an echo here of *hassatan*'s insinuation that profit may be the real motivation for Job's life of integrity toward God and people? In their superabundance of every good thing, the wicked lack the profit motive for righteousness! If they experienced Job's kind of loss, perhaps they would reconsider.) Verse 16 still puzzles interpreters, some of whom regard it as a kind of editorial aside added to the text by a later hand. The NRSV apparently understands verse 16a as Job's question: Are not the wicked "self-made men"? It is not inconceivable that 16b records Job's own revulsion against such gains and the means by which they were gotten.

Verses 17–21 sound like a rehearsal of several points made by the friends to shore up the doctrine of God's retribution against the wicked: The lamp of the wicked is put out (see 18:5–6); calamity comes upon them (see 18:12); they writhe in pain as a result of God's anger (see 15:20); they become like dead plants (see 8:13); their children suffer for their iniquity (see 5:4; 20:10). But Job demands evidence. How often, he asks four times, have you seen this retribution fall upon the wicked?"—implying that, actually, this rarely happens. If it is a question of divine retribution being delayed and then visited on their children, Job says, where is the justice in that? The wicked will experience nothing of this from the grave, and they are the ones who should be brought to justice (vv. 19–21).

Verse 22 may be another in this series of arguments that have been put forward by Job's friends from the beginning. Eliphaz set out to negate Job's right to raise questions about God's justice, not only because no mortal can be pure before God (4:17–21) but also because God's wisdom transcends all human wisdom (5:9; see 11:4–11; 15:8; 22:2). If verse 22 is indeed a sarcastic parroting of what Job has already heard from his friends, verses 23–26 represent his answer. Consider two parallel lives, says Job, one who has tasted the good life to the full and dies happy, the other who dies "in bitterness of soul, never having tasted of good." They are both ultimately united in the great democracy of death (v. 26; see 3:17–19), but the vast inequity of their respective days on earth is never redressed.

In verses 27–28, Job anticipates his friends' response to this case study. They have repeatedly appealed to their own observation (see 5:27; 15:17) and to the accumulated experience of ancient sages (see 8:8–10; 15:10, 18–19; 20:4) to prove God's unfailing justice in ordering the outcomes of human lives. The implication of 21:28 is that "the prince" and "the wicked" invariably reap the just reward for the evil they have sown (see 4:7–9).

In verse 29, however, Job calls up a different set of witnesses, sharp-eyed observers of the human scene who have no vested interest in sustaining abstract doctrines about divine justice in ordering human affairs. These are the people who travel the roads, people who are routinely exposed to what actually happens to people in real life, on a broad scale. Dare to see the world through realistic eyes, I hear Job saying, and you will discover that your religious "schemes" (v. 27) simply do not fit the harsh facts of real human experience. People really do "get away with murder" in this life, without ever being brought to account for their crimes or suffering the consequences of their actions (vv. 30–31). Death comes to them as a benediction, and they are borne to the tomb amid the solicitous acclamation of admiring crowds (vv. 32–33). In short, the "comfort" offered to Job by his so-called friends is no more than a tissue of self-serving lies, empty of all truth (v. 34).

JOB'S RESPONSE TO ELIPHAZ'S THIRD SPEECH
Job 23—24

The third cycle of arguments and counterarguments between Job and his friends began in chapter 21, with Job's response to Zophar's second speech. The familiar pattern continues smoothly enough with Eliphaz's third and final contribution in chapter 22. We have to brace ourselves for some rude surprises, however, as we try to follow the argument from chapters 23 through 27. A quick glance at these chapters reveals that Bildad's third speech is remarkably short (only six verses), that Job's reply to Bildad has two introductions (see 26:1, 27:1), and that poor Zophar is never even mentioned. The deeper problem, however, is that some of the passages assigned to Job in this third cycle seem to echo the orthodox ideas of his friends much more clearly than they echo anything we have heard Job say until now. At the very least, we must agree that the clearly defined arguments we have heard in chapters 3—22 break down rather badly in 23—27.

In scholarly circles, this state of affairs has led to the widespread conclusion that chapters 23—27 do not represent the original intention of the author of Job 3—22. We know that the present book of Job came down to us through a process of copying and recopying the text through many generations. Is it possible that some copyists felt compelled to edit or add new material to the text to reflect the copyist's own point of view?

One solution is to cluster all the materials in chapters 23—27 that sound "Joblike" and reconstruct two relatively clear speeches of Job (e.g., 23:1 through 24:17 and 26:1–4 plus 27:1–12). Out of the rest of the material, we could then cobble together enough "friends-like" material to constitute a respectable third speech for Bildad (e.g., 25:1–6; 26:5–14) and also for Zophar (who is not mentioned by name a third time; e.g., 27:13–23; 24:18–24). Such an attempt gets high marks for neatness, but there is no evidence that the "original" text of Job ever had this shape.

Other scholars have suggested that certain "non-Joblike" material in speeches assigned to Job can be taken as "quotations" from the friends' position, which a desperate Job now parrots in mocking despair. At least this honors the fact that the present text of Job, however puzzling it may be, is the only text of Job we have.

In chapters 28, 32—37, and 38—41 we encounter additional indications that the book of Job in its present form is not the work of a single author. This should not surprise us, since most books in the Bible show signs of having been edited and reedited by members of the faith communities who cherished the ancient texts, preserved them, and handed them on to future generations. The modern notion of "authors" who write "books" out of their own insights and ideas is almost completely alien to the communal tradition process by which most biblical texts came into being.

In the case of Job, the surprising thing is not that it shows signs of having been edited and reedited. The surprise lies rather in the strong evidence that a single author must have designed the remarkable literary architecture that still dominates the book of Job, regardless of the editorial interventions that resulted in the somewhat confusing state of the present text.

For Jewish and Christian faith communities who cherish the book of Job as Holy Scripture, however, the primary question is not what the "original author" may have intended or what the "original book of Job" may once have looked like (fascinating as that inquiry may be). Rather, it is how we will hear and respond to what we can understand from this remarkable witness to God in its present, somewhat tattered and cluttered form.

In that light, it is perhaps appropriate that the third round of disputations in chapters 21—27 should end in confusion and disarray. Does this suggest that we are not to look for an "answer" to the questions of Job on the philosophical or theological level? Perhaps the issue, rightly understood, was never a matter of whether Job or his friends turned out to be the winner in a debating contest. Over and over again we have heard Job saying that his controversy is with God, not with the "windy" ideas batted about between him and his friends. Perhaps "Who is right?" is always less interesting (and far less significant) than "Who is God?" for the community of faith. For an answer to that question, we (like Job) are ultimately dependent on God, rather than on our own cherished philosophical or theological constructs. If we could arrive at an intellectual resolution of the enormous issues raised by Job, God would be reduced to an idea, and there would be no need for a faith community or its Holy Scriptures.

In any case, the present text of Job 21—27 shows that the long disputations between Job and his friends do not come to a successful conclusion. As we have seen, the third cycle of arguments begins predictably enough, with Job's speech in chapter 21 and the reply of Eliphaz in chapter 22. Job's response to Eliphaz also continues the familiar pattern in chapters 23 and 24, at least as far as 24:12 and possibly as far as 24:17.

Job 23

23:1 **Then Job answered:**
2 **"Today also my complaint is bitter;**
   his hand is heavy despite my groaning.
3 **Oh, that I knew where I might find him,**
   that I might come even to his dwelling!
4 **I would lay my case before him,**
   and fill my mouth with arguments.
5 **I would learn what he would answer me,**
   and understand what he would say to me.
6 **Would he contend with me in the greatness of his power?**

No; but he would give heed to me.
7 There an upright person could reason with him,
    and I should be acquitted forever by my judge.

8 "If I go forward, he is not there;
    or backward, I cannot perceive him;
9 on the left he hides, and I cannot behold him;
    I turn to the right, but I cannot see him.
10 But he knows the way that I take;
    when he has tested me, I shall come out like gold.
11 My foot has held fast to his steps;
    I have kept his way and have not turned aside.
12 I have not departed from the commandment of his lips;
    I have treasured in my bosom the words of his mouth.
13 But he stands alone and who can dissuade him?
    What he desires, that he does.
14 For he will complete what he appoints for me;
    and many such things are in his mind.
15 Therefore I am terrified at his presence;
    when I consider, I am in dread of him.
16 God has made my heart faint;
    the Almighty has terrified me;
17 If only I could vanish in darkness,
    and thick darkness would cover my face!

In 23:2, Job alludes again to his experience of God as the oppressor, the enemy (see 16:7–17). Perhaps more powerfully in 23:3–10 than anywhere else in the book, however, Job expresses his upside-down trust by longing for a face-to-face encounter with this same God. In spite of the evidence that God has forsaken him, Job somehow dares to believe that this present experience of God's enmity cannot stand as God's last word about Job. If Job could only find God, if Job could ever lay out his case in God's own presence, if he could hear and understand what God would say to him . . . (vv. 3–5)! That would require a setting in which Job would not be simply obliterated by God's transcendent power, but somehow Job holds fast to the confidence that God may yet provide him with a hearing in just such a setting, where "an upright person could reason with [God]." Job's astonishing confidence in his own integrity, and more astonishing, in God's ultimate justice, is such that he is sure of the outcome: Job would "be acquitted forever by my judge" (vv. 6–7).

In the depths of Job's experience of the "real absence" of God, he searches in vain for this longed-for encounter (23:8–9). This strikes me as a refusal on Job's part to recognize the God he worships and longs for in the terrifyingly "real presence" of God the enemy he described so graphically in 16:7–17. He may indeed have experienced the "hand of God" upon him (23:2), but somehow Job knows he is not experiencing God's heart. God is surely "hidden" from Job in all this, but the God he longs for will vindicate Job's integrity as gold is tested in the crucible and found pure (vv. 10–12).

Again, Job is wholly ignorant of what has taken place between God and *hassatan* in the heavenly council chamber. He has no way of knowing that he is, in fact, being "tested" by this outrageous suffering. Nor does Job know what precipitated this "ungodly" test, namely, God's sovereign confidence that nothing can shake Job's integrity toward God and people, not even the experience of God's "real absence." In that light, *hassatan* must be nervous in the extreme to hear Job stumbling so near to the most closely guarded secret of the heavenly council chamber. With no evidence other than his own human integrity and his own human trust in God's ultimate justice, Job has almost uncovered the plot. In any case, Job still persists in his integrity, just as God has wagered God's own reputation that Job would (2:3).

In verses 13–17, it is clear that Job has neither uncovered the hellish/heavenly plot nor made some kind of spiritual breakthrough that eases his agony. Apart from his last-ditch confidence in his own integrity and his upside-down trust in God's ultimate justice, Job remains terrified in the real presence of God the enemy, whose will and purposes in all this not only elude Job's understanding but overwhelm him now and threaten him tomorrow (vv. 13–16). God has produced this dread in Job, making him long to take shelter in absolute darkness (v. 17; note that the psalmist in Psalm 139:11–12 has the same feeling, with no better luck than Job).

Job 24

24:1 **"Why are times not kept by the Almighty,**
   and why do those who know him never see his days?
 2 **The wicked remove landmarks;**
   they seize flocks and pasture them.
 3 **They drive away the donkey of the orphan;**
   they take the widow's ox for a pledge.
 4 **They thrust the needy off the road;**
   the poor of the earth all hide themselves.
 5 **Like wild asses in the desert**
   they go out to their toil, scavenging in the wasteland
   food for their young.
 6 **They reap in a field not their own**
   and they glean in the vineyard of the wicked.

⁷ They lie all night naked, without clothing,
and have no covering in the cold.
⁸ They are wet with the rain of the mountains,
and cling to the rock for want of shelter.

⁹ "There are those who snatch the orphan child from the breast,
and take as a pledge the infant of the poor.
¹⁰ They go about naked, without clothing;
though hungry, they carry the sheaves;
¹¹ between their terraces they press out oil;
they tread the wine presses, but suffer thirst.
¹² From the city the dying groan,
and the throat of the wounded cries for help;
yet God pays no attention to their prayer.

¹³ "There are those who rebel against the light,
who are not acquainted with its ways,
and do not stay in its paths.
¹⁴ The murderer rises at dusk
to kill the poor and needy,
and in the night is like a thief.
¹⁵ The eye of the adulterer also waits for the twilight,
saying, 'No eye will see me';
and he disguises his face.
¹⁶ In the dark they dig through houses;
by day they shut themselves up;
they do not know the light.
¹⁷ For deep darkness is morning to all of them;
for they are friends with the terrors of deep darkness.

¹⁸ "Swift are they on the face of the waters;
their portion in the land is cursed;
no treader turns toward their vineyards.
¹⁹ Drought and heat snatch away the snow waters;
so does Sheol those who have sinned.
²⁰ The womb forgets them;
the worm finds them sweet;
they are no longer remembered;
so wickedness is broken like a tree.

²¹ "They harm the childless woman,
and do no good to the widow.
²² Yet God prolongs the life of the mighty by his power;
they rise up when they despair of life.

^{23} He gives them security, and they are supported;
   his eyes are upon their ways.
^{24} They are exalted a little while, and then are gone;
   they wither and fade like the mallow;
   they are cut off like the heads of grain.
^{25} If it is not so, who will prove me a liar,
   and show that there is nothing in what I say?"

In chapter 24, Job, returns to the theme he struck in 21:7–34, with even greater power. In that passage, as well as here in 24:2–17, Job's concern focuses not on his own suffering but on the virulent injustice that rages in human affairs on a global scale.

Job's opening question in chapter 24 echoes the heartfelt cry of countless millions of people throughout all human history: If there is a God in heaven, why on earth does God not bring at least minimal justice to bear in human affairs? Why are malefactors not regularly held accountable before God, and why do God's true friends never see this happening (v. 1)?

In case that strikes us as an overly pessimistic view of the human condition, Job sets out to enumerate instances of egregious inhumanity that surround us every day: the ruthless expropriation and exploitation of land and property that rightly belong to others (v. 2); the victimization of persons who lack the wherewithal or the legal resources to fight back (v. 3); disregard for the starving poor of the earth, other than putting them out of sight and out of mind (vv. 4–5); the exploitation of cheap labor (v. 6), people who receive nothing but abject poverty in return for their efforts (vv. 7–8); children made economic pawns at the expense of helpless parents (v. 9); hungry people forced to produce food for the fat (v. 10); thirsty people treading out wine for the overindulged (v. 11). Cities resound with the outcries of the wounded and dying, and God disregards their prayers (v. 12; see 16:17).

I'm not sure the agony of the human condition can be put more sharply than that, whether in Job's time or in ours, where we have learned to accomplish most of these things legally and with much greater sophistication. Yet, according to Job, these are only the obvious injustices, the ones that can be observed in the light of day. Underneath the surface of human experience is a dark underworld whose motives and actions cannot stand the light of day and want nothing to do with it: murderers, predators of the poor, adulterers, and all others who regard darkness as dawn, those who are strangely at home with the terror of the night (vv. 13–17). At any given time, I suppose, that might include any of us who would frankly prefer that certain of our motives and actions never came to light.

It is just here, however, that the relatively predictable pattern of Job's protests appears to break down. It has occurred to some students of Job that this characterization of people who "rebel against the light" (vv. 13–17) would fit rather nicely into the conventional, orthodox picture of the wicked as represented by Job's friends. All that is lacking is the smug assurance that such wicked people face sure destruction at the unfailingly just hands of an angry God. Yet vv. 18–20 appear to supply just this orthodox assurance, in just the sort of language any of Job's friends might have used! What's more, verses 22–24 echo the theme most fully expressed by Zophar in chapter 20: The wicked may indeed appear to enjoy their ill-gotten gain for a time, but ultimately they "wither and fade"; in the end they are "cut off."

The passionate dare of verse 25 might fit equally well as the finale of many of the speeches we have heard so far, whether in the mouth of Job or that of one of his friends. I personally like the instinct of the editors of the *Jerusalem Bible*, who chose to understand it as an appropriate closing remark of Job after 24:2–17 (or possibly 24:1–12). In any case, Job 24:18–24 (and possibly vv. 13–24) sounds out of place in the context of Job's constant affirmation that this kind of retributive justice simply does not happen in real human experience. Has Job suddenly defected to the opposite side of the debate? Or is Job simply "quoting" what he knows his friends will say in response to the blistering accusations of 24:1–12? Or has Job simply "lost it," no longer able to distinguish his own harangues from those of his friends? Or has something happened in the transmission or editing of the text to produce this absurd mixture of contradictory affirmations in the same speech? The last alternative seems most likely, but on any reading the dialogues between Job and his friends have taken a surprising turn toward the absurd in chapter 24. What shall we make of that?

BILDAD'S THIRD SPEECH
Job 25

Job 25

25:1 **Then Bildad the Shuhite answered:**
   2 **"Dominion and fear are with God;**
      he makes peace in his high heaven.
   3 **Is there any number to his armies?**
      Upon whom does his light not arise?
   4 **How then can a mortal be righteous before God?**
      How can one born of woman be pure?

> ⁵ If even the moon is not bright
>   and the stars are not pure in his sight,
> ⁶ how much less a mortal, who is a maggot,
>   and a human being, who is a worm!"

Bildad's speech in chapter 25 does nothing to relieve our sense that something strange has happened to the familiar pattern of argument and counterargument that moved fairly predictably from chapter 3 through 24:12. For one thing, this speech comprises only four brief verses. (In his first speech in chapter 8, Bildad needed six verses just to get warmed up!) For another, the argument in verses 2–6 consists of brief variations on points already made by Eliphaz and Zophar. Since the utterly transcendent God finds even heavenly beings impure, no mere human can qualify as righteous before God. (It is not impossible that the "moon" and the "stars" of verse 5 were understood as visible signals or symbols of the presence of the "holy ones" referred to by Eliphaz in 5:1 and 15:15.)

JOB'S RESPONSE TO BILDAD'S THIRD SPEECH
Job 26—27

Job 26

> 26:1 Then Job answered:
> ² "How you have helped one who has no power!
>   How you have assisted the arm that has no strength!
> ³ How you have counseled one who has no wisdom,
>   and given much good advice!
> ⁴ With whose help have you uttered words,
>   and whose spirit has come forth from you?
> ⁵ The shades below tremble,
>   the waters and their inhabitants.
> ⁶ Sheol is naked before God,
>   and Abaddon has no covering.
> ⁷ He stretches out Zaphon over the void,
>   and hangs the earth upon nothing.
> ⁸ He binds up the waters in his thick clouds,
>   and the cloud is not torn open by them.
> ⁹ He covers the face of the full moon,
>   and spreads over it his cloud.
> ¹⁰ He has described a circle on the face of the waters,
>   at the boundary between light and darkness.
> ¹¹ The pillars of heaven tremble,

and are astounded at his rebuke.
¹² **By his power he stilled the Sea;**
by his understanding he struck down Rahab.
¹³ **By his wind the heavens were made fair;**
his hand pierced the fleeing serpent.
¹⁴ **These are indeed but the outskirts of his ways;**
and how small a whisper do we hear of him!
But the thunder of his power who can understand?"

Job's response in verses 2–4 echoes Job's often sarcastic but agonized rejection of his friends' advice in 6:24–27; 12:2–3; and 13:1–12, as elsewhere. The translation of verse 4 favored by the NRSV appears to raise questions about the true source of the confident theological judgments the friends have lodged against Job. Does such "wisdom" proceed from God, or does it breathe a different spirit? Job raised a similar question in 13:7–12, where he warns that God will hold the friends accountable if they "speak falsely for God" (13:7). But if the friends' judgments against Job do not stem from God, where do they come from? It would be a long stretch to suggest that the friends' skepticism about Job's integrity derives from *hassatan*, about whose role in the drama Job is entirely ignorant. We may note, however, that *hassatan*'s insinuations in chapters 1 and 2 find a strange echo in the accusation of Job's friends: No one, not even the incomparable Job, can lay claim to an integrity unsullied by self-interest. *Hassatan*'s insinuation and the friends' accusations are ultimately refuted by God in 42:7–8. At any rate, as the story turns out, God is surely *not* the source of the friends' "wisdom."

After this beginning, it is not easy to imagine Job singing the marvelous little hymn to God's inscrutable wisdom and power contained in 26:5–14. True, we have heard him say things like this before (see 9:4–13; 12:13–25), but always with the affirmation that just this cosmic wisdom and power make it impossible for the cause of human justice to be brought fairly before God (see 9:13–19). Is Job here echoing Bildad's "insight" of 25:2–3, going him one better by demonstrating how a proper hymn to God's transcendent wisdom and power in creation really ought to sound? Or is 26:5–14 better understood as a continuation of Bildad's speech in chapter 25, as many scholars suppose?

In either case, it is significant that the little hymn in 26:5–14 has nothing whatever to say about the burning issues of human integrity and justice that form the heart of Job's argument with his friends and his protest against God. In the mouth of Bildad, of course, the hymn suggests that the very grandeur of God's wisdom and power so dwarfs the human that no human being can "be righteous before God" (see 25:2–4). If Job sings this hymn, it is only a prelude to a renewed accusation that this immensely wise and powerful God has nevertheless "taken away my right" (27:2). Throughout the book Job refuses to be cowed, not even by God's overwhelming majesty, into surrendering his perhaps tiny but nevertheless genuine human integrity.

Whether from Job or from Bildad, however, the beauty of the hymn itself should not be ignored. The worldview reflected in the hymn includes a mysterious underworld—the place of chaotic waters (26:5; see Gen. 7:11), departed spirits, the bottomless abyss (26:5–6; Sheol, Abaddon). Yet even these uncanny depths are known to God, and their denizens tremble at God's presence. Over this unfathomable emptiness God stretched out Zaphon (literally, "the North"; in ancient Canaanite legend, the mountain where the gods assemble) and suspends the earth "upon nothing" (26:7). Verse 8 reflects ancient amazement that clouds contain such heavy volumes of water yet, by God's design, are not immediately rent asunder by the weight. More mysterious still is the full moon, which on an otherwise clear night may be suddenly eclipsed by "God's cloud" (v. 9), beyond which no human eye can penetrate. The horizon, which limits human sight in every direction at the edge of darkness and light, is a "circle on the face of the waters" drawn by God, possibly as a bulwark against the surrounding waters of chaos (v. 10; see 38:8–11). In any case, verses 11–13 clearly evoke the notion that God's work of creating and sustaining order involves conflict with awesome forces of chaos. The Hebrew word for sea, *yam* (v. 12), appears in ancient Canaanite texts as the name of such a chaos monster, defeated by Baal. Rahab (v. 13) obviously refers to a comparable being. (See Psalm 89:10; Isa. 51:9; and Job 7:12, where Job finds it ludicrous to be singled out for God's anger as if he were an opponent of the magnitude of *Yam* (Sea) or Rahab.) The "fleeing serpent" of verse 13 echoes a Canaanite designation for Leviathan, although this chaos monster is not named here (see Isa. 27:1 and the comments below on Job 41). Such notions of cosmic conflict are widespread in Near Eastern cultures, in striking contrast to what became Israel's normative tradition of God's establishment of order in the universe (Gen. 1:1–2:4a, where God's creative word is the sole agent in the cosmic drama). In the extravagant language of Israel's praise, however, ancient allusions to cosmic conflict are introduced to bear witness to God's incomparable wisdom and power, as they do in Job 26:11–14 (see Psalms 18:7–15; 74:12–17; 89:6–12).

Job 27

27:1 **Job again took up his discourse and said:**
2 **"As God lives, who has taken away my right,**
      and the Almighty, who has made my soul bitter,
3 **as long as my breath is in me**

and the spirit of God is in my nostrils,
⁴ my lips will not speak falsehood,
   and my tongue will not utter deceit.
⁵ Far be it from me to say that you are right;
   until I die I will not put away my integrity from me.
⁶ I hold fast my righteousness, and will not let it go;
   my heart does not reproach me for any of my days.

⁷ "May my enemy be like the wicked,
   and may my opponent be like the unrighteous.
⁸ For what is the hope of the godless when God cuts them off,
   when God takes away their lives?
⁹ Will God hear their cry
   when trouble comes upon them?
¹⁰ Will they take delight in the Almighty?
   Will they call upon God at all times?
¹¹ I will teach you concerning the hand of God;
   that which is with the Almighty I will not conceal.
¹² All of you have seen it yourselves;
   why then have you become altogether vain?

¹³ "This is the portion of the wicked with God,
   and the heritage that oppressors receive from the Almighty:
¹⁴ If their children are multiplied, it is for the sword;
   and their offspring have not enough to eat.
¹⁵ Those who survive them the pestilence buries,
   and their widows make no lamentation.
¹⁶ Though they heap up silver like dust,
   and pile up clothing like clay—
¹⁷ they may pile it up, but the just will wear it,
   and the innocent will divide the silver.
¹⁸ They build their houses like nests,
   like booths made by sentinels of the vineyard.
¹⁹ They go to bed with wealth, but will do so no more;
   they open their eyes, and it is gone.
²⁰ Terrors overtake them like a flood;
   in the night a whirlwind carries them off.
²¹ The east wind lifts them up and they are gone;
   it sweeps them out of their place.
²² It hurls at them without pity;
   they flee from its power in headlong flight.
²³ It claps its hands at them,
   and hisses at them from its place.

The opening line of chapter 27 offers yet another clue that the familiar pattern of alternating dialogues between Job and his friends has been broken in this third cycle. First we encountered a strangely un-Joblike passage in Job 24:18–24. Then we noticed how brief and unfinished Bildad's reply seems to be in 25:1–6. In chapter 26, we see no clear connection between Job's rejection of his friends' advice (vv. 1–4) and the hymn to God's transcendent wisdom and power that follows (vv. 5–14; do we have any indication that Job's friends would disagree with it or that it might not fit their point of view more comfortably than it would Job's?).

Now, in 27:1, the narrator who has introduced the words of each speaker so far (see 3:1; 4:1; 6:1) breaks into a speech of Job with what appears to be a fresh introduction. Scholars have noted that the Hebrew words translated "took up his discourse" are best understood as "made a solemn pronouncement," preparing us for the mouth-filling oath that follows. Yet it is difficult to see how the substance of what Job now says requires a special introduction. Job has uttered a number of outrageous affirmations and protestations already, none of which apparently required such an introduction by the narrator. At the very least, all these clues taken together generate a strong sense in the ordinary reader that this third cycle of discourses is moving toward a confusing dissonance, rather than a clear resolution.

The oath that Job takes in verses 2–6 is a momentous one on any reading. By beginning with the words "As God lives . . . ," according to ancient belief, Job does two things at once: He acknowledges God as the supreme arbiter of right and wrong, and he invites God to damn him if the oath he is making is not true. In the next breath, however, he identifies God as the one "who has taken away my right" and "made my soul bitter." The irony is complete. Not only must Job "appeal for mercy to my accuser" (see 9:15), but he is already suffering what his friends take to be the direct consequences, at God's hands, of untruthfulness before God.

The substance of Job's oath is the same avowal of innocence that underlies all his outcries (27:4–6; see, e.g., 6:10; 9:15; 10:7). For as long as God gives him breath (v. 3), Job will not falsely concede to his friends' accusations in order to curry favor with God, as they have urged him to do. To the death he will "persist in his integrity" (see 2:3), for his conscience is clear (vv. 4–6).

The prayer of imprecation against "my enemy," "my opponent," "the godless" in verses 7–10 sounds decidedly strange in Job's mouth at this point. For one thing, Job's self-sworn ethic, stated in 31:29–30 (see below), forbids him to "sin by asking for [his enemies'] lives with a curse." For another, the blithe certainty that God will "cut off" the godless and "take away their lives," refusing to "hear their cry when trouble comes upon them," sounds much more appropriate in the mouth of one of the friends than in Job's. This has led to the assumption among some scholars that verses 7–11 constitute a fragment from a lost third speech of Zophar. (Verse 12 would fit nicely as a conclusion to Job's affirmation in verses 2–6.) A more radical suggestion is that the speech is indeed from Job, and the terms *enemy* and *opponent* in verse 7 refer indirectly and almost blasphemously to God, whom Job has repeatedly identified as his real opponent (see, e.g., 6:4; 13:24; 16:7–17). It seems to me that verses 8–10 render this suggestion unlikely, since God clearly emerges here as the punisher of "the godless" (v. 8).

The closest parallel to 27:7–10 in Job's prior speeches is perhaps to be found in 13:4–11, where Job warns his friends that their lying "defense" of God's justice may one day incur the wrath of a just God. This corresponds to the apparently contradictory confidence Job expresses that in spite of all his wrongful suffering at God's hands, God must ultimately emerge as Job's just vindicator (see 9:34–35; 19:27; 23:3–7).

The sense of confusion produced by various possible interpretations of 27:7–12 is heightened further by verses 13–23. If we read these verses as a continuation of Job's speech, begun in 26:1 and renewed in 27:1, then Job is clearly parroting the friends' well-worn clichés about the "fate of the wicked" (Eliphaz: 15:20–35; Bildad: 18:5–21; Zophar: 20:4–11). If the words are indeed taken as Job's hysterical repetition of these threadbare slogans, the third cycle ends on a shrill note of despair, edging toward madness, signaling the end of any possible resolution of the issue between Job and his friends. The likelier option, as I see it, is that the entire block of material from 24:18 (perhaps from 24:9) through 27:23 has been rather hopelessly scrambled, whether deliberately or inadvertently, somewhere in the process of copying, preserving, editing, and transmitting the text. Whether anyone ever intended it or not, the Hebrew text that has come down to us allows the dialogues to end in utter confusion rather than resolution.

5. The Inaccessibility of Wisdom
Job 28

28:1 "Surely there is a mine for silver,
and a place for gold to be refined.
² Iron is taken out of the earth,
and copper is smelted from ore.
³ Miners put an end to darkness,
and search out to the farthest bound
the ore in gloom and deep darkness.
⁴ They open shafts in a valley away from human habitation;
they are forgotten by travelers,
they sway suspended, remote from people.
⁵ As for the earth, out of it comes bread;
but underneath it is turned up as by fire.
⁶ Its stones are the place of sapphires,
and its dust contains gold.

⁷ "That path no bird of prey knows,
and the falcon's eye has not seen it.
⁸ The proud wild animals have not trodden it;
the lion has not passed over it.

⁹ "They put their hand to the flinty rock,
and overturn mountains by the roots.
¹⁰ They cut out channels in the rocks,
and their eyes see every precious thing.
¹¹ The sources of the rivers they probe;
hidden things they bring to light.

¹² "But where shall wisdom be found?
And where is the place of understanding?
¹³ Mortals do not know the way to it,

and it is not found in the land of the living.
¹⁴ The deep says, 'It is not in me,'
     and the sea says, 'It is not with me.'
¹⁵ It cannot be gotten for gold,
     and silver cannot be weighed out as its price.
¹⁶ It cannot be valued in the gold of Ophir,
     in precious onyx or sapphire.
¹⁷ Gold and glass cannot equal it,
     nor can it be exchanged for jewels of fine gold.
¹⁸ No mention shall be made of coral or of crystal;
     the price of wisdom is above pearls.
¹⁹ The chrysolite of Ethiopia cannot compare with it,
     nor can it be valued in pure gold.

²⁰ "Where then does wisdom come from?
     And where is the place of understanding?
²¹ It is hidden from the eyes of all living,
     and concealed from the birds of the air.
²² Abaddon and Death say,
     'We have heard a rumor of it with our ears.'

²³ "God understands the way to it,
     and he knows its place.
²⁴ For he looks to the ends of the earth,
     and sees everything under the heavens.
²⁵ When he gave to the wind its weight,
     and apportioned out the waters by measure;
²⁶ when he made a decree for the rain,
     and a way for the thunderbolt;
²⁷ then he saw it and declared it;
     he established it, and searched it out.
²⁸ And he said to humankind,
     'Truly, the fear of the Lord, that is wisdom;
     and to depart from evil is understanding.' "

As if all of us needed a break from this long siege of arguments and counterarguments that finally lead nowhere, Job 28 offers us a calm moment of
reflection on the ultimately impossible human quest to find and comprehend the wisdom that belongs only to God. There are no obvious links between this poem and the three cycles of discourses that have just ended in
confusion. Nor is there a clear link to Job's magnificent summation for the
defense that follows in chapters 29—31. Job and his friends have agreed

that God's wisdom is unsearchable, but they have drawn opposite conclusions as to how this incontrovertible fact bears on Job's case (Eliphaz: 5:9–10; Zophar: 11:5–9; Job: 9:4–10).

In Job 28, however, the marvel of transcendent Wisdom is celebrated without reference to the argument that has raged between Job and his friends. The issue of God's justice in human affairs (that is, whether God metes out rewards and punishments in response to righteous or wicked behavior) is never touched on. This hymn to unsearchable Wisdom is apparently sung for any audience that cares to listen, without being addressed to anyone in particular. Theories abound as to whether chapter 28 is an integral part of the original book of Job or whether it was inserted by a later editor and, in either case, as to the purpose the poem was intended to serve in its present context. None of these theories is sufficiently strong to produce a major consensus among students of the book of Job. The one point of general agreement is that chapter 28 rather abruptly invites the present-day reader of Job to step back from everything that has been said so far and reflect on the ultimate limits that stand athwart the age-old human urgency to know, to understand, to find the way to authentic Wisdom. Such wisdom is not to be confused with either knowledge or information (let alone "data"). In the wisdom circles from which Job sprang, the ultimate Wisdom spoken of in chapter 28 includes more than comprehension of where things come from and how things work and how things are in nature and in human experience. More important, it includes the art of deliberately and successfully ordering life in full harmony with God, human beings, and nature.

The questions posed by chapter 28 are "Where shall [such] wisdom be found? And where is the place of understanding?" (vv. 12 and 20). To set up the question, however, the poet begins by celebrating the quite remarkable technologies human beings have developed to discover and exploit valuable things that were originally quite hidden from human sight. The place of precious metals is the mine, where gold, silver, iron, and copper can be extracted and refined (vv. 1–2). Verses 3 and 4 describe the remarkable skill and daring by which miners probe the darkness of the subterranean world, swaying on ropes into deep shafts opened in desolate places. (Archaeologists have found allusions here to the astonishingly sophisticated means by which ancient mining operations were carried out.) The surface of the earth is as commonplace as the grain it produces, but underneath, hidden from view, it is "turned up as by fire" (v. 5; a possible reference to an awareness of volcanism?), where precious stones and gold dust are to be found. (The "stones of fire" in Ezekiel 28:14 suggest a possible link in the ancient mind between subterranean fire and precious stones.)

Human capacity to discover the way to such subterranean treasures is the more astonishing since not even the sharpest eye in nature (the falcon's) nor the lordliest and widest-ranging of beasts (the lion and other proud denizens of remote places) have discerned a path to this hidden world (vv. 7–8).

Verses 10 and 11 conclude this celebration of the capacity of human technology with allusions to excavating and cutting through rock and probing the underground source of rivers, if necessary, to bring hidden and precious things to light. (The Hebrew text of verse 11a may indicate the "damming of rivers.")

Yet the import of verses 12–13 is that not even this remarkable, curiosity-driven human urge to explore and discover and exploit hidden things is capable of finding the place where "wisdom" and "understanding" are to be found. In a time of increasing cynicism about scientific and technological "progress," I think it would be a mistake to find comfort in this passage for an anti-intellectual, anti-scientific, anti-technological attitude. The poet stands quite frankly in awe before the human capacity to achieve such remarkable results. But verses 12–13 make the point that human cleverness, even at its best, is simply not capable of breaking through to the discovery and exploitation of what matters most: authentic wisdom with respect to God, human beings, and nature. The "place of understanding" (of this order at least) is simply not within the purview of anyone alive (v. 13). (What havoc has been wrought, in human history, by mortals convinced they know what is "wise" for the rest of us!) We should not feel bad, however, that the way to ultimate Wisdom lies beyond us, according to verse 14. Even "the deep" and "the sea" must confess that Wisdom is not to be found within them. Ancient readers may have understood each of these terms in the sense of divine or quasi-divine chaos monsters whose "depths" are quite literally unfathomable. Even if we could probe to the bottom of abysmal chaos, we should not find Wisdom there (not even in the last nanosecond before the big bang?). In this and other respects, Job 28 calls to mind the glorious personification of Wisdom in Proverbs 8:22–31: She was already there when God "established the fountains of the deep" (Prov. 8:28) and "assigned to the sea its limit" (8:29).

If no one can find the "place" of Wisdom, neither is Wisdom for sale (Job 28:15–19). While the precise meaning of several terms remains uncertain (especially the Hebrew words translated in the NRSV as "onyx," "sapphire" (lapis lazuli?), "coral," "crystal," "pearls," "chrysolite"), they obviously belong in a catalog of the most precious imaginable commodities. None of these things compares in value to Wisdom, and not even possession of vast treasures can empower the owner to purchase it. While wisdom literature in general often regards the acquisition of wisdom as the highest human goal (see Prov. 4:5–7; 16:16; 23:23), the ultimate Wisdom of which Job 28 speaks eludes all human capacities to search out and acquire. The dwelling place of transcendent Wisdom is permanently hidden from the sharpest eye, whether human or otherwise (vv. 20–21). Even death and the chaotic underworld, here personified, have at best heard rumors of Wisdom's place of origin (v. 22; see v. 14).

Earlier, we described chapter 28 as a hymn to unsearchable Wisdom, but verse 23 suggests that this is not quite accurate. Praise is due rather to God, who "understands the way to [Wisdom] and . . . knows its place" (v. 23), who "saw it and declared it," who "established it, and searched it out" (v. 27). Here, as in Proverbs 8:22–31, we are challenged to think that the primordial Wisdom by which the cosmos (including all humanity) is ordered is not merely identical with God, nor is it what theologians have typically called an "attribute" of God. According to Proverbs 8:22–29, Wisdom was "created," "set up," "brought forth" by God, before any of the now-discernible signs of God's creative activity came into being. According to Job 28:23–27, it is as if God "discovered" the place of Wisdom at the beginning of God's creative activity. It is perhaps easiest to understand both Job 28:23–27 and Proverbs 8:22–29 as metaphors for the transcendent Wisdom that belongs only to God. Yet both passages indicate a significant distance between God and the unsearchable "logic" that underlies all the realities of nature and history. Even if human beings could one day do the impossible and figure everything out, breaking through to some "grand unified theory" or "theory of everything" (as some contemporary physicists dream of doing), we should not yet have approached the ultimate grandeur of God. At best we should have stumbled across the traces of God's beloved agent, Wisdom, who is God's "master craftsman, delighting [God] day after day, ever at play in [God's] presence, at play everywhere in [God's] world, delighting to be with [the human race]" (Prov. 8:30–31, *Jerusalem Bible* translation).

This assessment is perhaps strengthened by God's definitive word to human beings in their insatiable hunger for wisdom in Job 28:28. Plumbing the depths of the cosmic order underlying all the processes of nature and history may indeed lie beyond human capacities, as 28:1–22 affirms. Yet the wisdom and understanding appropriate to God's human creatures are available to all, even to the simplest of us: wondering and trusting awe in the presence of God, "fear of the Lord," and the deliberate choice not to place one's own advantage higher than the justice due to one's neighbor ("to depart from evil"; my understanding of the meaning of this phrase in the context of Job is derived from the remarkably "secular" ethic that defines "evil" in this book, most notably apparent in Job 22:5–11 and in Job 31).

Regardless of how chapter 28 may have come to be in its present place in the book of Job, it makes a fine counterfoil to the rather frantic and confused ending of the dialogues in 24:18 through 27:23. If we read chapter 28 as an independent poem, its concluding verse sounds like a rather conventional corrective to all overheated efforts to comprehend the cosmic order (see Psalm 111:10 ; Prov. 1:7; and Eccl. 12:11–13). Whether intentional or unintentional, however, Job 28:28 takes on a special meaning when we listen to it in close connection with Job 1:1 and 2:3, where no less an authority than God declares Job to be a person who "feared God and turned away from evil." It is obvious from Job's speeches that he does not comprehend the hidden "wisdom" that has plunged him from a state of total blessedness into a state of utter godforsakenness "for no reason" (2:3). Yet it is not Job's understanding of this mystery that is at stake, according to chapters 1 and 2. The point at issue is whether Job will "persist in his integrity" toward God and people throughout this unaccountable plunge into wretchedness. From this perspective, Job 28:28 is a perfect lead-in to Job's final, magnificent affirmation of his integrity in chapters 29—31.

6. Job's Summation for the Defense
Job 29—31

There is a distinct danger, I think, that the full significance of Job 29—31 may be lost if we read these chapters as a lengthy continuation of the many speeches we have already heard from Job in chapters 3—27. In point of fact, Job sets out to do something in these three chapters that he has nowhere done before—not in this comprehensive and connected way—namely, to paint three dazzling self-portraits, each integrally connected to the other two. The first self-portrait conveys what it was like, from Job's viewpoint, to live an utterly blessed life in relation to God and people (chapter 29). The second self-portrait conveys what it is like, from Job's viewpoint, to plunge from utter blessedness to the absolute depths of human wretchedness (chapter 30). The third self-portrait conveys the state of Job's heart toward God and people (that is, his "integrity") before, during, and after this sudden "descent into hell."

It is important to recognize that we have already heard this before, not from Job's viewpoint but from the viewpoint of the ancient storyteller in chapters 1 and 2, one who observes Job only from the outside. With a few swift strokes, the storyteller paints an outsider's portrait of Job's wholly blessed life (Job 1:1–5, corresponding to Job 29). This is followed by an equally brief description of Job's two-stage plunge into wretchedness (1:13–19; 2:7–9, corresponding to chapter 30). We can hardly call four verses a "portrait," but 1:20–22 and 2:10 do provide an outsider's impression of what Job knows of himself according to chapter 31: Job's "integrity" remains constant before, during, and after the unimaginable reversal from God-blessedness to godforsakenness.

In one sense, the ancient story ends with Job's response in 1:20–21 and 2:10a. All outsiders may now marvel at Job's twice-demonstrated capacity to "persist in his integrity" throughout the ordeal, even though he has no inkling of the fact that both *hassatan* and God have risked their respective reputations on whether or not Job is capable of such a magnificent response. What the ancient story cannot do is take the listener deep inside Job's incomprehensible experience of this contrived "test" and disclose the titanic struggle of heart and mind by which this unparalleled persistence in human integrity is achieved. As I see it, most of the book of Job, from 2:11 through 31:40, is intended to explore precisely this interior dimension of Job's famous "endurance" (see James 5:11). Every speech of Job, in one way or another, explores the inner agony of truly innocent suffering or chronicles the profound interior refusal to surrender integrity toward God and people, even in the face of a terror Job can recognize only as the face of "God the enemy." Every speech of the friends, in one way or another, seduces Job to remove the terror of God the enemy by means of the convenient lie that the suffering God has brought on him is well deserved, that Job, not God, is in the wrong. As if Job could bribe God with such lying servility and so curry favor and gain restoration! As if God could be so bribed. We must bear in mind again that God's reputation rides on the conviction that neither terror nor seduction will shake the integrity of God's servant Job.

In the three self-portraits painted in chapters 29, 30, and 31, Job offers up, as with his last breath, his ultimate response to the crisis that has been thrust on him. Readers will note that these three chapters soar entirely above whatever theological haggling may have gone on between Job and his friends. What we encounter here are the brute facts of Job's experience and Job's response at the point of his incorruptible integrity.

TOTAL HARMONY WITH GOD
Job 29

Job 29
> 29:1 **Job again took up his discourse and said:**
> > 2 **"Oh, that I were as in the months of old,**
> > > **as in the days when God watched over me;**
> > 3 **when his lamp shone over my head,**
> > > **and by his light I walked through darkness;**
> > 4 **when I was in my prime,**
> > > **when the friendship of God was upon my tent;**
> > 5 **when the Almighty was still with me,**
> > > **when my children were around me;**
> > 6 **when my steps were washed with milk,**
> > > **and the rock poured out for me streams of oil!**
> > 7 **When I went out to the gate of the city,**

when I took my seat in the square,
⁸ the young men saw me and withdrew,
  and the aged rose up and stood;
⁹ the nobles refrained from talking,
  and laid their hands on their mouths;
¹⁰ the voices of princes were hushed,
  and their tongues stuck to the roof of their mouths.
¹¹ When the ear heard, it commended me,
  and when the eye saw, it approved;
¹² because I delivered the poor who cried,
  and the orphan who had no helper.
¹³ The blessing of the wretched came upon me,
  and I caused the widow's heart to sing for joy.
¹⁴ I put on righteousness, and it clothed me;
  my justice was like a robe and a turban.
¹⁵ I was eyes to the blind,
  and feet to the lame.
¹⁶ I was a father to the needy,
  and I championed the cause of the stranger.
¹⁷ I broke the fangs of the unrighteous,
  and made them drop their prey from their teeth.
¹⁸ Then I thought, 'I shall die in my nest,
  and I shall multiply my days like the phoenix;
¹⁹ my roots spread out to the waters,
  with the dew all night on my branches;
²⁰ my glory was fresh with me,
  and my bow ever new in my hand.'

²¹ "They listened to me, and waited,
  and kept silence for my counsel.
²² After I spoke they did not speak again,
  and my word dropped upon them like dew.
²³ They waited for me as for the rain;
  they opened their mouths as for the spring rain.
²⁴ I smiled on them when they had no confidence;
  and the light of my countenance they did not extinguish.
²⁵ I chose their way, and sat as chief,
  and I lived like a king among his troops,
  like one who comforts mourners.

As we approach the first of these self-portraits, it is perhaps in order to take a step back from Job the innocent sufferer and focus on the intention of the ancient poet in each of these portraits. We are apt to miss the point of each, I think, unless we understand what the poet is trying to achieve and give ourselves over to the poet's goal with our own powers of imagination.

If we don't do this in chapter 29, for instance, we are apt to dismiss this chapter as the nostalgic mouthings of a distressingly self-congratulatory old man. Yet the characterization of Job in 1:1–5 and the accolades God confers on him in 1:8 and 2:3 forbid any cynical or condescending reading of chapter 29. Whether the poet succeeds or not, there is no mistaking the artistic intention of this chapter: to describe an utterly blessed human life, one that reflects unmarred wholeness in relationship to God, people, and the environment. Every blessing God showers on Job, including awestruck recognition and honor accorded him by human contemporaries, is to be understood as a resounding yes! of God to the quality of Job's humanity. Every response Job makes to this supremely blessed existence is to be taken as a reflection of his complete integrity.

The poet faces formidable difficulties in such a task, not the least of which is our cynical human certainty that "nobody ever had it *that* good" and that "no human being ever *was* that good." Armed with that justifiable cynicism, any reader can easily discover flaws in this portrait of a person who embodies complete fidelity toward God and people, living in the best of all imaginable worlds. My own imagination balks at several points. The excellent people of my experience, for instance, never call attention to their own excellence. More disturbing, chapter 29 apparently relies on the model of an ancient Near Eastern autocrat—male, of course, endlessly wealthy and powerful—to convey the ultimate in human dignity, freedom, and benevolence. Persons who have best embodied for me what a life devoted to God and people might be like, in contrast, have been neither male nor autocratic nor wealthy nor powerful.

The question is whether I will allow these and other reservations to obscure what I take to be the poet's intention to provide a vivid and detailed picture of the kind of person described by God in Job 1:8: "There is no one like him on the earth, a blameless and upright man who fears God and turns away from evil."

The alternative is to enter into the poet's intention with all my powers of imagination, suspending disbelief where necessary, conspiring with the poet to conjure up a vision of human blessedness and integrity worthy of Job 1:1–5, 8 and 2:3. On that basis, the astonishing thing to me is not that the poem fails in this impossible task but that it so nearly succeeds. To test that estimate, we must turn now to the poem itself.

Job's reminiscences of how things were before his "descent into hell" begin with recalling the matchless intimacy of his former relationship with

God (vv. 2–5a). As concrete tokens of this intimacy with God, Job recalls the blessings of family (v. 5) and field (v. 6, using familiar biblical hyperboles to convey the presence, in abundance, of all life-sustaining and life-enriching commodities).

But a wholly blessed life, according to verses 7–11, cannot remain a merely private family affair. Public responsibilities and relationships (indicated by the terms *gate* and *square* in verse 7) must also be carried out with honor and dignity worthy of the ungrudging respect of the whole community. If not for verses 12–17, the response of the community might sound as if the abject deference of the whole community, old and young and nobles alike (vv. 8–11), were some kind of public relations coup, a "blessing" of public recognition and honor in its own right. In verses 12–17 we discover why it is that this superbly "blessed" human being commands such total respect and approval from the whole community, from top to bottom. It is because this blessed person has unswervingly taken the side of the helpless, the disenfranchised, the wretched, the oppressed, the blind, the lame, the needy, the resident aliens (vv. 12–16). If we are indeed talking about a "regal" person here, the royal regalia consist of God's own righteousness and justice lived out in a human life and worn as the sole badge of office (v. 14; compare Isa. 11:5). Only ungodly predators have anything to fear from the exercise of such royal power (v. 17).

Verses 21–25 strike me as a potent conclusion to this superb picture of God's "regal human being," begun in verses 7–17. These verses conjure up for me a scene in a human council chamber corresponding roughly to the scene in the heavenly council chamber described in chapters 1 and 2. Here, God's regal human being is surrounded by those who honor him extravagantly (vv. 8–11) because his record is so transparent of God's own justice and righteousness (vv. 12–17). Under his leadership, this earthly council is to develop the strategy and tactics appropriate to such a royal domain. Unlike the council scenes in Job 1 and 2, there is no *hassatan* here, no questioning or dissenting voice to becloud the issues. Instead, all members of the council only listen and wait in silence (v. 21). There are no counterproposals here, only a longing to hear comparable to the yearning of arid earth for water (vv. 22–23). The leadership of such an "autocrat" is exercised not to intimidate but to inspire confidence (v. 24a; the Hebrew of verse 24b can be interpreted variously, but it probably echoes the idea of verse 24a). The course of the future is established by God's regal human, as a king directs his hosts (v. 25a); yet an unlikely king, in that his goal is to comfort those who mourn (v. 25b).

How would the future look to such a person, so utterly blessed in all relationships to God and people (vv. 18–20)? With nothing and no one to fear, with the approbation of God resting so self-evidently on him, what is there to look forward to but a "good death," perhaps—who knows—a death like the fabulous phoenix from whose ashes another such marvelous bird may yet take wing? So, I think, the poet's portrait of an utterly blessed Job may have originally ended. To borrow a phrase from Pontius Pilate, "Ecce homo!"— and what a human being, surely deserving God's accolade in 1:8 and 2:3.

TOTAL GODFORSAKENNESS
Job 30

Job 30

30:1 "But now they make sport of me,
  those who are younger than I,
  whose fathers I would have disdained
  to set with the dogs of my flock.
 2 What could I gain from the strength of their hands?
  All their vigor is gone.
 3 Through want and hard hunger
  they gnaw the dry and desolate ground,
 4 they pick mallow and the leaves of bushes,
  and to warm themselves the roots of broom.
 5 They are driven out from society;
  people shout after them as after a thief.
 6 In the gullies of wadis they must live,
  in holes in the ground, and in the rocks.
 7 Among the bushes they bray;
  under the nettles they huddle together.
 8 A senseless, disreputable brood,
  they have been whipped out of the land.

 9 "And now they mock me in song;
  I am a byword to them.
 10 They abhor me, they keep aloof from me;
  they do not hesitate to spit at the sight of me.
 11 Because God has loosed my bowstring and humbled me,
  they have cast off restraint in my presence.
 12 On my right hand the rabble rise up;
  they send me sprawling,
  and build roads for my ruin.
 13 They break up my path,
  they promote my calamity;

    no one restrains them.
14 As through a wide breach they come;
    amid the crash they roll on.
15 Terrors are turned upon me;
    my honor is pursued as by the wind,
    and my prosperity has passed away like a cloud.

16 "And now my soul is poured out within me;
    days of affliction have taken hold of me.
17 The night racks my bones,
    and the pain that gnaws me takes no rest.
18 With violence he seizes my garment;
    he grasps me by the collar of my tunic.
19 He has cast me into the mire,
    and I have become like dust and ashes.
20 I cry to you and you do not answer me;
    I stand, and you merely look at me.
21 You have turned cruel to me;
    with the might of your hand you persecute me.
22 You lift me up on the wind, you make me ride on it,
    and you toss me about in the roar of the storm.
23 I know that you will bring me to death,
    and to the house appointed for all living.

24 "Surely one does not turn against the needy,
    when in disaster they cry for help.
25 Did I not weep for those whose day was hard?
    Was not my soul grieved for the poor?
26 But when I looked for good, evil came;
    and when I waited for light, darkness came.
27 My inward parts are in turmoil, and are never still;
    days of affliction come to meet me.
28 I go about in sunless gloom;
    I stand up in the assembly and cry for help.
29 I am a brother of jackals,
    and a companion of ostriches.
30 My skin turns black and falls from me,
    and my bones burn with heat.
31 My lyre is turned to mourning,
    and my pipe to the voice of those who weep.

Like chapter 29, chapter 30 is an invitation to join the poet in a shared work of imagination. The question here is how you would describe the absolute depths of human wretchedness. The story told in 1:13–19 and 2:7–8 gives us only a brief, external glance at the experience of the total loss of every good thing. Here the poet challenges us to experience Job's loss *with* Job, from within, with the unparalleled anguish of complete godforsakenness. The unspoken question behind chapters 29 and 30, taken together, is: How would it be if the best and most blessed person imaginable were suddenly plunged, for no reason, to the absolute depths of all human misery? How would such a person respond? For Job's response we must wait until chapter 31, but it is already clear that the test of Job's integrity devised in the heavenly council chamber (1:11–12 and 2:5) is being described from Job's side, without Job's being given any hint that *hassatan*'s reputation and God's are riding on how he responds to this most extreme imaginable plunge from the heights to the depths of human experience.

In some respects, chapter 30 places more severe demands on modern imaginations than chapter 29 does. For the first time in all human history, twentieth-century people have been confronted with utterly graphic and appalling images of real human suffering on a global scale. To think of anything "worse" is not only beyond our powers of imagination, it is frankly more than we can stand. Yet we lose all access to chapter 30, I think, unless we allow the poet to take us by the hand and lead us into the interior experience of the "worst-case scenario" of all human suffering. Just as there was "no one like Job" in his experience of God-blessedness (1:8; 2:3), we are now to believe that there is none like him in the experience of godforsakenness. Again, it is not surprising that the poet's words fail to convey this unimaginable wretchedness in all its stark reality. No words could. But again, it is the reader's task to recognize the poet's intention and "piece out the poem's imperfections with our thoughts" (with apologies to the Chorus in the opening speech of Shakespeare's *Henry the Fifth*), in order to approach its goal as nearly as possible.

The first obstacle to my imagination comes in the depiction of the "scum of the earth" in 30:1–8. I should like to think that the "blessed" Job of chapter 29 would have taken a less harsh and uncaring view of people on the bottom rungs of human society than this: They are the insolent offspring of worthless fathers (vv. 1–2); they bray like animals from their pangs of hunger (v. 7); they are "senseless," no-account outcasts from decent society (v. 8). On the strength of these estimates, it almost sounds as if their starvation and homelessness (vv. 3–7) were somehow their own fault (an opinion, alas, that is still met with in our own times).

Yet the poet discloses the point of this bleak, uncharitable description in verses 1 and 9–11. We are to imagine the starving and homeless outcasts

of society in the direst terms we can and then imagine these wretches looking down on Job, as one who is utterly beneath their "dignity"! They make
jokes at Job's expense (v. 1); they mock him and invent slurs based on his
wretched condition (v. 9); they turn their backs on him, they spit at the
sight of him (v. 10; some scholars translate this to mean "spitting in Job's
face"; see Isa. 50:6). It is one thing to be among the outcasts of this world.
It is quite another to be beneath them, to be despised and rejected even by
the dregs of humanity. We are to imagine Job at the rock bottom of the
worst imaginable human wretchedness. For Job, however, the agony goes
deeper still. He perceives God as the one who has caused his distress (an
accurate judgment, according to 1:12 and 2:6), and this is what has given
license to his tormentors (v. 11).

It is possible that the onslaught of "the rabble" in verses 12–14 is to be
understood as a continuation of Job's oppression at the hands of the outcasts of verses 1–11, their scorn now turning to violence. Yet the language
of verses 12–19 recalls the terrifying description of God as Job's enemy,
leading troops against him (see 16:11–14). In any case, the conclusion of
verses 12–19 identifies God as the one who is implicated in and has ultimately caused all Job's suffering (see vv. 18–19). Perhaps this, more than
any other anguish, is what makes Job's experience of suffering unique,
somehow beneath the worst of all human distress: It is the unaccountable
loss of the "friendship of God" (29:4) on the part of one whose whole being
was turned toward God with unmatched fidelity and integrity (Job 1:1, 8;
2:3).

Not even this ultimate distress, however, prevents Job from calling God
"you" (vv. 20–23). I take this to mean that Job "persists in his integrity"
(2:3) toward God, even in the face of his experience of God as the enemy.
The only way Job can maintain his side of the relationship with God, under these circumstances, is to continue laying his case before God with
complete honesty. Like certain laments in the Psalms, the language of
verses 20–23 is accusatory (see Psalms 10:1–13; 13:1–4; 88:6–18). Yet to
address these accusations directly to God ("you") carries the implication
that the relationship with God is still intact from the human side. By holding God accountable for God's side of the relationship, Job affirms in the
only way left to him that God somehow will yet hear Job's cry and will yet
answer him (what we have called upside-down trust).

"Out of the depths," then (see Psalm 130:1), Job honors his integrity toward God (and so honors God) by holding God accountable for the unjust
suffering that has befallen him. Yet the very hopelessness of Job's outcry
to God, against God, in verses 20–23 measures the true depth that makes

Job's suffering reprehensible even by the standards of ordinary human compassion (vv. 24–25). God's abandonment of Job is outrageous, leaving Job in utter darkness (v. 26), filled with turmoil (v. 27), bereft of justice (v. 28), as cut off from companionship and a fair hearing as the lonely animals of the desert (v. 29), in utter ruin of body and grief of soul (vv. 30–31).

Perhaps one of us could paint a more vivid and telling portrait of a human being who has reached the greatest imaginable depth of human suffering and humiliation. Job 30 has set a remarkable standard, however, and serves notice that the task will not be easy.

TOTAL INTEGRITY
Job 31

Job 31

31:1 **"I have made a covenant with my eyes;**
    how then could I look upon a virgin?
  2 **What would be my portion from God above,**
    and my heritage from the Almighty on high?
  3 **Does not calamity befall the unrighteous,**
    and disaster the workers of iniquity?
  4 **Does he not see my ways,**
    and number all my steps?

  5 **"If I have walked with falsehood,**
    and my foot has hurried to deceit—
  6 **let me be weighed in a just balance,**
    and let God know my integrity!—
  7 **if my step has turned aside from the way,**
    and my heart has followed my eyes,
    and if any spot has clung to my hands;
  8 **then let me sow, and another eat;**
    and let what grows for me be rooted out.

  9 **"If my heart has been enticed by a woman,**
    and I have lain in wait at my neighbor's door;
 10 **then let my wife grind for another,**
    and let other men kneel over her.
 11 **For that would be a heinous crime;**
    that would be a criminal offense;
 12 **for that would be a fire consuming down to Abaddon,**
    and it would burn to the root all my harvest.

¹³ "If I have rejected the cause of my male or female slaves,
  when they brought a complaint against me;
¹⁴ what then shall I do when God rises up?
  When he makes inquiry, what shall I answer him?
¹⁵ Did not he who made me in the womb make them?
  And did not one fashion us in the womb?

¹⁶ "If I have withheld anything that the poor desired,
  or have caused the eyes of the widow to fail,
¹⁷ or have eaten my morsel alone,
  and the orphan has not eaten from it—
¹⁸ for from my youth I reared the orphan like a father,
  and from my mother's womb I guided the widow—
¹⁹ if I have seen anyone perish for lack of clothing,
  or a poor person without covering,
²⁰ whose loins have not blessed me,
  and who was not warmed with the fleece of my sheep;
²¹ if I have raised my hand against the orphan,
  because I saw I had supporters at the gate;
²² then let my shoulder blade fall from my shoulder,
  and let my arm be broken from its socket.
²³ For I was in terror of calamity from God,
  and I could not have faced his majesty.

²⁴ "If I have made gold my trust,
  or called fine gold my confidence;
²⁵ if I have rejoiced because my wealth was great,
  or because my hand had gotten much;
²⁶ if I have looked at the sun when it shone,
  or the moon moving in splendor,
²⁷ and my heart has been secretly enticed,
  and my mouth has kissed my hand;
²⁸ this also would be an iniquity to be punished by the judges,
  for I should have been false to God above.

²⁹ "If I have rejoiced at the ruin of those who hated me,
  or exulted when evil overtook them—
³⁰ I have not let my mouth sin
  by asking for their lives with a curse—
³¹ if those of my tent ever said,
  'O that we might be sated with his flesh!'—
³² the stranger has not lodged in the street;
  I have opened my doors to the traveler—

³³ if I have concealed my transgressions as others do,
   by hiding my iniquity in my bosom,
³⁴ because I stood in great fear of the multitude,
   and the contempt of families terrified me,
   so that I kept silence, and did not go out of doors—
³⁵ Oh, that I had one to hear me!
   (Here is my signature! let the Almighty answer me!)
   Oh, that I had the indictment written by my adversary!
³⁶ Surely I would carry it on my shoulder;
   I would bind it on me like a crown;
³⁷ I would give him an account of all my steps;
   like a prince I would approach him.

³⁸ "If my land has cried out against me,
   and its furrows have wept together;
³⁹ if I have eaten its yield without payment,
   and caused the death of its owners;
⁴⁰ let thorns grow instead of wheat,
   and foul weeds instead of barley."

   The words of Job are ended.

Now comes the third, massive self-portrait in Job 29—31. We have moved from a picture of ultimate God-blessedness to a picture of ultimate god-forsakenness. The point of this most extreme imaginable reversal, according to the story told in 1:1 through 2:10, was to discover the answer to *hassatan*'s question in 1:9: "Does Job fear God for nothing?" According to 2:3, the answer hinges entirely on whether Job will "persist in his integrity" even if all his fortunes are reversed, even if Job is faced with catastrophic evidence that his famous integrity carries with it no personal gain or reward whatsoever.

As we have seen, chapter 29 can be understood as the "inside story," from Job's viewpoint, of the idyllic picture of Job's former blessedness described in 1:1–5. In a similar way, chapter 30 provides the inside story of Job 1:13–19 and 2:7–8, taken together as a single picture of absolute suffering and loss. Chapter 31, on this reading, provides the inside story of Job's deceptively serene and pious affirmation of God, out of the depths of his overwhelming distress, in 1:20–22 and 2:10b.

At first glance, chapter 31 appears to have nothing to do with the unshakable trust described in 1:20–22 and 2:10b: the capacity to accept whatever comes from God's hands in life, the bad with the good, in the mode of humble acceptance and praise. Within the framework of the story told in 1:1–2:10, Job's pious affirmations indicate that he has passed the twofold test proposed by *hassatan* in 1:11 and 2:5. Job's mind and heart have not been changed by this unparalleled loss, not even by the experience of what appears to be the enmity of God. (Note Job's willingness to assign his distress directly to the "hand of God" in 1:21 and 2:10.)

Job 2:3 and 2:9, however, indicate that more is at stake in Job's pious submission than his feelings and attitudes toward God. First God and then Job's wife describe Job's faithful endurance as the unaccountable will to "persist in his integrity." Job 1:1; 1:8; and 2:3 make it clear that this "integrity" includes Job's conduct toward his fellow human beings as well as toward God. The distinction contemporary people sometimes make between "faith" (or "piety") and "ethics" is absent in this characterization of Job. Faithfulness and justice in dealing with people *is* faithfulness toward God, and vice versa. Job's affirmation of God in 1:21 and 2:10b hinges directly on his capacity to maintain the same "blameless" conduct toward people after his devastating loss as he did before.

This is the point of chapter 31. Especially now, after all communications between Job and God have been cut off (chap. 30), only one avenue is left by which Job can prove that this relationship with God is still intact—from Job's side at least, if not from God's. He can still affirm his unswerving commitment to the way of life he believes God always intended for human beings.

In this way, chapter 31 indeed explores the interior dimension of the breathtaking faithfulness so simply expressed in 1:20 and 2:10b. Once again, the poet of chapters 29 and 30 challenges us to imagine the extreme case. If a completely God-blessed person experienced complete godforsakenness and yet "persisted in his integrity," how should this magnificent persistence of heart and will be described?

Of the three self-portraits in 29—31, this one is the most difficult for contemporary readers of Job to visualize. The form in which this manifesto of integrity is cast is alien to modern tastes and sensibilities. The form itself is widely attested in the ancient Near East, from Egypt to Mesopotamia: the "oath of clearance" or "oath of purity," in which one declares oneself innocent of attitudes or actions understood to be offensive to God (or the gods). Exodus 22:7–11 provides an example of the possible use of this form in a practical legal setting. With remarkable similarities to the prebiblical Code of Hammurabi, Exodus 21:2–23:8 includes a variety of cases at law, together with prescribed penalties and restitutions to be paid by the person who is found liable. Exodus 22:7–11, however, raises the question of what is to be done in cases where accusations or suspicions of wrongdoing are present but no corroborating witness or evidence exists that could establish guilt. In such a case, Exodus 22:11 specifies that the accused shall take "an oath before the Lord" (presumably an "oath of innocence"), and the accuser must accept this oath in lieu of restitution. The implication is clear: Such an oath invites the retribution of God against the accused in the event the oath is sworn falsely. The form such an oath might have taken is indicated in texts such as Ruth 1:17 and 1 Samuel 3:17; 14:44: "May God [or 'the gods' in 1 Kings 19:2; 20:10] do so to me and more also if . . ."

In a society where words are cheap, perjury is routine, and oaths are lightly sworn, it is difficult to imagine the life-and-death seriousness with which Job's oaths of innocence in chapter 31 are meant to be taken. Every time Job pronounces the word *if* (sixteen times in chapter 31) we are to understand that he is literally placing his life on the line before God to affirm his innocence with respect to the attitudes and actions named in each oath.

The reason for Job's mighty affirmation of innocence is that he stands accused. *Hassatan* has called Job's motivation in question, insinuating that raw self-interest underlies all his attitudes and actions (1:9–11; 2:4–5). The friends accuse Job of having sinned against God and people so flagrantly that his suffering is no more than due punishment (see Job 22:4–11). If it is true that God visits suffering upon people in just proportion to their wickedness (an assumption Job denies), then Job concedes that his very wretchedness accuses him (see 16:8).

Chapter 31, then, envisions a courtroom scene in which Job responds to his accusers with his ultimate "cross my heart and hope to die" declaration of innocence. We are being asked to imagine what it might mean to persist in one's integrity in its most extreme form: on the part of one who has been cast down from unparalleled God-blessedness to unparalleled godforsakenness "for no reason" (2:3).

For modern readers, the intended impact of chapter 31 may strike us more forcefully if we look away from the ancient oath formula and concentrate on the positive ethic Job affirms as characterizing a genuinely "innocent" human life. If we regard Job's affirmations as symptoms of virulent self-righteousness, we join the friends in their accusations (see 11:4–6). Job 1:8; 2:3; and 42:7–8, however, compel us to take Job at his word. We are to consider each affirmation as entirely grounded in Job's life, free of all lip service and self-righteousness. What emerges is a portrait of a human being who is genuinely righteous; one who is not motivated by self-interest; one whose interior moral compass holds true course regardless of external seductions or pressures (even from the side of God). Regarded as a catalog of "virtues," Job 31 contains nothing so very different from similar characterizations of righteous living common throughout the ancient Near East (including that of Job's friends). What sets it apart from any comparable passage in ancient Near Eastern literature (to my knowledge) is the question of motivation for the moral life. The standard answer in the ancient Near East to *hassatan*'s question "Does Job fear God for nothing?" was "Of course not!" Without the "carrot" of future blessing for the righteous and the "stick" of punishment for the wicked, the very basis of the moral life collapses. (Eliphaz appears to affirm this in 15:4.) Job's friends reflect the well-nigh universal view in the ancient Near East, both in and outside the Bible, that righteous living is simply the highest form of "enlightened self-interest." Wickedness is not merely wrong, it is ultimately counterproductive.

By the time we arrive at chapter 31, however, Job has made it abundantly clear that he is not motivated by hope of future reward. Fear has also lost its motivating power, since the worst has already happened: "Truly the thing that I fear comes upon me, and what I dread befalls me" (3:25). All that is left to him is to "persist in his integrity" beyond hope or fear. His affirmations of innocence proclaim his unswerving integrity toward people; that these affirmations are addressed to God and no other (31:35–37) expresses his unswerving integrity toward God.

The single thread that runs throughout Job's oath of innocence is a human center of thinking and deciding and acting that is simply not influenced by the kinds of external seductions and pressures that so easily nudge ordinary people morally off course. The opening oath (31:1–5) illustrates this vividly. The decision to use another person for one's own sexual gratification begins with an interior willingness, here symbolized by an ogling eye. Simply to look at another person with lustful intent, thinks Job, already transforms the other into a dehumanized instrument of one's own self-indulgence. Did Jesus have Job 31:1 in mind when he spoke about the adulterous heart in Matthew 5:28? We do not require the public confession of a pious former president (Jimmy Carter) on this point to recognize what a towering personal ethic Job claims when he affirms that he has struck a nonnegotiable deal with his "eyes" to cut off the crime of sexual exploitation at its source—not at the deed but at the interior disposition toward the other that makes the deed thinkable.

What follows in verses 2–4 sounds very much like the standard rationale for morality that is well-nigh universal in the ancient Near East: God is watching (v. 4), and all manner of evil consequences befall people who stray from the straight and narrow (vv. 2–3). What renders this so ironic here is that every conceivable evil consequence has already befallen Job (chap. 30), as if he were guilty of this and every other moral failure. Yet this is the very implication Job has resolutely refused to draw from his suffering! Is Job merely mocking God's justice here, or is he affirming out of the depths of his own undeserved suffering that somehow God must be unalterably opposed to sexual exploitation of the other, must confirm the "ethic of the eyes" that Job has made fundamental to his own humanity, regardless of the counterevidence in human experience. If we choose the second option, then Job 31:1–4 constitutes a further instance of what I have called Job's upside-down trust that God is, that God knows, and that God cares, even though the hard realities of human existence (and Job's own experience) appear to deny it daily.

The key words in verses 5–9 are *falsehood*, *deceit*, and *spot* (v. 7), the last of which almost certainly refers to the acceptance of a bribe. The common denominator among these very generalized "sins" is the diverse strategies by which people contrive to gain personal advantage in social, political, and economic relationships, while "the way" (v. 7) of integrity toward God and people clearly forbids such strategies. The agonized parenthetical cry in verse 6 expresses the only "gain" Job desires: a just weighing of his claim to innocence, so that his integrity is acknowledged by God. The self-imprecation of verse 8, by which Job affirms his innocence in this regard, must again strike us as ironic. At this point, Job has literally nothing left to lose.

Job's third oath of innocence (vv. 9–12) returns to the theme of sexual purity. For people committed to the cause of equal justice, rights, and dignity for women, extreme patience is required to discern a contemporary standard of moral excellence in the painfully sexist conceptuality that dominates this affirmation. The notion of woman as the evil seducer of hapless males (see Prov. 6:23–35; 7:4–27) is here combined with the equally sexist understanding of adultery primarily as a crime against the deceived husband's "property rights."

Until the last vestiges of such destructive attitudes toward women are rooted out of society, it is perhaps too soon to look for some "harmless" or "neutral" way of evaluating the sexual ethic to which Job swears in verses 9–12. The author's intent throughout chapter 31 can nevertheless be traced here also: to describe human integrity that cannot be thrown off course by any external impulse to self-aggrandizement. And once again, the ruin Job holds to be the just end of the adulterous life (v. 12) has already overtaken him. If Job is indeed innocent, he has nevertheless been "punished" as if he were guilty. To make matters worse, Job's self-imprecation in verse 10 discloses a despicable notion of just retribution for the "heinous" crime of adultery against one's (male) neighbor: that Job's *wife* should become the sexual plaything of other males.

Like any number of biblical texts, verse 13 accepts slavery as an unobjectionable institution within the social order. Apparently, a slave was able to register a complaint of ill treatment against his or her owner, but the implication of verse 13 is that it is the owner's choice whether to accept or reject the legitimacy of the slave's complaint. As in all slaveholding societies, owners might earn reputations as "good" masters or "hard" masters, depending on their sensitivity to the conditions under which their slaves lived and worked. By this standard of measure, Job is perhaps claiming no more for himself here than that he has always been a "good" master. Yet the grounds on which Job bases this treatment of his slaves is breathtaking: the common humanity of slave and master alike as creatures of God. This does not permit us to characterize Job as an "abolitionist" millennia ahead of his time, but the principle enunciated here was surely destined to call the institution of slavery itself into question. In any case, Job here holds himself accountable to God (v. 14) for just treatment of his slaves and affirms his innocence. While the usual self-imprecation is missing here, verse 14 hints at the dire consequences of mistreating even the least of one's sisters and brothers. As a footnote to verses 13–15, it is perhaps worth remembering that God designates Job as "my servant"—using the same word translated "slave" in verse 13—in 1:8; 2:3; and 42:7–8. The irony may be unintentional, but the whole question of the book of Job turns on whether or not God will "accept the cause" of God's "slave" Job, as Job lays out his "complaint." Will God deal as justly with God's slave Job as Job has dealt with his own slaves?

This quality of concern for powerless and vulnerable people is affirmed further in verses 16–23. The "poor," the "widow," the "orphan," and the "naked" or shelterless (see vv. 19–20) are all code words for people without resources or legal rights of their own. If they are to receive justice or even survive, the intervention of caring people is required. It is a bit surprising how widely this compassion for vulnerable people is extolled in ancient Near Eastern literature, from Egypt to Mesopotamia (especially in the wisdom literature of various cultures). As far as we can tell, however, such charitable concern was universally regarded as a private and individual matter. Demonstrating the upright heart of the benefactor was at least as important as alleviating the distress of the poor and powerless. In ancient Near Eastern literature generally, the motivation for such attitudes and actions toward the needy lay in the hope of proving oneself acceptable to God or the gods, thus avoiding divine retribution and winning divine blessing. Job appears to affirm this conventional motivation in verse 23: "For I was in terror of calamity from God, and I could not have faced [God's] majesty."

Yet as chapter 30 has made so devastatingly clear, Job has already experienced "calamity from God" and the terror of God's majesty (as the enemy) in the most extreme imaginable degree, as if he were guilty on all the points enumerated here and elsewhere in chapter 31. (Eliphaz has drawn just this conclusion, on the evidence of Job's suffering, in 22:5–11.) In that light, 31:23 may indicate Job's last-ditch confidence, in spite of everything, that the life of compassion and justice lived on behalf of the vulnerable is indeed rooted in the very character of God. In the context of the book of Job, however, it cannot possibly reflect Job's motivation for persisting in his integrity (2:3). The very point of chapter 31 in its entirety is simply this: Beyond all fear of what God may do to him (the worst has already happened), and beyond all hope of achieving the blessed life because of his innocence (God has destroyed him "for no reason," 2:3), Job still refuses to relinquish his integrity, as if this were the quality of life God should approve, regardless of what has befallen him. "Does Job fear God for nothing?" *Hassatan*'s pivotal question in 1:8 is being answered in chapter 31 with Job's last defiant breath: "Yes, without hope of gain or fear of punishment!" The dire self-imprecation that guarantees this oath of innocence (v. 22) is bitterly ironic in view of the far more catastrophic calamities Job has already endured as a "reward" for his integrity.

Job declares himself innocent of two apparently quite different means by which people attempt to gain a competitive edge over their neighbors: money and magic (vv. 24–27). To put one's confidence in either, Job affirms, is to play false with God (v. 28). The proper use of money, together with whatever power and acclaim may accompany it, has already been indicated by Job in 29:12–17: to use it and all other resources at one's disposal on behalf of the poor, the orphan, the wretched, the widow, the blind, the lame, the needy, and the stranger, as well as to overpower those who oppress them. The opposite use, which Job denounces in this oath of innocence, is to place one's confidence in the possession of money in its own right, as one's heart's delight, one's badge of individual accomplishment.

Perhaps this is not far removed from the sin of idolatrous superstition described in verses 26–27. In both cases, the temptation is to place one's individual well-being higher than any other value and to concentrate all one's energies on the most effective means of securing it. Human imaginations have always been stirred by the mysterious and the unknown, by forces beyond our ken that appear to shape human destinies. Magic and priestcraft have always flourished (they still do!) because of their promise that mysterious powers can be induced to pay off for people schooled in the proper attitudes and rituals. "Idolatry" is perhaps too pale and abstract a word to cover what Job describes as the "secret seduction" (v. 27) to blow on the dice, to say the magic word, to align one's life with the stars, all in the interest of achieving good fortune.

Job then declares himself innocent of vindictiveness, inhospitality, and moral cowardice (vv. 29–34). In each case the question is whether external impulses and pressures are able to throw Job's moral compass off course. The ethic Job affirms in verses 29–30 is nothing short of heroic by ordinary human standards. How should one react when one's favorite enemy suffers ruin and calamity? Job is governed by an attitude toward others that forbids him either to rejoice over their misfortune or to lash out against them with curses, regardless of malicious actions they may have taken against him. This may fall a bit short of Jesus' shocking command to love one's enemy (see Matt. 5:44; Luke 6:27), but the grace that finds no delight in the enemy's comeuppance is surely kin to it. (Job's ethic on this point will be sorely tested in 42:7–9.) For Job, it is a betrayal of one's own heart to permit the enemy to trigger a response that apes the enemy's own viciousness.

Verses 31–34 have proven difficult for scholars to translate and interpret. What seems clear is that verses 31–32 refer to the virtue of hospitality that was so highly prized in the ancient Near Eastern world (and still is, especially among bedouin of the Near East). Genesis 18:1–8 portrays Abraham as a paragon of hospitality in his extravagant solicitude for the needs of the "strangers" who appear before his tent without forewarning.

The most extreme imaginable violation of this ideal appears to have been gang-style sexual assault upon a stranger who lacks the protection of a willing and resolute host. Genesis 19:1–11 (see Heb. 13:2) and Judges 19:16–30 describe this enormity all too gruesomely. The language of Job 31:31 has been understood to refer to this supreme test of hospitality, and some interpreters have understood all of verses 31–34 in the light of such a test. If so, the reference is so oblique (or discreet?) that it cannot be clearly demonstrated from the present text.

Verses 33–34 can be read as Job's claim to innocence on the point of hypocrisy, refusing to conceal any wrongdoing of his out of fear of popular opinion and the loss of reputation. As the textual note in the NRSV indicates, the Hebrew text of verse 33 reads "as Adam did" instead of "as others do." Some interpreters read this as a direct allusion to the story of

Adam's attempt to conceal himself and his sin in Genesis 3:7–12. The translators of the NRSV have conjectured a more generalized reading, possibly on the grounds that such a specific reference to a particular biblical story is unparalleled elsewhere in Job. Job's rejection of concealment and deceit is equally clear in either case.

Taken together, verses 31–34 claim at least this much for Job: Neither the liabilities and risks of costly hospitality nor the pressure of public opinion with its implied threat is sufficient to alter Job's behavior or his commitment to compassion and candor.

Like many interpreters of Job, I find the climax of chapter 31 in verses 35 through 37. This mighty succession of ethical affirmations cries out for just the kind of ultimate challenge to God contained in these verses. Is it possible that the oath of innocence contained in verses 38–40 originally belonged together with verses 1–34, coming before the climactic challenge of verses 35–37? Verse 35 speaks of an "indictment written by my adversary," presumably charging Job with guilt on each of the ethical points he has sworn to or perhaps rejecting Job's description of his humanity out of hand. The oath form of verses 38–40 surely implies that treatment of the land under his ownership is another in the series of points on which Job claims innocence. The "indictment" Job calls for in verse 31 must surely include this point as well.

For that reason, I choose to attempt an interpretation of verses 38–40 before turning to verses 35–37. The key to these difficult verses appears to be the conception of a direct link between human behavior and the fruitfulness of the land on which human life depends. Genesis 3:17–19 and 4:10–12 suggest such a link; Hosea 4:1–3 makes it explicit: When there is no faithfulness and loyalty and knowledge of God in the land, when there is swearing, lying, murder, stealing, adultery, and violence, "the land mourns." What Job seems to be saying in verses 38–40 is that he is innocent of the kind of rapacity and ruthlessness that would cause his land to cry out against him. If this is not true, so goes the oath, then Job wishes on himself the curse of Adam (see Gen. 3:18; again, we cannot be sure this is a direct allusion).

Taken together, verses 1–34 and 38–40 provide an interior description of what it means to say that Job "was blameless and upright, one who feared God and turned away from evil" (1:1, 8; 2:3). Job is not superman. The code of ethics to which he swears corresponds to notions of humaneness, justice, and rectitude that are honored in almost every culture, in one form or another. It is a standard most of us want to achieve—or at least, we want to want to. The book of Job makes only two shocking claims about

Job in this regard: (1) that he actually embodies this homely ethic flaw-lessly, unlike the rest of us, so that "there is no one like him on the earth" (1:8; 2:3); (2) that he "persists" in this magnificent integrity even after God turned against him, that is, without hope of reward or fear of punishment, without recognition from God or from the human community. *Ecce homo.*

But how is Job's "fear of God" ("sincere worship," "awe-filled devo-tion") demonstrated in all this? We have already noted a partial answer to this question in the notion that integrity toward people is, in itself, in-tegrity toward God and vice versa. But this leaves out Job's passionate longing for an intact relationship with God and Job's upside-down trust that somehow, in spite of the hellish injustice he has suffered, God must approve such a life as Job's, must grant him a fair hearing, must vindicate his humanity.

It is in this longing, in this strange confidence, that Job discloses the in-terior meaning of "fearing God." This dimension of the "fear of God" finds its final and most shocking expression in 31:35–37: "Oh, that I had one to hear me! (Here is my signature! let the Almighty answer me!)" It is as if Job's whole life of integrity were a written testament that Job signs and lays before God, whatever the consequences may be. "Oh, that I had the indictment written by my adversary!" Job's longing for a hearing be-fore God is expressed here in a comparable way, asking God to provide a similar "testament" indicating God's estimate of Job's declaration of in-nocence. Does God accept or reject Job's claim of innocence, vindicate or condemn the life Job has lived?

The word translated "indictment" in the NRSV is intriguingly ambigu-ous. The Hebrew word simply means "scroll" or "document," with no in-dication of its contents. Is it a bill of indictment, condemning Job? Or is it perhaps a writ of acquittal, indicating Job's vindication by his "adversary" in this long, hellish trial?

The latter possibility is the less shocking of the two. Job would wear God's vindication as if it were a piece of royal regalia; he would pour out to God a faithful account of all his thoughts and actions; he would ap-proach God with the confidence of God's regal human being (see chap. 29), one whose relationship with God is perfectly intact, from both sides.

If, in contrast, we understand God's "document" as a rejection of Job's claim to integrity, the words of verses 36 and 37 take on a shockingly de-fiant character, a more than Promethean tone of defiance. The effect then is to say that if there is a God in heaven who faces down and rejects Job's kind of humanity, then Job is prepared to wear that indictment like a crown of honor, to throw a full account of his integrity into God's face, to stand like a regal human being before such an unjust God without flinching or groveling! In short, daring God *not* to be the God who affirms the humanity of "God's servant Job!"

Of these two possibilities, surely the defiant response to rejection corresponds most dramatically to God's accolade in 2:3: "He still persists in his integrity, although you have incited me against him for no reason." Job affirms his merely human integrity even if it leads him to the edge of blasphemy and beyond. Now the final words of Job 31 are fully in order: "The words of Job are ended." There is nothing more to say. Or as Job himself might have put it, "It is finished!"

7. The Speech of Elihu
Job 32—37

Chapters 29, 30, and 31 leave the reader yearning to hear God's "answer" (31:35) to Job's profoundly moving and outrageous summation for the defense of his humanity. Surely the time is past for any further human discussion of the merits of the case. According to 32:1, even Eliphaz, Bildad, and Zophar have had the good sense to fall silent. For that reason, many students of Job are convinced that the long and windy speech of Elihu in chapters 32—37 was not a part of the "original" book of Job. If Elihu was meant to be one of the major players in this great drama, why does he not appear in the prologue, and why is he not named among the friends who are scolded by God in 42:7–9? And what does Elihu have to say that is not said or implied somewhere in chapters 3—31, typically more than once?

Yet it is not the task of the community of faith to interpret the book of Job as it may once have been. Regardless of how chapters 32—37 may have come to be in their present place, the fascinating question is what we shall make of these words, as they are, as an integral part of the only book of Job we actually find in the Hebrew Bible.

There is no doubt that Elihu's speech snaps the dramatic tension that has come to a superb climax in chapters 29—31. Whether or not we are prepared to do so, this long speech demands that we back off from Job's outrageous challenge to God and return to the mundane debating chamber where people endlessly swap ideas about the ways of God and the ways of people and how they may relate to one another. Weary as the reader is by now of such arguments, Elihu at least provides a certain relief, perhaps even comic relief, from the apparently irresolvable issues raised in chapters 29—31.

Indeed, one characteristic way of perceiving Elihu is that he is a clown figure, a ridiculous caricature of all human pretensions to have found answers to questions about God and human existence—questions that can never be domesticated to the uses of human understanding. But this estimate of Elihu may be premature. Let us go to the text and let it shape our notions of what may be going on here.

Job 32:1–33:7

32:1 So these three men ceased to answer Job, because he was righteous in his own eyes. 2 Then Elihu son of Barachel the Buzite, of the family of Ram, became angry. He was angry at Job because he justified himself rather than God; 3 he was angry also at Job's three friends because they had found no answer, though they had declared Job to be in the wrong. 4 Now Elihu had waited to speak to Job, because they were older than he. 5 But when Elihu saw that there was no answer in the mouths of these three men, he became angry.

6 Elihu son of Barachel the Buzite answered:
"I am young in years,
   and you are aged;
therefore I was timid and afraid
   to declare my opinion to you.
7 I said, 'Let days speak,
   and many years teach wisdom.'
8 But truly it is the spirit in a mortal,
   the breath of the Almighty, that makes for understanding.
9 It is not the old that are wise,
   nor the aged that understand what is right.
10 Therefore I say, 'Listen to me;
   let me also declare my opinion.'

11 "See, I waited for your words,
   I listened for your wise sayings,
   while you searched out what to say.
12 I gave you my attention,
   but there was in fact no one that confuted Job,
   no one among you that answered his words.
13 Yet do not say, 'We have found wisdom;
   God may vanquish him, not a human.'
14 He has not directed his words against me,
   and I will not answer him with your speeches.

15 "They are dismayed, they answer no more;
   they have not a word to say.
16 And am I to wait, because they do not speak,
   because they stand there, and answer no more?
17 I also will give my answer;
   I also will declare my opinion.

¹⁸ **For I am full of words;**
the spirit within me constrains me.
¹⁹ **My heart is indeed like wine that has no vent;**
like new wineskins, it is ready to burst.
²⁰ **I must speak, so that I may find relief;**
I must open my lips and answer.
²¹ **I will not show partiality to any person**
or use flattery toward anyone.
²² **For I do not know how to flatter—**
or my Maker would soon put an end to me!

33:1 **"But now, hear my speech, O Job,**
and listen to all my words.
² **See, I open my mouth;**
the tongue in my mouth speaks.
³ **My words declare the uprightness of my heart,**
and what my lips know they speak sincerely.
⁴ **The spirit of God has made me,**
and the breath of the Almighty gives me life.
⁵ **Answer me, if you can;**
set your words in order before me; take your stand.
⁶ **See, before God I am as you are;**
I too was formed from a piece of clay.
⁷ **No fear of me need terrify you;**
my pressure will not be heavy on you.

Job 32:1–5 confronts us with a unique figure in ancient Near Eastern wisdom literature: an angry young man. As Elihu well knows, the proper attitude of the young in that ancient thought structure was silent docility and deference to one's elders. Yet his anger at what he has been hearing is so intense that he is finally compelled to break all traditional restraints and speak his mind—anger at Job for putting himself in the right and God in the wrong; anger at the three friends because their "answers" to Job have proven wholly inadequate to resolve the issue.

It is difficult for contemporary readers not to side with Elihu, at least initially, because we tend to place high value on the courage of the young to speak out against outworn ideas, whether of old-style conservatives or old-style revolutionaries, when none of those ideas appears adequate to the future the young must enter. When Elihu says, "It is not the old that are wise, nor the aged that understand what is right," our society is conditioned to say, "Right on!" This may obscure something of the scandal ancient sages may have registered on hearing such words. Whether Elihu's brashness is to be taken as outrageously comical or merely outrageous will ultimately depend on the substance of what is said. Job 32:6–33:7 tips the scale toward the comical, since Elihu goes to extraordinary lengths to bolster his right and his urgency to speak before saying anything of substance. When Elihu says, "I am full of words" (32:18), the reader can only concur. The young man is not only on the point of bursting with words and ideas (32:19), but he also harbors an inordinately high estimation of his own worth (32:21–22; 33:3, 7).

Job 33:8–33

⁸"Surely, you have spoken in my hearing,
　and I have heard the sound of your words.
⁹ You say, 'I am clean, without transgression;
　I am pure, and there is no iniquity in me.
¹⁰ Look, he finds occasions against me,
　he counts me as his enemy;
¹¹ he puts my feet in the stocks,
　and watches all my paths.'

¹² "But in this you are not right. I will answer you:
　God is greater than any mortal.
¹³ Why do you contend against him,
　saying, 'He will answer none of my words'?
¹⁴ For God speaks in one way,
　and in two, though people do not perceive it.
¹⁵ In a dream, in a vision of the night,
　when deep sleep falls on mortals,
　while they slumber on their beds,
¹⁶ then he opens their ears,
　and terrifies them with warnings,
¹⁷ that he may turn them aside from their deeds,
　and keep them from pride,
¹⁸ to spare their souls from the Pit,
　their lives from traversing the River.
¹⁹ They are also chastened with pain upon their beds,
　and with continual strife in their bones,
²⁰ so that their lives loathe bread,
　and their appetites dainty food.
²¹ Their flesh is so wasted away that it cannot be seen;
　and their bones, once invisible, now stick out.
²² Their souls draw near the Pit,
　and their lives to those who bring death.

[23] Then, if there should be for one of them an angel,
  a mediator, one of a thousand,
  one who declares a person upright,
[24] and he is gracious to that person, and says,
  'Deliver him from going down into the Pit;
  I have found a ransom;
[25] let his flesh become fresh with youth;
  let him return to the days of his youthful vigor.'
[26] Then he prays to God, and is accepted by him,
  he comes into his presence with joy,
 and God repays him for his righteousness.
[27] That person sings to others and says,
 'I sinned, and perverted what was right,
  and it was not paid back to me.
[28] He has redeemed my soul from going down to the Pit,
  and my life shall see the light.'

[29] "God indeed does all these things,
  twice, three times, with mortals,
[30] to bring back their souls from the Pit,
  so that they may see the light of life.
[31] Pay heed, Job, listen to me;
  be silent, and I will speak.
[32] If you have anything to say, answer me;
  speak, for I desire to justify you.
[33] If not, listen to me;
  be silent, and I will teach you wisdom."

What interests us, of course, is how Elihu will answer the questions posed by Job's suffering, Job's protests, and the counsel offered by the three friends. In 33:8–11, the young man finally comes to the point. He begins by accurately restating Job's claim to innocence and Job's accusation that God has moved against him for no reason. Like Job's three friends, of course, Elihu has no way of knowing that God has chosen to do precisely this in the heavenly council chamber (2:3). Like them, Elihu is persuaded that God could never take such a course.

The problem lies in the infinite difference between God and "mortals." Job has not been able to discern God's answer because he is not open to the mysterious variety of ways in which God may speak, for example, through night visions (vv. 12–18; Eliphaz has made this point in 4:12–21) and the chastisement of pain (vv. 19–22; see 5:17–26).

Like Eliphaz (see 5:1), Elihu points to the possibility of an advocate in the heavenly court who might plead the sufferer's case before God. Unlike Eliphaz, Elihu extends to Job the hope that "one of a thousand" (that is, one of God's innumerable courtiers) might indeed take Job's part (vv. 23–26). In verses 27–28, however, it is clear that such gracious mediation is available only to persons prepared to confess that the fault lies within themselves and that God's restoration is purely gracious. It is precisely this admission that God is in the right and Job is in the wrong that the three friends have attempted to coerce from Job all along.

Elihu concludes this discourse by rehearsing another recurring theme from the friends' argument: While God is invariably just, God's sometimes mysterious way of speaking to sinners is in fact motivated by God's intent to spare them (vv. 29–30).

Job 34

34:1 **Then Elihu continued and said:**
  2 **"Hear my words, you wise men,**
        and give ear to me, you who know;
  3 **for the ear tests words**
        as the palate tastes food.
  4 **Let us choose what is right;**
        let us determine among ourselves what is good.
  5 **For Job has said, 'I am innocent,**
        and God has taken away my right;
  6 **in spite of being right I am counted a liar;**
        my wound is incurable, though I am without transgression.'
  7 **Who is there like Job,**
        who drinks up scoffing like water,
  8 **who goes in company with evildoers**
        and walks with the wicked?
  9 **For he has said, 'It profits one nothing**
        to take delight in God.'

  10 **"Therefore, hear me, you who have sense,**
        far be it from God that he should do wickedness,
        and from the Almighty that he should do wrong.
  11 **For according to their deeds he will repay them,**
        and according to their ways he will make it befall them.
  12 **Of a truth, God will not do wickedly,**
        and the Almighty will not pervert justice.
  13 **Who gave him charge over the earth**
        and who laid on him the whole world?
  14 **If he should take back his spirit to himself,**

and gather to himself his breath,
¹⁵ all flesh would perish together,
    and all mortals return to dust.

¹⁶ "If you have understanding, hear this;
    listen to what I say.
¹⁷ Shall one who hates justice govern?
    Will you condemn one who is righteous and mighty,
¹⁸ who says to a king, 'You scoundrel!'
    and to princes, 'You wicked men!';
¹⁹ who shows no partiality to nobles,
    nor regards the rich more than the poor,
    for they are all the work of his hands?
²⁰ In a moment they die;
    at midnight the people are shaken and pass away,
    and the mighty are taken away by no human hand.

²¹ "For his eyes are upon the ways of mortals,
    and he sees all their steps.
²² There is no gloom or deep darkness
    where evildoers may hide themselves.
²³ For he has not appointed a time for anyone
    to go before God in judgment.
²⁴ He shatters the mighty without investigation,
    and sets others in their place.
²⁵ Thus, knowing their works,
    he overturns them in the night, and they are crushed.
²⁶ He strikes them for their wickedness
    while others look on,
²⁷ because they turned aside from following him,
    and had no regard for any of his ways,
²⁸ so that they caused the cry of the poor to come to him,
    and he heard the cry of the afflicted—
²⁹ When he is quiet, who can condemn?
    When he hides his face, who can behold him,
    whether it be a nation or an individual?—
³⁰ so that the godless should not reign,
    or those who ensnare the people.

³¹ "For has anyone said to God,
    'I have endured punishment; I will not offend any more;
³² teach me what I do not see;
    if I have done iniquity, I will do it no more'?

³³ Will he then pay back to suit you,
　　because you reject it?
　For you must choose, and not I;
　　therefore declare what you know.
³⁴ Those who have sense will say to me,
　　and the wise who hear me will say,
³⁵ 'Job speaks without knowledge,
　　his words are without insight.'
³⁶ Would that Job were tried to the limit,
　　because his answers are those of the wicked.
³⁷ For he adds rebellion to his sin;
　　he claps his hands among us,
　　and multiplies his words against God."

If one can imagine Job listening to this renewed harangue, especially after he has uttered his ultimate cry for an "answer" from God (not a human debating partner; see 31:35 and compare 13:1–12), then Elihu's demand to be heard in 33:31–33 sounds insufferably arrogant and empty. This impression is heightened in 34:1–3, where Elihu lightly diverts his attention from Job the silent sufferer to the other bystanders, for whom Job's response to his fate poses a hypothetical but potentially serious religious problem. Job once satirized such superficial ideological word games by saying, "Does not the ear test words as the palate tastes food?" (12:11). In 34:3, however, Elihu appears to repeat the old saying quite seriously, as if it were up to the "wise" (v. 2) to sort these questions out intellectually and "determine among ourselves what is good" (v. 4).

The starting point for theological discussion is Job's outrageous claim that he is in the right and God is in the wrong in this case (vv. 5–6). Like all the friends, Elihu knows from the start that this places Job in the company of scoffers, evildoers, the wicked (vv. 7–8). The most outrageous of all Job's claims is that taking delight in God does not pay dividends (v. 9)! Apparently, Elihu cannot conceive of a "delight in God" that is not based on the confidence that such devotion is rewarded. To think otherwise strikes Elihu as blasphemous. Yet *hassatan*, in the heavenly council chamber, raised the question "Does Job fear God for nothing?" on the opposite assumption: If Job's "delight in God" is driven by the "profits" that derive from it, then his legendary righteousness is only a self-serving charade. Unwittingly, Elihu has probed near the heart of the mystery of Job's suffering.

In verses 10–30, Elihu restates themes that the friends have consistently stressed: that God is righteous and just and that God requites evil with sovereign wisdom and power, never showing partiality toward people of rank or privilege. Verse 33 suggests that verses 31–32 refer directly to Job: Has Job repented of his iniquity? If not, the implication of verse 33 is that unless Job makes some such confession, his cause is lost. From Elihu's viewpoint, all truly wise people must concur that Job's words are ignorant as well as wicked. He is arrogantly flying in the face of God (vv. 34–37).

Job 35

35:1 **Elihu continued and said:**

2 **"Do you think this to be just?**
   You say, 'I am in the right before God.'
3 **If you ask, 'What advantage have I?**
   How am I better off than if I had sinned?'
4 **I will answer you**
   and your friends with you.
5 **Look at the heavens and see;**
   observe the clouds, which are higher than you.
6 **If you have sinned, what do you accomplish against him?**
   And if your transgressions are multiplied, what do you do to him?
7 **If you are righteous, what do you give to him;**
   or what does he receive from your hand?
8 **Your wickedness affects others like you,**
   and your righteousness, other human beings.

9 **"Because of the multitude of oppressions people cry out;**
   they call for help because of the arm of the mighty.
10 **But no one says, 'Where is God my Maker,**
   who gives strength in the night,
11 **who teaches us more than the animals of the earth,**
   and makes us wiser than the birds of the air?'
12 **There they cry out, but he does not answer,**
   because of the pride of evildoers.
13 **Surely God does not hear an empty cry,**
   nor does the Almighty regard it.
14 **How much less when you say that you do not see him,**
   that the case is before him, and you are waiting for him!
15 **And now, because his anger does not punish,**
   and he does not greatly heed transgression,
16 **Job opens his mouth in empty talk,**
   he multiplies words without knowledge."

In 35:2–3, Elihu returns to what he takes to be a basic flaw in Job's protest. Job has said there is neither advantage for the blameless nor disadvantage for the wicked in God's ordering of human affairs (see 9:22; 10:3; 21:7–26).

In his own case, Job makes this the basis of his claim to be "in the right before God," that is, that there is no just reason for the suffering that has befallen him. (God concurs in 2:3.) From Elihu's point of view, Job's cry for a trial before God in which his case can be fairly adjudicated expresses a woeful misunderstanding of God's absolute transcendence. God is so exalted above all petty human affairs that individual actions and attitudes do not move God one way or the other. Such attitudes and actions affect only other human beings for good or ill (vv. 4–8; Eliphaz has made a comparable point in 22:2–3; Zophar concurs in 11:6–11).

For Job, it is just this awesome transcendence of God that thwarts his human appeal for justice (see 9:2–20; 13:20–21; 14:13–17). The delicious secret in the heavenly council is that God cares intimately and personally about God's servant Job, and that Job's hellish ordeal is ultimately related to God's unqualified approval of Job's life. Is it possible that God is both infinitely more transcendent and infinitely more personally engaged with human beings than either Elihu or Job has any way of knowing?

Like Job, Elihu is aware that distressed people cry out to God (v. 9) and that God does not answer (v. 12; see 24:12). But Elihu knows a reason for that: It is because those who cry out want relief from suffering, not a trusting relationship with God (vv. 10–11). Absent this wondering trust, their cry is "empty," and God does not regard it (v. 13).

On these grounds, Job is doubly guilty. Not only is his cry "empty," but he has had the audacity to lay his case before God and fault God for failure to appear at trial (v. 14)! Moreover, Job has taken advantage of the fact that God is not affected by human transgressions (see vv. 5–8) to indulge in empty and ignorant tirades. Apparently, Elihu's basic premise, hinted at in verses 12 and 13, is the same as the one Eliphaz relies on in 4:12–21: God's infinite transcendence of the merely human means that no human being can claim to be righteous in the presence of God (see also 25:4–6). The proper course for suffering people under these circumstances, according to Elihu, is perhaps indicated in verses 10–11: to intensify one's reliance on God, "who gives strength in the night" and who plants hints of God's transcendent wisdom even in the natural order.

The Hebrew text of verse 11 can also be translated to mean that God teaches us "by" or "through" the animals and birds, rather than the comparative "more than." This notion is firmly rooted in wisdom literature (see 12:7–25, where Job learns from the animals lessons that are quite different from those Elihu has in mind; see also Proverbs 6:6; Isa. 1:3; and Jer. 8:7). This seems to run parallel to the advice of Eliphaz in 5:8–16, where people who are inherently unrighteous before God are nevertheless encouraged to commit their cause to God, whose ways are beyond human comprehension but whose justice is sure.

Job 36

36:1 **Elihu continued and said:**

2 **"Bear with me a little, and I will show you,**
 for I have yet something to say on God's behalf.
3 **I will bring my knowledge from far away,**
 and ascribe righteousness to my Maker.
4 **For truly my words are not false;**
 one who is perfect in knowledge is with you.

5 **"Surely God is mighty and does not despise any;**
 he is mighty in strength of understanding.
6 **He does not keep the wicked alive,**
 but gives the afflicted their right.
7 **He does not withdraw his eyes from the righteous,**
 but with kings on the throne
 he sets them forever, and they are exalted.
8 **And if they are bound in fetters**
 and caught in the cords of affliction,
9 **then he declares to them their work**
 and their transgressions, that they are behaving arrogantly.
10 **He opens their ears to instruction,**
 and commands that they return from iniquity.
11 **If they listen, and serve him,**
 they complete their days in prosperity,
 and their years in pleasantness.
12 **But if they do not listen, they shall perish by the sword,**
 and die without knowledge.

13 **"The godless in heart cherish anger;**
 they do not cry for help when he binds them.
14 **They die in their youth,**
 and their life ends in shame.
15 **He delivers the afflicted by their affliction,**
 and opens their ear by adversity.
16 **He also allured you out of distress**
 into a broad place where there was no constraint,
 and what was set on your table was full of fatness.

17 **"But you are obsessed with the case of the wicked;**
 judgment and justice seize you.

¹⁸ Beware that wrath does not entice you into scoffing,
    and do not let the greatness of the ransom turn you aside.
¹⁹ Will your cry avail to keep you from distress,
    or will all the force of your strength?
²⁰ Do not long for the night,
    when peoples are cut off in their place.
²¹ Beware! Do not turn to iniquity;
    because of that you have been tried by affliction.
²² See, God is exalted in his power;
    who is a teacher like him?
²³ Who has prescribed for him his way,
    or who can say, 'You have done wrong'?

²⁴ "Remember to extol his work,
    of which mortals have sung.
²⁵ All people have looked on it;
    everyone watches it from far away.
²⁶ Surely God is great, and we do not know him;
    the number of his years is unsearchable.
²⁷ For he draws up the drops of water;
    he distills his mist in rain,
²⁸ which the skies pour down
    and drop upon mortals abundantly.
²⁹ Can anyone understand the spreading of the clouds,
    the thunderings of his pavilion?
³⁰ See, he scatters his lightning around him
    and covers the roots of the sea.
³¹ For by these he governs peoples;
    he gives food in abundance.
³² He covers his hands with the lightning,
    and commands it to strike the mark.
³³ Its crashing tells about him;
    he is jealous with anger against iniquity.

In 36:1–4 it is again difficult to avoid the sense that Elihu is being presented to us as a ludicrous caricature of all religious or intellectual arrogance. He not only proposes to marshal all his wide-ranging researches to make the case for God's righteousness (v. 3; see 13:7–12) but also boasts that he is "perfect in knowledge." The Hebrew word translated "perfect" here comes from the same root as the word translated "blameless" in 1:1, 8 and 2:3. It is as if we are being deliberately invited to contrast Job's truly "blameless" life of innocent suffering with the unbounded arrogance of an unscarred pip-squeak who claims "perfection" for his religious grasp of Job's suffering and its cause.

This impression is strengthened in verses 5–33, where this "perfect" understanding is expressed in a tiresome rerun of religious clichés of the sort we have heard from Eliphaz, Bildad, and Zophar *ad nauseam:* God's transcendent power and wisdom are invariably exercised against the wicked and on behalf of the afflicted, the righteous (vv. 5–7). Experiences of oppression and affliction are visited on people to teach them the error of their arrogant ways, to restore them to docile obedience (vv. 8–10). If they acknowledge their guilt and serve God faithfully, they are rewarded with the good life, but if not, they are doomed to die in their ignorance (vv. 11–12). Anger is an indelible symptom of such godlessness. (Job's passionate outcries are no doubt a case in point; see 5:2.) Refusal to "cry for help" demonstrates unwillingness to recognize God's chastisement and throw oneself on God's mercy (as opposed to Eliphaz's advice in 5:8; Job cries out to God not for "help" in this sense but for a just hearing before God). The inevitable result of such "anger" and obduracy is shameful ruin (vv. 13–14). God's intent, however, is to use the experience of adversity and affliction as a teaching tool, designed to deliver the afflicted from their affliction (v. 15; see 5:17–18).

The Hebrew text of verse 16 presents serious difficulties for translators. The translation offered in the NRSV appears to run counter to the story told in Job, where God leads Job from blessedness into distress, not vice versa. In the context of 36:8–11 and 15, it seems likely that verse 16 refers not to God's past treatment of Job but to God's intention, through Job's present distress, to "allure" him toward repentance and thus toward the blessed life.

In Elihu's judgment, however, Job has turned his back on God's gracious "wooing" (through catastrophe), by insisting (wickedly) on pressing his case (v. 17). Verses 18–21 also present difficulties for translators, but there is considerable agreement that Job is being warned here that persistence in pressing his case amounts to nothing less than scoffing at God; that no conceivable resources of wealth or influence are sufficient to win the case and avert the distress with which God has justly afflicted him; that Job's "longing for the night" (see 3:3–9) is futile; and that it is just such "iniquity" that has brought God's chastising affliction upon him.

In all this, God demonstrates power and wisdom of such transcendent magnitude that no lesser being can instruct God or determine God's course or challenge God's action (vv. 22–23). The only proper course for "mortals" is to sing praises to God in all generations and in all places (vv. 24–25). God's grandeur and eternity defy all human understanding (v. 26); witness the mystery by which God causes the rain to fall, governs storm clouds and thunder and lightning, rules in human affairs, provides good, and sends thunderbolts to their targets, revealing in thunder God's jealous wrath against evil (vv. 27–33).

Although Elihu makes no significant additions here to the argument of Job's three friends, it is perhaps worth noting again that something very like this piety has sustained literally millions of faithful Jews and Christians through times of incomprehensible distress. God is surely greater, infinitely greater, than our understanding. None of us is able to claim for ourselves that we are above reproach or that God somehow owes us immediate relief or instant gratification. Faith itself depends on the conviction that God is both loving and just, that "whatever God ordains is right," that our duty is not to comprehend but to accept what comes and trust in God's wise mercy and merciful wisdom.

The revolutionary aspect of the book of Job, however, is that it asks us to imagine a human being who really is innocent, who really does reflect God's intention for human life in relation to God and people, and who really does experience catastrophe at God's hand "for no reason" (2:3). On the surface, Job appears to accept his fate with just the kind of trusting submission Job's friends and now Elihu prescribe for him (see 1:20–22; 2:10). But the issue being explored in the dialogues goes beyond all conventional ways of understanding such submission and trust. For Job to deny his innocence under the pressure of suffering, for Job to pretend that some fault in himself has made his suffering just, for Job to seek relief from God by pretending guilt—this would be for Job to surrender his integrity (2:3). Nor does Job conceive it possible to honor God by pretending that God is in the right and Job is in the wrong in this matter. If this means "charging God with wrongdoing" (1:22; see 2:10b), so be it. Yet Job's passion has never been to malign God as an evil deity. It is *because* Job holds fast to God's inherent justice and righteousness that he lays out his case against God with such ruthless honesty. He refuses to accept the notion that what he has endured reflects God's true character or God's estimate of Job.

This is why all Job's outcries ultimately come to focus in his relentless longing to secure a fair hearing in God's own presence. The God Job worships simply must take Job's side in such an encounter, even though the evidence of Job's suffering seems to disclose God as Job's enemy (see 9:34–35; 13:3, 16–24). To affirm God's justice, for Job, means to proclaim honestly the injustice of innocent human suffering, both his own and that of others (see 24:1–12). To attempt to curry God's favor by pretending otherwise (as Elihu and the friends have urged) would be to conceal the truth with a lie and so to surrender Job's own integrity. It would also impugn God as one who extorts submission from human beings on false grounds.

Job 37

37:1 "At this also my heart trembles,
and leaps out of its place.
² Listen, listen to the thunder of his voice
and the rumbling that comes from his mouth.
³ Under the whole heaven he lets it loose,
and his lightning to the corners of the earth.
⁴ After it his voice roars;
he thunders with his majestic voice
and he does not restrain the lightnings when his voice is heard.
⁵ God thunders wondrously with his voice;
he does great things that we cannot comprehend.
⁶ For to the snow he says, 'Fall on the earth';
and the shower of rain, his heavy shower of rain,
⁷ serves as a sign on everyone's hand,
so that all whom he has made may know it.
⁸ Then the animals go into their lairs
and remain in their dens.
⁹ From its chamber comes the whirlwind,
and cold from the scattering winds.
¹⁰ By the breath of God ice is given,
and the broad waters are frozen fast.
¹¹ He loads the thick cloud with moisture;
the clouds scatter his lightning.
¹² They turn round and round by his guidance,
to accomplish all that he commands them
on the face of the habitable world.
¹³ Whether for correction, or for his land,
or for love, he causes it to happen.

¹⁴ "Hear this, O Job;
stop and consider the wondrous works of God.
¹⁵ Do you know how God lays his command upon them,
and causes the lightning of his cloud to shine?
¹⁶ Do you know the balancings of the clouds,
the wondrous works of the one whose knowledge is perfect,
¹⁷ you whose garments are hot
when the earth is still because of the south wind?
¹⁸ Can you, like him, spread out the skies,
hard as a molten mirror?
¹⁹ Teach us what we shall say to him;
we cannot draw up our case because of darkness.
²⁰ Should he be told that I want to speak?

> **Did anyone ever wish to be swallowed up?**
> 21 **Now, no one can look on the light**
>   **when it is bright in the skies,**
>   **when the wind has passed and cleared them.**
> 22 **Out of the north comes golden splendor;**
>   **around God is awesome majesty.**
> 23 **The Almighty—we cannot find him;**
>   **he is great in power and justice,**
>   **and abundant righteousness he will not violate.**
> 24 **Therefore mortals fear him;**
>   **he does not regard any who are wise in their own conceit."**

Elihu's closing argument, which begins in 36:24–33, continues passionately and at length in chapter 37. If Job will simply open his eyes to God's overwhelming wisdom and power, everywhere evident in the natural order, he will surely stop being "wise in [his] own conceit" and will collapse before God in wonder, as all "mortals" should (see 37:24). Elihu almost goes into such a collapse himself, just thinking about it (37:1)! Job 36:24–37:24 can be understood as a unified hymn to God manifest in nature, with two alternating themes: (1) the wisdom of God perceived in the mysterious regularities of nature that make life possible for human beings (see 36:27–29; 37:6–11, 14–17); and (2) the threat of God's power in unpredictable and ungovernable storms (see 36:30–33; 37:2–5), understood as instruments of God's wrath (36:32–33). By this alternation of gift and threat in nature, God "governs peoples" (36:31). By God's guidance, these two aspects of nature serve to "accomplish all that [God] commands them . . . whether for correction, or for [God's] land, or for love" (37:12–13). Understood in this way, the workings of nature possess a moral content. Beyond all possibilities of human understanding or control, nature points beyond itself to God, who "is great in power and justice" and who will not violate righteousness (37:23).

If Job wishes to complain of God's injustice, let him measure his own paltry wisdom and power by comparison with God's (37:14–18). If Job can equal God in these respects, perhaps his "lawyers" might be able to make his case before God. Otherwise they are in the dark (37:19). Is Job really prepared to press charges under these circumstances (v. 20)?

Suppose Job *were* to encounter God directly, as he has repeatedly said he longs to do. From Elihu's point of view, given the overwhelming majesty of God's wisdom and power, it would be as if Job were to stare directly into the sun on a clear day, something no human can endure (v. 21).

Yet it is not the blinding noonday sun Job has to fear, according to verse

22, but the awesome splendor of God's own appearing. The phrase "out of the north" almost certainly refers to an ancient Canaanite conception of Zaphon, a "mountain of assembly of the gods," that is, the place of God's dwelling. While the conception itself is polytheistic and extrabiblical, it has left its traces in Isaiah 14:13 ("the mount of assembly on the heights of Zaphon," or "in the far north," since the word *Zaphon* is also used in Hebrew to indicate geographical north). (Note that the prophet uses this extra-Israelite tale of an insurrection among the gods as an illustration of the arrogance of the very human "king of Babylon" [14:4] and his sure destruction.) In Psalm 48:2, it appears that Israel appropriated the phrase "in the far north" (or "the heights of Zaphon"), stripped of its polytheistic connotations, as a desgination for God's dwelling place on Mount Zion.

Ezekiel 1:4 may well allude to this conception of Zaphon as the place of God's dwelling when the prophet describes the vision of God's appearing with the words "a stormy wind came out of the north [*zaphon*], a great cloud with brightness around it and fire flashing forth continually, and in the middle of the fire, something like gleaming amber."

Such texts recall other vivid biblical passages describing God's appearing in human affairs to execute divine wrath against God's enemies and to vindicate God's faithful. (See Psalms 18:4–19; 50:1–6; 77:16–20; Hab. 3:3–15. In Hab. 3:16 the poet's response resembles that of Elihu in Job 37:1.) Taken together, Job 36:30–33; 37:1–5, 9–13, and 21–22 appear to threaten Job with just such an "appearing" of God, when God's ultimate judgment falls against all who are "wise in their own conceit" (37:24). If so, then 36:29–37:24 serves as a kind of distant early warning signal for Job 38—41, where the altogether unimaginable thing happens: Job finds himself a solitary, utterly vulnerable human being in the unshielded presence of Almighty God!

8. God's "Answer" and Job's Response
Job 38:1–42:6

It is just here, in God's speeches and in Job's twofold response, that overall interpretations of the book of Job differ from one another so widely. Every interpreter makes the point that the speeches of God almost never touch on the issue that has been so important to Job, to Job's friends, or to Elihu, namely, whether God's transcendent wisdom and power do or do not ultimately produce justice in God's ordering of human affairs. The major emphasis appears to rest on the chilling contrast between God's wisdom and power on the one hand and Job's paltry "wisdom" and "power" on the other. This contrast alone renders it laughable that Job "darkens counsel by words without knowledge" (38:2), or that he should "condemn [God] so that [Job] may be justified" (40:8; see 40:2). In 38:12–15 does God allude, rather indirectly, to the fact that God's providential order exposes the wicked, withholds light from them, and breaks their "uplifted arm"? Job 40:10–14 suggests that if Job were truly God's equal in glory, wisdom, and power, then Job, like God, would be justified in pouring out his anger, bringing the proud and wicked low, consigning them to the netherworld. Only then would God acknowledge that Job's "own right hand can give [him] victory." On the points of whether the innocent suffer unjustly (so important to Job) and whether God ultimately rewards the righteous (so important to Job's friends), the speeches of God have nothing to say.

This strange "answer" to Job has typically driven interpreters in one of three directions. Particularly among modern people who dismiss both the quest for God and the quest for some larger meaning in human life as absurd, the speeches of God in chapters 38—41 constitute a deliciously comic climax to the whole absurd "drama" of Job. Job has accused God of being a cosmic bully who cares nothing at all about human notions of justice and righteousness (see Job 12:13–25 and 24:1–12). Yet, absurdly, Job hangs on to the hope that he can one day come face to face with God and these matters can be sorted out between them. In chapters 38—41, Job is granted this longed-for encounter with God—and guess what? God turns out to be exactly the sort of cosmic bully Job thought he was! Job's "repentance" in 42:2–6 can then be paraphrased for modern people in the "prayer" of Robert Frost: "God forgive my little jokes on Thee and I'll forgive Thy great big one on me" ("In the Clearing," 1962). Obviously, this kind of interpretation requires us to dismiss the prologue as a kind of stage-setting device and the epilogue as a "happy ending" designed to make this outrageous tale palatable for pious believers.

The second general approach honors the marvelous poetry of Job 38–41 as the poet's attempt to communicate the "infinite qualitative difference" between God and human beings. Of course God's glory and wisdom and power elude all human efforts to comprehend God, let alone to make God conform to human notions about how the universe ought to be run. This is why God faults Job for finding fault with God (40:2, 8), and Job's repentance reflects his own astonished awareness, now that he is face to face with Almighty God, that he never had any right to carry on so about his own "innocence" or the "outrage" of innocent human suffering (42:2–6). It is at least a little troubling for this interpretation that it sounds rather like the point of view of Job's friends and of Elihu, at least on the point of whether it is "right" for Job to protest as he has. This approach, like the first, requires us to sit loose to the demands of the prologue, where God expresses unconditional approbation of "my servant Job," and the epilogue, where God tells the friends, "You have not spoken of me what is right, as my servant Job has" (42:7–8).

The third approach, rather like the second, makes a great point of Job's words "I had heard of you by the hearing of the ear, but now my eye sees you" (42:5). This represents Job's conversion from a "religion of the head" to a "religion of the heart," in which the believer's willingness to trust in a "personal relationship with God" makes it unnecessary to understand the whys and hows of God's providence. Like the second, this interpretation ultimately faults Job for his arrogant impiety and makes it difficult to comprehend God's initial (1:8; 2:3) and final (42:7–8) approbation of Job. According to the second and third approaches, God's lavish restoration of Job's blessings in 42:10–17 sounds like direct confirmation of the friends' position: Drop the protest, acknowledge God's inscrutable providence as just, and God will reward your piety beyond your wildest dreams.

We noted at the outset that any interpretation of the book of Job typically reveals more about the interpreter's frame of mind and heart than it does about Job. The three general lines of interpretation noted above, together with their many variations, prove the rule. By this time, readers here may well have broken through to an interpretation of Job that is significantly different from any of the three approaches sketched above. So have I. But perhaps the special function of this marvelous book in the Jewish and Christian canons of Holy Scripture is to provoke this whole range of reactions. Long after all these interpretations have proven threadbare, including yours and mine, the book of Job will still be there, with all its mysteries, challenging people to think again about God's righteousness and ours and to reject anyone's canned answers as the final word. Neither Jewish nor Christian faith has grown up until it has faced Job's questions with the full seriousness that human experience of people and of God demands.

Apart from attitudes of mind and heart of which I am probably not fully aware, the following interpretation of Job 38—41 is offered not as the last word but as a provocative suggestion for how these disquieting speeches of God may be understood in the context of the present book of Job. Three considerations dominate this interpretation: (1) I choose to take God's accolade to Job in 1:8; 2:3; and 42:7–8 at face value. Let us suppose that God approves not only who Job is but what Job says about himself and about God. (2) If that is so, then the very fact that God answers Job "out of the whirlwind" (38:1) is to be understood as God's vindication of Job's humanity, as attested by God in 1:8 and 2:3 and by Job in chapter 31. Job has demonstrated that he does indeed "serve God for nothing" (1:9), that is, without any self-interested motive. God's "answer" to Job is a personal validation of God's judgment that Job "still persists in his integrity" in spite of having been compelled to encounter God as the enemy "for no reason" (2:3). (3) If the speeches of God in Job 38—41 sound far more like an attack on Job than words of vindication, we must also remember that Job's speeches to God sound more like an attack on God than what we tend to think of as the "right" way to speak about God. In the unique case of Job, however, given the hellish test to which Job has been put, God thinks otherwise (42:7–8)! Through his angry speeches Job has not only persisted in his own human integrity; more important, by laying the justice of his case directly before God, Job has demonstrated what we have called upside-down trust that behind the rank injustice of Job's innocent suffering is a God who must approve the kind of human being Job is and who will ultimately vindicate Job's integrity.

As we noted at the outset, however, God's integrity is also called in question by hassatan's question "Does Job fear God for nothing?" Has God showered Job with blessings as a bribe, calculated to elicit from him the "blameless" and "upright" human life in which God takes such obvious delight? Do the "angry" speeches of God demonstrate the integrity of God in a comparably "upside-down" way? If Job does not require God's goodwill in order to "persist in his integrity," perhaps God does not require Job's goodwill in order to persist in *God*'s integrity. Perhaps it is in just this inverse way that the book of Job affirms the integrity of Job and the integrity of God beyond all question of self-serving motivation on either side. Job is Job, and God is not. God is God, and Job is not. Job's angry speeches are the means by which Job has maintained his integrity toward God and people—*against* God, if it comes to that! Perhaps God's angry speeches are the means by which God maintains God's integrity toward Job—*against* Job if it comes to that! But this makes sense only if the fact of God's "answer" to Job—before God's angry speeches begin—constitutes in itself God's unconditional vindication of Job's humanity, God's everlasting yes to the kind of human being God has declared Job to be (1:8; 2:3), to the kind of human being Job has declared himself to be, with his last breath (Job 31).

GOD'S FIRST SPEECH AND JOB'S RESPONSE
Job 38:1–40:5

Job 38:1–40:5

38:1 **Then the LORD answered Job out of the whirlwind:**
   2 **"Who is this that darkens counsel by words without knowledge?**
   3 **Gird up your loins like a man,**
      I will question you, and you shall declare to me.

   4 **"Where were you when I laid the foundation of the earth?**
      Tell me, if you have understanding.
   5 **Who determined its measurements—surely you know!**
      Or who stretched the line upon it?
   6 **On what were its bases sunk,**
      or who laid its cornerstone
   7 **when the morning stars sang together**
      and all the heavenly beings shouted for joy?

   8 **"Or who shut in the sea with doors**
      when it burst out from the womb?—
   9 **when I made the clouds its garment,**
      and thick darkness its swaddling band,
  10 **and prescribed bounds for it,**
      and set bars and doors,
  11 **and said, 'Thus far shall you come, and no farther,**
      and here shall your proud waves be stopped'?

¹² "Have you commanded the morning since your days began,
    and caused the dawn to know its place,
¹³ so that it might take hold of the skirts of the earth,
    and the wicked be shaken out of it?
¹⁴ It is changed like clay under the seal,
    and it is dyed like a garment.
¹⁵ Light is withheld from the wicked,
    and their uplifted arm is broken.

¹⁶ "Have you entered into the springs of the sea,
    or walked in the recesses of the deep?
¹⁷ Have the gates of death been revealed to you,
    or have you seen the gates of deep darkness?
¹⁸ Have you comprehended the expanse of the earth?
    Declare, if you know all this.

¹⁹ "Where is the way to the dwelling of light,
    and where is the place of darkness,
²⁰ that you may take it to its territory
    and that you may discern the paths to its home?
²¹ Surely you know, for you were born then,
    and the number of your days is great!

²² "Have you entered the storehouses of the snow,
    or have you seen the storehouses of the hail,
²³ which I have reserved for the time of trouble,
    for the day of battle and war?
²⁴ What is the way to the place where the light is distributed,
    or where the east wind is scattered upon the earth?

²⁵ "Who has cut a channel for the torrents of rain,
    and a way for the thunderbolt,
²⁶ to bring rain on a land where no one lives,
    on the desert, which is empty of human life,
²⁷ to satisfy the waste and desolate land,
    and to make the ground put forth grass?

²⁸ "Has the rain a father,
    or who has begotten the drops of dew?
²⁹ From whose womb did the ice come forth,
    and who has given birth to the hoarfrost of heaven?
³⁰ The waters become hard like stone,
    and the face of the deep is frozen.

³¹ "Can you bind the chains of the Pleiades,
    or loose the cords of Orion?

³² Can you lead forth the Mazzaroth in their season,
    or can you guide the Bear with its children?
³³ Do you know the ordinances of the heavens?
    Can you establish their rule on the earth?

³⁴ "Can you lift up your voice to the clouds,
    so that a flood of waters may cover you?
³⁵ Can you send forth lightnings, so that they may go
    and say to you, 'Here we are'?
³⁶ Who has put wisdom in the inward parts,
    or given understanding to the mind?
³⁷ Who has the wisdom to number the clouds?
    Or who can tilt the waterskins of the heavens,
³⁸ when the dust runs into a mass
    and the clods cling together?

³⁹ "Can you hunt the prey for the lion,
    or satisfy the appetite of the young lions,
⁴⁰ when they crouch in their dens,
    or lie in wait in their covert?
⁴¹ Who provides for the raven its prey,
    when its young ones cry to God,
    and wander about for lack of food?

39:1 "Do you know when the mountain goats give birth?
    Do you observe the calving of the deer?
² Can you number the months that they fulfill,
    and do you know the time when they give birth,
³ when they crouch to give birth to their offspring,
    and are delivered of their young?
⁴ Their young ones become strong, they grow up in the open;
    they go forth, and do not return to them.

⁵ "Who has let the wild ass go free?
    Who has loosed the bonds of the swift ass,
⁶ to which I have given the steppe for its home,
    the salt land for its dwelling place?
⁷ It scorns the tumult of the city;
    it does not hear the shouts of the driver.
⁸ It ranges the mountains as its pasture,
    and it searches after every green thing.

⁹ "Is the wild ox willing to serve you?
    Will it spend the night at your crib?

¹⁰ Can you tie it in the furrow with ropes,
    or will it harrow the valleys after you?
¹¹ Will you depend on it because its strength is great,
    and will you hand over your labor to it?
¹² Do you have faith in it that it will return,
    and bring your grain to your threshing floor?

¹³ "The ostrich's wings flap wildly,
    though its pinions lack plumage.
¹⁴ For it leaves its eggs to the earth,
    and lets them be warmed on the ground,
¹⁵ forgetting that a foot may crush them,
    and that a wild animal may trample them.
¹⁶ It deals cruelly with its young, as if they were not its own;
    though its labor should be in vain, yet it has no fear;
¹⁷ because God has made it forget wisdom,
    and given it no share in understanding.
¹⁸ When it spreads its plumes aloft,
    it laughs at the horse and its rider.

¹⁹ "Do you give the horse its might?
    Do you clothe its neck with mane?
²⁰ Do you make it leap like the locust?
    Its majestic snorting is terrible.
²¹ It paws violently, exults mightily;
    it goes out to meet the weapons.
²² It laughs at fear, and is not dismayed;
    it does not turn back from the sword.
²³ Upon it rattle the quiver,
    the flashing spear, and the javelin.
²⁴ With fierceness and rage it swallows the ground;
    it cannot stand still at the sound of the trumpet.
²⁵ When the trumpet sounds, it says 'Aha!'
    From a distance it smells the battle,
    the thunder of the captains, and the shouting.

²⁶ "Is it by your wisdom that the hawk soars,
    and spreads its wings toward the south?
²⁷ Is it at your command that the eagle mounts up
    and makes its nest on high?
²⁸ It lives on the rock and makes its home
    in the fastness of the rocky crag.
²⁹ From there it spies the prey;

        its eyes see it from far away.
³⁰ **Its young ones suck up blood;**
        and where the slain are, there it is."

40:1 **And the LORD said to Job:**
² **"Shall a faultfinder contend with the Almighty?**
        Anyone who argues with God must respond."

³ **Then Job answered the LORD:**
⁴ **"See, I am of small account; what shall I answer you?**
        I lay my hand on my mouth.
⁵ **I have spoken once, and I will not answer;**
        twice, but will proceed no further."

For this interpretation, Job 38:1 takes on pivotal significance. What does it mean to say, "Then the LORD *answered* Job out of the whirlwind"? One thing is certain: The "whirlwind" is not to be confused with any mere natural phenomenon, such as a killer tornado or a category 5 hurricane. The evidence is clear that this whirlwind is nothing less than a mighty signal of a *theophany*, that is, God's own immediate appearing in the midst of human affairs. From the texts cited above (see p. 156), it is clear that God's decisive appearing, according to the Bible, always happens for the purpose of delivering God's people and confounding God's enemies. The theophany of Job 38:1 immediately raises the question: Is God appearing on Job's side, for his vindication, or against Job, as the enemy, to annihilate him? In a variety of ways, both Job's friends and Elihu have warned him that if such a direct encounter between Job and God ever took place, Job would be unmasked as God's enemy, fully deserving the utter annihilation that must ensue. God's angry speeches against Job seem to indicate that Job's friends and Elihu are right about that. Yet Job *survives* this encounter with God. Not only this, but God affirms, later on, that Job was in the right all along, and Job's friends were in the wrong (42:7–8). Odd. What's going on here?

    It is just this question that drove me to take a closer look at the Hebrew word translated "answer" in Job 38:1. The word itself is as common in Hebrew as it is in English. But when you look for instances in the Bible where people ask for an "answer" from God or where God is said to "answer" human beings, the texts become very interesting. In the Psalms, for instance, people who cry out for an answer from God (or who report the absence of such an answer) are invariably innocent people who are in need or under attack from false accusers (see Psalms 4:1; 13:3; 22:2). When such people anticipate or have received such an answer from God, the outcome is invariably an act of vindication or deliverance by God (see Psalms 3:4; 17:6; 20:1). In Psalm 91:15, God promises to "answer" God's people when they call, to "be with them in trouble," to "rescue them and honor them" (see Isa. 49:8; Zech. 10:6). In Psalm 18:41, in contrast, God's refusal to "answer" the cries of the psalmist's enemies indicates God's utter rejection of their cause (see Micah 3:4, 7).

The Hebrew text of Psalm 22 offers a striking instance of an innocent, Joblike sufferer for whom God's answer constitutes a complete vindication of the sufferer's cause. Like Job, the psalmist has been unaccountably abandoned by God, subjected to torment not only by physical suffering but by mockery and accusations of "evildoers" (v. 16; see vv. 6–8; 12–18). Like Job, the psalmist has cried out repeatedly to God, receiving no answer (v. 2). Like Job, the psalmist finds this state of affairs incomprehensible, since he remembers times past in which those who trusted God were not "put to shame" (vv. 3–5; see Job 29). Like Job, the psalmist is also puzzled by the mystery that this suffering should happen to one whose birth and nurture have indicated God's intention for his well-being (Psalm 22:9–10; see Job 10:3, 8–13, 18).

Beginning in verse 22, however, Psalm 22 suddenly changes from a psalm of lamentation to a psalm of extravagant praise and thanksgiving to God, clearly from the lips of one who has experienced God's vindication and deliverance (see v. 24). This change is so abrupt that many scholars have understood verses 22–31 as a deliberate corrective added to this otherwise quite hopeless-sounding psalm of lament. A very minor emendation of the Hebrew text of verse 21b helps make this separation complete. Earlier editions of the RSV chose this option, following ancient Greek and Syriac manuscripts, and translated verse 21 "Save me from the mouth of the lion, my afflicted soul from the horns of the wild oxen!" Yet the footnote in these earlier editions of the RSV dutifully indicates that the Hebrew text does not read "my afflicted soul" at this point. The consonants of the Hebrew text are very similar to this reading, but what the Hebrew text actually says is "You have answered me!" The NRSV follows the lead of several contemporary scholars by preferring the present Hebrew text over the usual emendation based on ancient Greek and Syriac translations. The result is that the break between the psalm of lament (22:1–21a) and the psalm of praise and thanksgiving (22:21b–31) now takes place in the middle of verse 21: "From the horns of the wild oxen you have rescued me." Again, the footnote indicates that the phrase "you have rescued me" is literally, in Hebrew, "you have answered me."

By using the word *rescue* instead of *answer*, the NRSV translators are stressing the point that God's answer consists of a deed of vindication and deliverance, not an explanation or a discourse in words. This is entirely consistent with the great majority of biblical texts which speak of God's "answer" to faithful people. In every one of the texts cited above, the word *answer* could be translated "rescue" or "vindicate" or "deliver" or "stand by the side of" with no loss of meaning. In none of the texts cited above can God's answer be understood as a verbal response.

On these grounds, then, I offer the suggestion that Job 38:1, all by itself, before the speeches of God ever begin, may be understood as God's unqualified yes, spoken to God's servant Job after Job has "persisted in his integrity" to the very end (chap. 31), even though he has been put to the test of confronting God as his enemy. Job has proved that he truly "serves God for nothing," that is, even at the unimaginable personal cost of challenging God directly in order to make the point. If 38:1 all by itself constitutes God's yes to Job, then all the "angry" speeches of God that follow are addressed to a *vindicated* Job, one who has already been granted God's unqualified approval. Perhaps even more important, as we shall see, the words of submission and repentance in Job 40:3–5 and 42:1–6 come from the lips of a *vindicated* Job, one who has now had the unimaginable experience of being vindicated in a direct encounter with Almighty God, amid the overwhelming display of God's transcendent wisdom and power.

The reader should know that this line of interpretation is only one among many and that it represents a tiny fragment of scholarly opinion. At best it may serve as a stimulus for readers to work out their own understandings of Job, not as any sort of definitive "answer" to the urgent questions of faith Job raises in every generation. For what it is worth, however, the following is an attempt to work out an interpretation of Job 38—42 as if 38:1 constitutes God's complete vindication of Job.

The difficulties of this interpretation are immediately obvious in 38:2–5. Why would a God who has just vindicated Job by answering him "out of the whirlwind" now identify Job as one who "darkens counsel by words without knowledge" (v. 2)? Why should this "vindicating" God now sarcastically challenge Job to a ludicrous test of their respective wisdom and power (vv. 3–5)? Why overwhelm this "vindicated" Job with a series of questions that Job cannot possibly answer and a series of feats that Job cannot possibly equal (38:5–39:30)?

One point on which almost all students of Job agree is that chapters 38—41 are the poet's attempt to describe the transcendent and inscrutable wisdom and power of God in the creation and governance of the universe.

Insofar as the poet succeeds, the reader is left in a state of wide-eyed, open-mouthed, slack-jawed wonder at the unapproachable splendor and majesty of God as reflected in nature and in God's mastery of chaotic powers.

Modern readers, for whom scientific explanations are commonplace and for whom an authentic sense of wonder is rare, must engage all their powers of imagination to capture anything of the awe these magnificent speeches of God are meant to convey. This is now the sixth occasion on which the author of Job has asked us to imagine the unimaginable, the other occasions being:

1. In 1:1–5, 8, 20–22 and 2:7–10, we are asked to imagine that there once was a supremely righteous and supremely blessed human being who remained utterly faithful in spite of the unaccountable loss of every good and comforting thing.
2. In 1:6–12 and 2:1–6, we are asked to imagine what it might be like to eavesdrop in the very council chamber of God, where an unimaginable test is contrived for God's servant Job.
3. In chapter 29, we are asked to imagine what a human life would be like if every experience reflected perfect *shalom* (intactness, harmony, peace) between God and a particular human being.
4. In chapter 30, we are asked to imagine what it would be like if the *shalom* of chapter 29 were unaccountably shattered, and this same person experienced the absolute depths of human deprivation, humiliation, and suffering, for no reason.
5. In chapter 31, we are asked what it would be like if the person described in chapter 29 went through the inexplicable pain described in chapter 30 and then affirmed this notion of a human integrity worth living and dying for, no matter what.

In chapters 38—41 we are being asked to imagine an even less imaginable thing: What would it be like for a mere human being (even a human being like Job, who enjoys God's unconditional approval; see 1:8; 2:3; 42:7–8) to stand unshielded and totally vulnerable in the absolute cosmic splendor of God's immediate presence? If the poet's appeal to images of God's wisdom and power in creating and ordering the universe and overcoming chaos do not accomplish that for us, then I think it is up to us to supply our own images to achieve nothing less. If Job's angry speeches are designed to tell God, "Look, I am a 100 percent human being and you are not!" perhaps God's angry speeches are designed to tell Job, "Look, I'm 100 percent God and you are not!" Yet neither collection of angry speeches makes sense unless both God and Job are united at the irreducible point. In spite of the "infinite qualitative difference" between Almighty God and the merely human, Job and God concur on the definition of a quality of life that is both fully human and worthy of the unconditional approval of Almighty God. The unimaginable differences between Job and God on the points of wisdom and power do nothing to compromise that.

Job has had his chance to call God to account for Job's side of this astonishing equation. Now it is God's turn to call Job to account for God's side of the same equation. Job has challenged God. Now God challenges Job! Job has no clue as to what was on God's mind when the foundations of the earth were sunk (38:4), when "the morning stars sang together . . . for joy" at God's creation (38:7). Job was nowhere to be found when God set ultimate bounds to the chaos waters when they burst forth, threatening to wipe out everything (38:8–11). Job had no part in regulating the alternation of day and night or setting ultimate limits to human wickedness (38:12–15). God alone has plumbed the mysteries of the deep; Job has not (38:16–18). Speak to me of the origins of light and darkness, says God; surely you are the firstborn of all creation; surely you were around when all these things were arranged (38:19–21; see Job 15:7–8 and Prov. 8:22–31, where only the personified Wisdom of God was privy to the secrets of creation).

Job 38:39–39:30 rings the changes on the dazzling phenomena of animal life on earth (the habits and characteristics of the lion, the raven, the mountain goat, the wild ass, the wild ox, the ostrich, the warhorse, the hawk, the eagle, the vulture), none of which fits into rational human schemes or can be finally bent to human control. Even people schooled in modern zoological science can still catch something of the ancient poet's wonder at the sheer variety (and perhaps even whimsicality) of animal forms, some of which appear to be designed for efficiency, some for beauty, and some just for fun (see 39:13–18). (Modern zoologists, however, tell us that the ostrich is rather badly misrepresented in this delightful caricature!) Yet these are only the "outskirts of [God's] ways" (see 26:14), behind which lie a wisdom and a power in God's creating and ordering of the universe that go infinitely beyond the capacities of human reason. Of course Job cannot expect to read the character or purposes of God from the incomprehensible vagaries of nature, history, or human experience. God is God, and Job is not! This seems to me to be the point of the renewed challenge to Job with which God's first mighty speech ends (40:1–2).

If the poet's intention in 38:1–39:30 was to convey the unimaginable splendor of a direct encounter with Almighty God, Job's response in 40:3–5 indicates the effect the poet hopes to achieve in the mind of the reader: sheer dumbstruck awe before the living presence of God. Job now understands at complete depth that God is God, and Job is not; therefore, there is nothing left to say.

Job's silent submission in 40:3–5 can be understood in two quite different ways, depending on how we interpret 38:1. If the answer Job receives is limited to the angry speech of God in 38:2–40:2, then Job's submission in 40:3–5 indicates that he has simply been overwhelmed by this pyrotechnic demonstration of God's transcendent wisdom and power. To confess that he is "of small account" then suggests that all Job's protestations of innocence, all his outcries against injustice, all his demands for a hearing before God are now disclosed to have been both arrogant and trivial. God is so overwhelmingly wise and powerful that all such petty human concerns are beneath God's transcendent dignity, and Job was foolish to attempt to call God's attention to them. If this is indeed God's answer to Job, then God has placed Job in the wrong, just as Job's friends and Elihu predicted all along. As we have noted, the only reference to what might be called the moral issues in God's first speech occurs in 38:12–15, a rather vague suggestion that God's cosmic order somehow works to the disadvantage of the wicked. There is no indication whatever that God has any positive regard for instances of human integrity and faithfulness. This would no doubt have been disappointing to Job's friends and to Elihu, but at least they could have taken delight in God's humiliation of Job.

To maintain that God's answer to Job consists of this scathing reduction to absurdity of everything Job has said ("Who is this who darkens counsel?"), it is obviously necessary to disregard what is said in 1:8; 2:3; and 42:7–8. Scholars have typically done this by making an important distinction between the prose framework of Job (chaps. 1—2 and 42:7–17) and the mighty poem that stretches from 3:1 to 42:6. Perhaps this prose material reflects nothing more than a rather conventional piety according to which God ultimately rewards the patient sufferer (see 42:12–17). It is often argued that this pious "framework" is all that made the otherwise outrageous poem in any way acceptable to subsequent conventional faith communities. Indeed, it is quite unimaginable that any faith community based on the Hebrew Bible would ever have cherished as Holy Scripture a document portraying God as sublimely indifferent to issues of human justice, righteousness, and compassion.

The situation is altogether different, however, if the *fact* of God's answer to Job "out of the whirlwind" (38:1) constitutes God's unconditional yes to Job's life of selfless integrity as epitomized in chapter 31, which I suggest it may. Then Job's abject wonder in 40:3–5 has two sources, not one. The obvious source is the unimaginable wonder of a direct encounter with God in all God's transcendent glory (conveyed by God's "angry" speeches in 38:2–39:30). But surely the greater wonder, for such a man as Job, is that this utterly transcendent God, in all God's infinite mystery, should deign to take Job seriously, to hear him, to *answer* him—to stand by him, with him, for him—to vindicate his fragile human life of integrity toward God and people. That is a wonder capable of rendering even so persistent and fearless a man as Job quite speechless. (Note Psalm 8, where the ultimate source of wonder is not God's overwhelming grandeur, manifested in the starry heavens, but the fact that God pays attention to and cares about fragile "earthlings" such as us. The Job of 40:3–5 is now in a position to understand that psalm quite differently from the way he apparently did in 7:17.)

GOD'S SECOND SPEECH AND JOB'S RESPONSE
Job 40:6–42:6

Job 40:6–42:6

40:6 Then the LORD answered Job out of the whirlwind:
　　⁷ "Gird up your loins like a man;
　　　　I will question you, and you declare to me.
　　⁸ Will you even put me in the wrong?
　　　　Will you condemn me that you may be justified?
　　⁹ Have you an arm like God,
　　　　and can you thunder with a voice like his?

　　¹⁰ "Deck yourself with majesty and dignity;
　　　　clothe yourself with glory and splendor.
　　¹¹ Pour out the overflowings of your anger,
　　　　and look on all who are proud, and abase them.
　　¹² Look on all who are proud, and bring them low;
　　　　tread down the wicked where they stand.
　　¹³ Hide them all in the dust together;
　　　　bind their faces in the world below.
　　¹⁴ Then I will also acknowledge to you
　　　　that your own right hand can give you victory.

　　¹⁵ "Look at Behemoth,
　　　　which I made just as I made you;
　　　　it eats grass like an ox.
　　¹⁶ Its strength is in its loins,
　　　　and its power in the muscles of its belly.

¹⁷ It makes its tail stiff like a cedar;
    the sinews of its thighs are knit together.
¹⁸ Its bones are tubes of bronze,
    its limbs like bars of iron.

¹⁹ "It is the first of the great acts of God—
    only its Maker can approach it with the sword.
²⁰ For the mountains yield food for it
    where all the wild animals play.
²¹ Under the lotus plants it lies,
    in the covert of the reeds and in the marsh.
²² The lotus trees cover it for shade;
    the willows of the wadi surround it.
²³ Even if the river is turbulent, it is not frightened;
    it is confident though Jordan rushes against its mouth.
²⁴ Can one take it with hooks
    or pierce its nose with a snare?

41:1 "Can you draw out Leviathan with a fishhook,
    or press down its tongue with a cord?
² Can you put a rope in its nose,
    or pierce its jaw with a hook?
³ Will it make many supplications to you?
    Will it speak soft words to you?
⁴ Will it make a covenant with you
    to be taken as your servant forever?
⁵ Will you play with it as with a bird,
    or will you put it on leash for your girls?
⁶ Will traders bargain over it?
    Will they divide it up among the merchants?
⁷ Can you fill its skin with harpoons,
    or its head with fishing spears?
⁸ Lay hands on it;
    think of the battle; you will not do it again!
⁹ Any hope of capturing it will be disappointed;
    were not even the gods overwhelmed at the sight of it?
¹⁰ No one is so fierce as to dare to stir it up.
    Who can stand before it?
¹¹ Who can confront it and be safe?
    —under the whole heaven, who?

¹² "I will not keep silence concerning its limbs,
    or its mighty strength, or its splendid frame.

13 Who can strip off its outer garment?
　　Who can penetrate its double coat of mail?
14 Who can open the doors of its face?
　　There is terror all around its teeth.
15 Its back is made of shields in rows,
　　shut up closely as with a seal.
16 One is so near to another
　　that no air can come between them.
17 They are joined one to another;
　　they clasp each other and cannot be separated.
18 Its sneezes flash forth light,
　　and its eyes are like the eyelids of the dawn.
19 From its mouth go flaming torches;
　　sparks of fire leap out.
20 Out of its nostrils comes smoke,
　　as from a boiling pot and burning rushes.
21 Its breath kindles coals,
　　and a flame comes out of its mouth.
22 In its neck abides strength,
　　and terror dances before it.
23 The folds of its flesh cling together;
　　it is firmly cast and immovable.
24 Its heart is as hard as stone,
　　as hard as the lower millstone.
25 When it raises itself up the gods are afraid;
　　at the crashing they are beside themselves.
26 Though the sword reaches it, it does not avail,
　　nor does the spear, the dart, or the javelin.
27 It counts iron as straw,
　　and bronze as rotten wood.
28 The arrow cannot make it flee;
　　slingstones, for it, are turned to chaff.
29 Clubs are counted as chaff;
　　it laughs at the rattle of javelins.
30 Its underparts are like sharp potsherds;
　　it spreads itself like a threshing sledge on the mire.
31 It makes the deep boil like a pot;
　　it makes the sea like a pot of ointment.
32 It leaves a shining wake behind it;
　　one would think the deep to be white-haired.
33 On earth it has no equal,
　　a creature without fear.
34 It surveys everything that is lofty;
　　it is king over all that are proud."

42:1 **Then Job answered the LORD:**
  2 **"I know that you can do all things,**
      and that no purpose of yours can be thwarted.
  3 **'Who is this that hides counsel without knowledge?'**
    Therefore I have uttered what I did not understand,
      things too wonderful for me, which I did not know.
  4 **'Hear, and I will speak;**
      I will question you, and you declare to me.'
  5 **I had heard of you by the hearing of the ear,**
      but now my eye sees you;
  6 **therefore I despise myself,**
      and repent in dust and ashes."

Strangely enough, God has not yet finished the angry speeches; neither does Job remain completely silent. Job 40:6 is identical with 38:1, and the whole encounter appears to begin afresh, even though the themes familiar to us in 38:1–40:5 are repeated using different imagery. Did the "original" book of Job really reach its climax with two slightly different accounts of this divine-human encounter? Or is 40:6–42:6 to be regarded as an addition incorporated into the text later on, in the process of its transmission and editing?

As we have seen, both Job 28 and Job 32—37 are often considered to be later additions of this kind, and the book contains other passages that may reflect editorial changes. Our approach throughout, however, has been to try to interpret the whole book as it has actually come down to us in the Jewish and Christian canons of Holy Scripture.

In that spirit, what shall we make of this second salvo of God's cosmic artillery against Job, and what shall we make of Job's second (and even more puzzling) response? Job 40:8 leaps out at us because it appears to level a specific charge against Job, a charge that is far more serious than anything we remember from 38:2–40:2. Verse 8 not only accuses Job of having spoken what is *not* right about God (against 42:7–8) but does so in language that might have come straight out of a speech by Eliphaz (see 15:12–13) or Elihu (see 32:2; 33:12–13; 34:5–6). For that matter, Job has, in fact, said that to maintain his own integrity, he *must* assert that God is not in the right (see 27:5). It will prove difficult, if not impossible, to reconcile 40:8 with the notion that God's answer vindicates Job from the outset. Interestingly enough, however, nothing in this second speech of God asserts that Job was wrong to justify himself (= "persist in his integrity"?). The objection of verse 8 is that Job felt compelled to put *God* in the wrong in order to do so. This is a dicey argument on God's part if we relate 40:8 to 2:3, where God effectively admits to having destroyed Job "for no reason." Is Job expected to have somehow "intuited" that God's unjust attack against him was an expression of God's supreme confidence in and approbation of Job? How could Job have thought otherwise than that either he or God was in the wrong in this extraordinary instance? Let's keep this question open.

God quickly moves from the question of Job's "justification" to a sarcastic hypothetical instance in which Job might legitimately have the right to call God in question. All Job needs to do is to demonstrate that he has "an arm like God" and "can . . . thunder with a voice like [God's]" (40:9). The premise of verses 10–14 is that Job would have to prove that he is God's full equal to earn the acknowledgment of God that Job's "own right hand" can prove him victorious in this dispute. Once again, the implication is that God is God and Job is not, but this time with a disturbing twist. Verses 11–13 suggest that if Job were God's equal, then Job, like God, would give the "proud" their comeuppance and dispatch the "wicked" to the netherworld. This sounds all too similar to the hackneyed doctrine of Job's friends that God invariably punishes the wicked. (Zophar devotes an entire speech to this theme in chapter 20. Job refutes it at length in 21:7–34.) Job knows well the "overflowings of [God's] anger" and what it means to be abased by God (v. 11). Job knows what it is to be brought low by God, to be trodden down (v. 12), to be consigned to the netherworld (v. 13). Is he to infer from verses 11–13 that God identifies Job as one of the "proud" and the "wicked"? If so, then Job's friends have surely spoken what is right about Job (and therefore, about God), contrary to God's estimation in 42:7–8. Is there any alternative way to understand the harsh words of God in 40:8–14?

God's second speech concludes with poems describing two quite indescribable "beasts" or "monsters" that have puzzled biblical interpreters for the better part of two millennia. Who is "Behemoth" (40:15–24)? Who is "Leviathan" (41:1–34)? Vivid and complex as these twin poems are, their import in the context of God's speech to Job is simple in the extreme: They are surely to be taken, in the first line, as variations on the theme that God is God and Job is not. Job is expected to be overwhelmed by the sheer power and terror of these beings, but even more so by the fact that they exist as signs of God's overarching power, which includes them, in all their chaotic terror, but also controls them.

If Behemoth is to be understood as the hippopotamus, as many scholars think, then its description in 40:15–24 suggests dimensions of awesomeness and mystery that go far beyond the merely animal (see 40:19, 23). If the description of Leviathan suggests the crocodile (see 41:13–17,

23, 30), this beast also transcends anything ever observed in nature (see 41:18–21, 25, 31–34). At the very least, Behemoth and Leviathan symbolize uncontrollable and terrifying power before which human beings stand utterly helpless. Studies in ancient Egyptian, Mesopotamian, and Canaanite traditions have persuaded many scholars that conceptions of primeval chaos monsters underlie both of these descriptions, even though characteristics of the hippo and the crocodile may have colored the descriptions of Behemoth and Leviathan respectively.

In any case, neither description is identical with that of such monsters as depicted in any ancient Near Eastern mythology of record. The name Leviathan denotes a serpentine monster in a Mesopotamian text and in Canaanite myth. The former text suggests the power of a conjurer to unleash Leviathan's destructive power, recalling Job 3:8. In Canaanite myth, this serpentine Leviathan is a sea monster against whom the god Baal does battle. In the tradition of Israel, traces of this myth appear in the notion of God's primordial (Psalm 74:14) and ultimate (Isa. 27:1) victory over the powers of chaos (see also Psalms 18:7–15; 89:9–10; Isa. 51:9).

In Job 41, however, God challenges Job to deal with Leviathan in the almost playful manner in which God does, angling for it (v. 1), putting a rope in its nose (v. 2), bending it to the role of a servant (v. 4), playing with it as a pet (v. 5; see Psalm 104:26), and so on. At its fiercest, Leviathan poses no threat to God (the word *creature* in verse 33 indicates that it was "made" by God), no matter how unmanageable and terrifying it appears to Job.

After God's first speech, Job was struck dumb with wonder (40:3–5). After the second speech of God, Job is moved to break his awed silence, but only to make his submission to God complete by words of total humility and repentance (42:1–6). In this direct encounter with God, Job perceives as never before that God's purposes in the creation and governance of the world are sure, regardless of the way things may appear from a merely human perspective (42:2). It was a lack of that perception that led Job to "hide counsel without knowledge" (quoting God's question to Job in 38:2) and to say things that Job now knows he did not understand, "things too wonderful" to lie within his ken (42:3). Job marvels at the fact that God has indeed deigned to speak to him face to face, challenging him to precisely the kind of encounter Job had always longed for (42:4, quoting God's words from 38:3 and 40:7; see 9:32–35; 13:20–25; 14:13). Everything Job had thought to know of God before is disclosed as mere hearsay, now eclipsed by the utterly overwhelming experience of beholding God directly, face to face (42:5). The only appropriate response to this unimaginable encounter is abject humility and the withdrawal of all complaint against God (42:6).

The Hebrew text of verse 6 is open to a variety of interpretations. There appears to be a consensus among recent interpreters, however, that Job does not here recant his claims to innocence and integrity, which God nowhere calls into question in 38—41. At the critical point, however, there was always something Job did not know or failed to understand about God's role in Job's story, which led to all those passionate outbursts against God as the enemy. What Job could not have known, yet somehow should have known, is that God staked God's own reputation on Job's integrity toward God and people.

That God's transcendent wisdom and power defy all human capacities is not a new idea for Job, even though he now experiences these realities face to face, in a direct, personal encounter with God. What is incomparably new for Job is the awesome discovery that God was always with him and for him throughout his tragic ordeal, even when the course of events seemed to disclose God only as the enemy of Job, as well as of all innocent victims of injustice (see 24:1–12). In this light, both Job's defense of his integrity and his protests against injustice disclose God's own character, through the fragile means of a human being who "persists in his integrity" (2:3). In the face of the worst imaginable experience of life, what eluded Job before was the possibility that God's true attitude toward Job could *not* be read from the chaotic and amoral character of the catastrophes that have befallen him. What reduces him now to repentance "in dust and ashes" is the shocked awareness that authentic human integrity toward God and people can *only* be expressed in a morally neutral setting, one in which there can be no suspicion that this integrity is based on the prospect of personal advantage.

The question of *hassatan* ("Does Job fear God for nothing?") has now received a twofold answer. Job's integrity stands proven beyond any suspicion that his "fear of God" is motivated by the self-interested desire to receive God's blessings. God's action toward Job, climaxed by the angry speeches to Job in 38—41, has exonerated God from *hassatan*'s implied charge that the blessings initially showered on Job (see 1:1–5 and 29:1–6) were designed to seduce Job toward exhibiting the kind of humanity in which God takes such pride and delight (1:8; 2:3).

Both sets of angry speeches (God's as well as Job's) establish the mutual integrity of God and Job at the irreducible point: God's heart toward Job and Job's heart toward God are one, free from ulterior motives on either side. Job has "persisted in his integrity" to his next-to-last breath, in the absence of any token that God knows or cares about how things are with him. God has ultimately vindicated Job (38:1), not only enduring the wholly undeserved suffering of "my servant Job" but approving the well-nigh blasphemous accusations by which Job has expressed God's own outrage against all injustice and innocent suffering.

Once Job has encountered God as his vindicator, the pyrotechnic display of God's transcendent wisdom and power produces not terror but absolute wonder. Secure in the knowledge that God has stood with him and for him throughout the whole ordeal, Job is ready now to withdraw all his charges against God in abject humility and submission. Now he can concede willingly that God's inscrutable ordering of the universe will forever elude human understanding. What terrifies human beings as sheer chaos is nevertheless under God's control. But this awareness is possible for Job only on the basis of what Job *can* understand: that God stands irrevocably on the side of human life that is authentically devoted to God and people. This, I think, is the "too wonderful" thing that has eluded Job's understanding until this face-to-face encounter with God. For Job, this is what it means to "see" God with his own eyes, disclosing all his previous theological thoughts to be mere hearsay.

If this is so, then Job's repentance in 42:6 has nothing to do with knuckling under to the display of God's incomprehensible wisdom and power. If it did, then the story of Job is only another example of right being overwhelmed by might, a phenomenon all too common in human experience. But if Job now sees God, in all God's transcendent glory, standing on the side of Job's humanity, then Job's repentance contains nothing of servility. Rather, it is the only appropriate mode of tardy adoration.

9. Job's Last Test
Job 42:7–10

Job 42:7–10

42:7 **After the Lord had spoken these words to Job, the Lord said to Eliphaz the Temanite: "My wrath is kindled against you and against your two friends; for you have not spoken of me what is right, as my servant Job has. ⁸Now therefore take seven bulls and seven rams, and go to my servant Job, and offer up for yourselves a burnt offering; and my servant Job shall pray for you, for I will accept his prayer not to deal with you according to your folly; for you have not spoken of me what is right, as my servant Job has done." ⁹ So Eliphaz the Temanite and Bildad the Shuhite and Zophar the Naamathite went and did what the Lord had told them; and the Lord accepted Job's prayer.**

¹⁰ **And the Lord restored the fortunes of Job when he had prayed for his friends; and the Lord gave Job twice as much as he had before.**

The prose epilogue of Job is frequently understood as a pious addition to the mighty poems of Job 3—41, tacked on to affirm the conventional notion that piety ultimately pays off in superabundant blessings from God. If that is the case, then this "happy ending" simply confirms what Eliphaz, Bildad, Zophar, and Elihu have been saying all along. Job's repentance in 42:1–6 can then be taken as the essential turning point that qualifies Job to receive God's blessing in even greater measure than he enjoyed before.

The line of interpretation we have been following thus far, however, opens the way for a different reading of the epilogue. First of all, verses 7–9 appear to demolish any idea that the conventional reward-and-punishment theology of Job's friends is vindicated here. On the contrary, the worst imaginable fears of Eliphaz, Bildad, and Zophar are realized in verse 7. (Note that Elihu is not mentioned in the epilogue.) Until now they had been supremely confident that a direct encounter between God and Job would prove Job wrong and confirm the rightness of their own orthodoxies. It was in this confidence that Zophar wished for Job "that God would . . . open [God's] lips to you" and "tell you the secrets of wisdom" (see 11:1–6). Imagine the friends' consternation when God speaks these devastating words directly to *Eliphaz:* "My wrath is kindled against you and against your two friends; for you have not spoken of me what is right, as my servant Job has."

Surely this constitutes the most complete role reversal in literature. Job's accusers now stand accused not by Job but by the very God in whose name they had smugly warned Job of the consequences of God's wrath. The speeches of Job that the friends had found so blasphemous are now declared to be the *right* way to speak of God. The artful arguments by which the friends had thought to "plead the case for God" (13:8) and condemn Job are now declared to be utterly wrong, incurring the wrath of God against *them*. Eliphaz, Bildad, and Zophar are now the ones sitting on a spiritual ash heap, condemned not on the evidence of their suffering but by the solemn verdict of God. Job now stands as the one approved by God, not by his mere human assertion of being right but by God's own vindicating "answer."

It is easy to imagine that if *hassatan* were still around (he also is not mentioned in the epilogue), he might seize on this most complete imaginable reversal of roles to put Job's integrity to the ultimate test. "Remember how these people have treated you," he might have said to Job. "Now that God is unmistakably on your side and against them, this is surely the perfect time to get even, or at least to say, 'I told you so!' "

In the event, it is God and not *hassatan* who confronts Job with this most subtle and exquisite of temptations. But God arranges a dual test, first for the friends and then for Job. First, they must offer a sacrifice to God in the presence of Job, in token of their profound sorrow for having dishonored God by their arguments against Job. Not an easy penance; but there is more. They must then ask Job, whom they have accused and humiliated, to pray to God, on their behalf, not to deal with them "according to [their] folly" (v. 8).

Job has had quite a lot to say, negative and positive, about the duty of friends toward one who is in distress, even if those friends think the sufferer is in the wrong (see Job 6:14–23; 19:2–6). More important, however, he knows himself bound by a self-sworn ethic not to rejoice "at the ruin of those who hated me" or to exult "when evil overtook them," not to "let my mouth sin by asking for their lives with a curse" (31:29–30). In 42:9, Job once again "persists in his integrity," rejecting even this most exquisite temptation to serve himself by getting even.

The words of Job's prayer are not recorded, but their essential content is already suggested in verse 8. They can hardly have been other than "O Lord, forgive them, do not deal with them according to their folly."

Christians can hardly avoid thinking about the words of an ancient variant text that has become a permanent part of the church's lore about the crucifixion of Jesus: "Father, forgive them, for they do not know what they are doing" (Luke 23:34; see also Stephen's prayer in Acts 7:60).

In any case, this dual test of Job and his friends is passed with flying colors, as indicated by the cryptic note at the conclusion of verse 9: "The LORD accepted Job's prayer."

Perhaps the most astonishing thing about verses 8–9 is that they break open a new way in which human beings may relate positively to God, one that is nowhere hinted at in Job 1:1–42:7. The friends have argued that the only way for mortal (and therefore sinful) human beings to win God's blessing is to affirm God's absolute justice in all that occurs, even if human reason is incapable of discerning the hidden wisdom of God by which this justice is meted out. Apparently unwarranted instances of human suffering may then be understood as God's (just) chastisement, designed to warn us away from utterly destructive unrighteousness. Only an arrogant and persistent unrighteousness evokes the wholly destructive wrath of God that signals the ultimate victory of God's justice against all unrighteousness. Righteous people recognize this, throw themselves on God's mercy, and bend every effort to conform their lives to God's justice. The blessed life in relation to God is assured to all those who conform to this view of things and who persistently struggle to embody it in their lives. Those who refuse this option are simply "wicked," and their ultimate end is destruction and death. In either case, God's justice is confirmed in the details of human experience, even when the transcendent wisdom of God's providence eludes human understanding.

Job's story discloses a quite different conception of how a human being may relate positively to God. We are asked to imagine a circumstance in which the experiences of life neither demonstrate God's justice nor disclose God's true estimation of the persons involved (see 1:8–12; 2:3–7). The world as Job experiences it is a place where "bad things happen to good people" and good things happen to bad people, without any evidence of God's justice in human affairs. Insofar as God is understood to be the ordainer of "whatever things come to pass," then God emerges as the ruthless enemy of the innocent (see 16:7–17 and 24:1–12).

The question of the book of Job is whether even the most faithful imaginable person could maintain a life of integrity toward God and people under these hellish conditions. If God's "answer" to Job in 38:1 is indeed God's vindication of Job's integrity, then the life approved by God turns out to be Job's life of unswerving commitment to God and people, in the absence of any sign that such commitment offers Job any personal comfort or any promise of future blessedness.

Chapter 31, in the context of Job's summation of his case in chapters 29—31, is intended to demonstrate the unshakable ethic on which Job orders his relationships to God and people, even though his experience of life (chap. 30) has shown him that this exalted ethic has spared him nothing of the world's suffering and humiliation. Job's devotion to God throughout his ordeal, however, is far less clear. We have pointed to those texts in which Job expresses his longing for relationship with God, implying confidence that his hellish experience of life does not—*cannot*—express either God's true character or God's estimate of Job's humanity. But what shall we make of Job's passionate accusation against God and against the overwhelming evidence of injustice in human affairs?

The shocking implication of 42:7–8 is that God not only vindicates Job's life of integrity toward God and people but also approves what Job has spoken! In what sense can all Job's passionate and well-nigh blasphemous outbursts constitute the "right" way to speak of God? Taken together, all the speeches of Job express a human outrage against whatever diminishes, cripples, or destroys human life; a human outrage against all oppression, injustice, and unrighteousness in human affairs; a human outrage against innocent suffering; and finally, human outrage against God, on the supposition that God is the one who causes or allows such things to happen.

Is it possible that God concurs with Job so completely that Job's words of anguish and outrage express God's own anguish and outrage, not "out of the whirlwind" but from the lips of God's servant Job? We may risk this conjecture on the grounds of God's unqualified approval of Job in 1:8 and 2:3, climaxed by God's vindicating answer in 38:1. If a merely human heart can be so congruent with God's heart, then perhaps Job's frail words on the points of justice and righteousness and compassion can bring God's own mind to expression, even in a chaotic, terrifying world where there is no other sign that God knows or cares how things are with the human family.

But what of Job's accusations against God, in which he contends not only that God's justice does not prevail on earth but that God has singled him out and attacked him as the enemy? How can those words be understood as "right" speech about God? At the simplest level, according to the story told in 1:6–12 and 2:1–6, God can only concur that the accusation is true. Not until Job 38:1 does Job discover that the God he has encountered as the enemy has been with him and for him throughout his ordeal, confident that not even the experience of utter alienation from God is capable of shattering Job's integrity toward God and people. If God's justice, righteousness, and compassion are evident nowhere else in a morally formless universe, God's own reputation is staked on the possibility that they will nevertheless come to expression in the outraged speech of God's servant Job. In that light, however, perhaps God can even concur in Job's accusations against the one who acted against him, "to destroy him for no reason" (2:3). To rail boldly against *this* God while never relinquishing his quest for relationship with the God Job *knows* will vindicate him—this is surely the ultimate evidence that Job "persists in his integrity" toward God.

In God's estimate, "there is no one like him on the earth" (1:8; 2:3). This is terrifying news for Eliphaz, Bildad, and Zophar, whose nicely calculated prescription for winning God's favor has now been declared wrong by the very mouth of God. Their situation is utterly hopeless, unless—unless there is a third way of relating positively to God that has not been proposed anywhere in Job 1:1–42:7 (although Job 1:5 may contain the subtlest hint of it). It is the shocking possibility that intercession by God's uniquely righteous servant, on behalf of utterly failed sinners, may yet restore sinners to the grace and peace of God.

Voltaire once said something to the effect that "the dear Lord will forgive; it's God's thing." Yet this trite formula for "cheap grace" is miles away from the ultimate test to which Job is put here, and the test to which Eliphaz, Bildad, and Zophar are put in order to receive it. Just as God's justice, righteousness, and compassion took shape in Job's incredibly costly human devotion to God and people, so God's forgiveness is now to take shape in the costly act of Job's human forgiveness. Job must now demonstrate again that he "fears God for nothing." Not even his longed-for moment of vindication in the presence of Almighty God is to be cherished as a personal "reward" that somehow makes all the suffering worthwhile. Rather, what he has achieved is to be expended on behalf of others who have not deserved it. As one who has the right to lord it over those who have made his life miserable, he now takes their part before God, standing with them and for them even in their utter bankruptcy before God.

Eliphaz, Bildad, and Zophar now have a friend before God—the very friend from whom they have withheld friendship (see 6:14–23) when their situations were apparently reversed. Yet the forgiveness Job's friends are to receive carries certain costs of its own. It is no easy thing to surrender cherished orthodoxies, especially when the whole theme of religious commitment is based on the personal advantages to be derived from it. To receive Job's forgiveness, they must first acknowledge that his way of selfless commitment to God and people is right and their notion of religion as "enlightened self-interest" is simply wrong. To ask forgiveness from a friend like Job is to undertake a life of devotion like his, devotion to God and people regardless of the cost to oneself. Let it be said of Eliphaz, Bildad, and Zophar that they found grace and courage to do just that.

"And the LORD restored the fortunes of Job when he had prayed for his friends" (42:10a)—that is, after Job has dispelled the last shadow of doubt that his integrity toward God and people is motivated by self-interest of any kind. Job does not need any of the blessings of this life in order to be God's kind of human being. God's willingness to confront Job with the worst imaginable experiences of life and the angry speeches God addresses to a vindicated Job have demonstrated that God has not seduced Job into righteousness by showering him with blessings. God does not need an idyllic relationship with Job to recognize him as God's servant. The integrity of Job toward God and God's integrity toward Job have already been established at the irreducible point. What shall we then make of Job 42:10b–17?

10. Happy Ever After?
Job 42:10b–17

Job 42:10b–17

42:10b **and the LORD gave Job twice as much as he had before.** [11] **Then there came to him all his brothers and sisters and all who had known him before, and they ate bread with him in his house; they showed him sympathy and comforted him for all the evil that the LORD had brought upon him; and each of them gave him a piece of money and a gold ring.** [12] **The LORD blessed the latter days of Job more than his beginning; and he had fourteen thousand sheep, six thousand camels, a thousand yoke of oxen, and a thousand donkeys.** [13] **He also had seven sons and three daughters.** [14] **He named the first Jemimah, the second Keziah, and the third Keren-happuch.** [15] **In all the land there were no women so beautiful as Job's daughters; and their father gave them an inheritance along with their brothers.** [16] **After this Job lived one hundred and forty years, and saw his children, and his children's children, four generations.** [17] **And Job died, old and full of days.**

As I have indicated, many scholars regard this "happy ending" of Job as a pious addition designed to confirm a widely held popular belief (not only in Judaism and Christianity but in many extrabiblical religious traditions), namely, that unswerving devotion to God pays off extravagantly in the end. The friends of Job made this a fundamental pillar of their appeal to Job (see Job 5:17–26; 8:5–7; 11:13–20; see also Elihu's argument in 33:24–28). If the wrath of God is the terrifying stick that coerces believers toward righteousness, the hope of future reward is the carrot that makes their righteous endurance worthwhile. It can never be said that such people "fear God for nothing." God has programmed them, by negative and positive reinforcement, to live the kind of life approved by God. The motives that drive such religious performance are fear, shame/guilt, and self-interest.

In the case of Job, however, chapters 1, 2, and 29 open the way for an alternative understanding of 42:10–17. In Job 1:1–5 we are asked to envision a human being who already enjoys the blessed life and whose "blameless and upright" character would appear to exempt him from fear of God's wrath. The question posed by *hassatan* in the heavenly council goes directly to the question of motivation (1:6–12; 2:1–6). Suppose such a person were stripped of all God's blessings and forced, "for no reason," to experience God only as an angry destroyer. If Job is able to "persist in his integrity" under those hellish conditions, then (and only then) will his legendary righteousness toward God and people prove genuine, generated wholly from within, impervious to fear, unswayed by self-interest. God's complicity in the dreadful conspiracy to submit Job to this test puts the "blessedness" Job enjoyed according to Job 1:1–5 in an interesting light. If Job passes the test, it will become evident that it was never the enjoyment of the blessed life that prompted Job toward faithfulness. It will also become evident that God has not showered blessings on Job in order to seduce him to be God's kind of human being.

Job's idyllic reminiscence about the "days when God watched over" him (chap. 29) throws additional light on the "blessed life" he once enjoyed. Job does indeed long for the days "when the friendship of God was upon [his] tent." But it becomes apparent that this friendship was far more important to Job than any other blessing he enjoyed. Job regards all these external blessings as gifts that empowered him to give wise counsel and leadership to others; to stand with and for the poor, the orphan, the wretched, the widows, the blind, the lame, the needy, the resident alien; and to stand resolute against their oppressors. In short, God's gifts are to be expended on behalf of others, not clutched to one's breast as a reward for righteous achievements.

On the interpretation of Job 38:1–42:9 proposed here, any question of Job's motivation (or God's) with respect to his former enjoyment of the blessed life has been completely removed. Job does not need such blessings in order to be faithful to God and people. God does not need to shower blessings upon Job in order to win from him the quality of human life in which God delights.

If this be so, there can be no talk of "reward" (or even reparation) in the redoubled blessings that God now showers upon him. The only alternative left is to suppose that God, for lover's reasons, *wants* to bestow them. The contrived absence of any external token of God's favor was capable of demonstrating that neither Job nor God needs such tokens to express mutual integrity at the irreducible point. But the mutual pain of this absence is not capable of expressing the richness and fullness of life God wants for God's beloved servant—not to make him "happy" but to make him useful.

The Job we have come to know in this book, especially in chapter 29, can be calculated not to revel in his unexpected season of restored affluence, as if these blessings made him better than or better off than others. Unless he is to prove false to the integrity that sustained him throughout his near-fatal alienation from God, from people, and from the good things of life, these renewed gifts will also be received as God's gracious empowerment to serve God and people.

Interestingly enough, the first of Job's restored blessings to be specifically named is reconciliation with other human beings (42:11), well ahead of the double number of sheep, camels, oxen, and donkeys (42:12; see 1:3). What a questionable crew of people it is with whom Job now breaks bread in his house! They are identified only as "all his brothers and sisters and all who had known him before." This would include Eliphaz, Bildad, and Zophar, and perhaps Elihu as well. During his time of alienation, Job mentioned the attitude of unnamed others who were "treacherous" (6:15); who made Job their "laughingstock" (12:4); who mocked him, struck him, massed together against him (16:10; see 17:2); who spit before him as a sign of rejection and disgust (17:6); who were wholly estranged from him (19:13); who failed him (19:14); who forgot his former hospitality to them and regarded him as an alien (19:15)—including servants who were suddenly deaf to his call (19:16), children who despised him and gossiped behind his back (19:18), intimate and beloved friends who turned against him (19:19), mocking youngsters from the dregs of society (a senseless, disreputable brood, outcasts from decent company) who abhorred him, who couldn't stand his presence, who spit at the sight of him (30:1, 8–10), even though Job had wept for those whose day was hard, even though Job's soul had grieved for the poor (30:25).

Perhaps not all these people were at Job's reconciliation banquet. It seems likely that the author of 42:11 is making only a general reference to those who had known Job in the halcyon days described in 1:1–5. Even so, Job has made it plain that not a single human being stood by him and offered him comfort during his trial by suffering. Yet whoever these people may have been, and however they may have signaled their rejection of Job, here they sit together at Job's table, caught up in a wild celebration of reconciliation in the midst of an unparalleled outburst of God's *shalom! Now* they sympathize with him; *now* they comfort him for "all the evil that the LORD had brought upon him." (The Hebrew word for "evil" can mean "misfortune" or "affliction" as well as moral evil. The former sense is undoubtedly intended here. Have these people tumbled to the fact that God's affliction of Job was grounded in God's supreme confidence in Job's faithfulness to God and people?) Such sympathy and comfort are easily given when the crisis is over and there is no longer any risk of guilt by association.

We are also told that each gave Job a piece of money and a gold ring. A cynic might suspect that this is either guilt money or a desperate attempt to curry favor with one who not only stands vindicated by God but is under way toward becoming again "the greatest of all the people of the east" (1:3). Job, however, has demonstrated that his love for God and people is not for sale. His self-sworn ethic in chapter 31 discloses a heart of such integrity that it is simply not governed by the actions of other people toward him, whether for good or ill. The best clue as to how Job regards all the guests at his party is given in 42:9: However rank their failures may have been before (and perhaps, however questionable their motives may be now), Job's prayer for them is that the Lord not "deal with [them] according to [their] folly." Obviously, the meaning of God's forgiveness for them is that they are allowed to participate with Job in God's vindication of Job's superb humanity.

The icing on Job's cake is the gift of seven sons and three new daughters. Once again, the male-dominated culture from which Job sprang is disclosed in the author's attempt to describe an ideal family. In ancient Near Eastern numerology, the numbers seven and three frequently connote completeness, wholeness, perfection. The "right" number of children, however, requires more than twice the number of sons as daughters. That the daughters are exceptionally beautiful, that they bear correspondingly alluring names (in translation, Dove, Spice, and Eye Shadow), and that they are included with their brothers as heirs of the family estate—all this suggests their father will have no problem finding suitable husbands for them. Moreover, the rather essential role of the woman who bore these ideal children is not even mentioned. It's a man's world, and this lovely family emerges as not only Job's glory but his prized possession. Once again, it is up to the reader to allow this flawed imagery to conjure up a further image of the ultimate in human blessedness.

To complete the picture of perfect restoration, the author depicts Job coming to his grave "in a ripe old age, as a shock of grain comes up to the threshing floor in its season" (see Job 5:18–26), surrounded by four generations of his offspring. Comparison of Job 42:12–17 with Job 5:18–26 shows that both descriptions, of a happy ending and of a good death, belong to a common cultural stereotype. The author's purpose is to evoke the ultimate instance of human blessedness as God's purpose for God's uniquely faithful and beloved servant Job.

Works Consulted

Habel, Norman C. *The Book of Job*. Old Testament Library. Philadelphia: Westminster Press, 1985.

Janzen, J. Gerald. *Job*. Interpretation: A Bible Commentary for Teaching and Preaching. Atlanta: John Knox Press, 1985.

Newsom, Carol A. *The Book of Job. New Interpreter's Bible*. Vol. 4. Nashville: Abingdon Press, 1996.

Pfeiffer, Robert H. *Introduction to the Old Testament*. New York: Harper & Brothers, 1941.

Pope, Marvin H. *Job*. 3d ed. Anchor Bible. Garden City, N.Y.: Doubleday Co., 1979.

Terrien, Samuel. *The Book of Job: Introduction and Exegesis*. New York and Nashville: Abingdon Press, 1954.

For Further Reading

Frost, Robert. "A Masque of Reason." In *Complete Poems of Robert Frost*, pp. 587–606. New York, Chicago, San Francisco, Boston: Holt, Rinehart and Winston.

Gutiérrez, Gustavo. *On Job: God-Talk and the Suffering of the Innocent.* Translated by M. J. O'Connell. Maryknoll, N.Y.: Orbis Books, 1987.

Kushner, Harold S. *When Bad Things Happen to Good People.* New York: Avon Books, 1988.

MacLeish, Archibald. *J.B. A Play in Verse.* Boston: Houghton Mifflin, 1956. Reprint, New York: Holt, Rinehart & Winston, 1964.

Wiesel, Elie. *The Trial of God: A Play in Three Acts.* Translated by M. Wiesel. New York: Schocken Books, 1979.